# NEARBY
# HISTORY

# Nearby History

## Exploring the Past Around You

David E. Kyvig

Myron A. Marty

**ALTAMIRA**
PRESS

*A Division of Sage Publications, Inc.*
Walnut Creek • London • New Delhi

*Published in cooperation with the*
*AMERICAN ASSOCIATION FOR STATE AND LOCAL HISTORY*

*For information contact:*

AltaMira Press
A Division of Sage Publications, Inc.
1630 North Main Street, Suite 367
Walnut Creek, California 94596 U.S.A.

Sage Publications Ltd.
6 Bonhill Street
London EC2A 4PU United Kingdom

Sage Publications India Pvt. Ltd.
M-32 Market
Greater Kailash 1
New Delhi 110 048 India

PRINTED IN THE UNITED STATES OF AMERICA

**Library of Congress Cataloging-in-Publication Data**

Kyvig, David E.
    Nearby history : exploring the past around you / David E. Kyvig, Myron A. Marty.
      p.  cm. — (American Association for State and Local History book series)
    Originally published: Nashville, Tenn. : American Association for State and
    Local History, c1982.
    Published in cooperation with the American Association for State and Local History.
    Includes bibliographical references and index.
    ISBN 0-7619-9158-1 (pbk: alk. paper)
    1. United States—History, Local. I. Marty, Myron A. II. American Association for
State and Local History. III. Title IV. Series.
E180.5.K98    1996
973—dc20                               95-52746
                                                        CIP

1996    1997    1998    1999   10  9  8  7

Publication of this book was made possible in part by funds from the sale of the Bicentennial State Histories, which were supported by the National Endowment for the Humanities.

Designed by Gary Gore.

# A WORKER READS HISTORY

Who built the seven towers of Thebes?
The books are filled with names of kings.
Was it kings who hauled the craggy blocks of stone?
And Babylon, so many times destroyed,
Who built the city up each time? In which of Lima's houses,
That city glittering with gold, lived those who built it?
In the evening when the Chinese wall was finished
Where did the masons go? Imperial Rome
Is full of arcs of triumph. Who reared them up? Over whom
Did the Caesars triumph? Byzantium lives in song,
Were all her dwellings palaces? And even in Atlantis of the legend
The night the sea rushed in,
The drowning men still bellowed for their slaves.

Young Alexander plundered India.
He alone?
Caesar beat the Gauls.
Was there not even a cook in his army?
Philip of Spain wept as his fleet
Was sunk and destroyed. Were there no other tears?
Frederick the Great triumphed in the Seven Years War. Who
Triumphed with him?

Each page a victory,
At whose expense the victory ball?
Every ten years a great man,
Who paid the piper?

So many particulars.
So many questions.

—*Bertolt Brecht*

# The Nearby History Series

David E. Kyvig, *Series Editor*
Myron A. Marty, *Consulting Editor*

*Nearby History: Exploring the Past Around You*
by Kyvig and Marty (1982)

VOLUME 1
*Local Schools*
by Ronald E. Butchart (1986)

VOLUME 2
*Houses and Homes*
by Barbara J. Howe, Dolores A. Fleming,
Emory L. Kemp, and Ruth Ann Overbeck (1987)

VOLUME 3
*Public Places*
by Gerald A. Danzer (1987)

VOLUME 4
*Places of Worship*
by James P. Wind (1990)

VOLUME 5
*Local Businesses*
by K. Austin Kerr, Amos J. Loveday, and
Mansel G. Blackford (1990)

# Contents

# Preface

SEVERAL YEARS AGO WE WROTE A SMALL BOOK INTENDED for students in history courses and persons with an independent interest in exploring their own past. We were convinced that students, accustomed to looking at history as a series of national and world events, could benefit from examining a single family. At the same time, we wished to show genealogists concerned with single families that their work could be enriched by considering the experiences of others. We sought to demonstrate to everyone that most historical research techniques could be mastered by any literate person. Finally, we particularly wanted to make clear that accurate knowledge of the past, whether gained from one's own efforts or the work of others, could be not only interesting for its own sake but also useful in understanding the present.

Whether *Your Family History: A Handbook for Research and Writing* (Arlington Heights, Ill.: AHM, 1978) met our objectives is for others to decide. But whatever the judgment, interest in the book persuaded us that the goals, at least, were worth pursuing. We therefore decided to carry our endeavor further by expanding our focus to include the widest possible range of subjects within the realm of ordinary individual, family, and community life. This book is the result.

*Nearby History* seeks to bring together historical studies of the family, the community, and material culture. So much unites these fields that artificial divisions should not be allowed to persist. Each area influences the others, and all involve everyone's immediate world. We attempt to demonstrate the excitement and value that may be derived from exploring this world. Both to clarify the range of opportunities and to suggest specific possibilities, we offer an extensive list of questions for investigating the family, buildings, neighborhoods, institutions, and communities as a whole. Thereafter, several chapters describe methods for using evidence from the nearby world, such as written documents, oral testimony, visual records, material objects, buildings, and landscapes. These chapters may be used independently or in any sequence, depending upon the nature of the topic under study. Next, we offer some ideas for organizing and sharing the results of a personal inquiry into the past. In a final chapter, we describe the work of academic historians in the fields of family and community history. By underscoring the fact that academic and nonacademic historians share interests, we hope to promote greater communication and cooperation among them.

When we began research for this book, we were conscious of the distinctions frequently drawn between amateur and professional historians. The conventional widsom says that amateurs rework the local past, while professionals are more concerned with national and world history. The argument continues: the concerns of amateurs are relatively unimportant and frequently too personal to be taken seriously; professionals work on important issues with a sense of detachment and clinical skill that deserves respect; amateurs are driven by nostalgia, professionals by a desire to find the truth; amateurs think in parochial terms, whereas professionals use terms cosmic in character and part of a universal language.

As our work progressed, these distinctions blurred. Many professionals have found value in the detailed consideration of a single community or a local institution, while many amateurs show sensitivity to the larger picture. Although we are by training academic historians and have spent most of our careers in college and university settings, we have been led by a variety of experiences to see the futility of trying to draw sharp lines between historians of one sort and those of another. These experiences have included teaching adult students, participating in the activities of state and local historical associations, doing family history, working in archives, and serving in an agency that supports a full range of activities in history.

As the differences between kinds of historians became less clear, we realized that while there are unquestionably many varieties of interests, there is really only one audience. Some members make their living as historians; others do so in different ways. This is about the only clear-cut distinction between professionals and amateurs.

Consequently, we have written a book that seeks to answer the questions of all historians, no matter how they earn their living. Indeed, given the nature of the times, it may well be that some who are trained as historians will need to make their living in other ways; conversely, some who now pursue history avocationally or as students may someday profit financially from their historical work. Whatever the direction of their movement, we believe that this book will remain useful to them.

Having said this much, we must stress two points. First, we do not wish to minimize the necessity for historians to develop special competencies for specific work. This book is an introduction, and almost any of the topics with which it deals could be developed in much greater detail and depth. For that reason we have provided extensive bibliographies at the end of most chapters.

Second, we believe that there is an important difference in methods and concerns between historians of the close at hand and historians of the world out there. The former, we believe, have tended to focus on the specific. They know about this person and that place, this building and that organization. The latter are good at identifying, describing, analyzing, and interpreting the universals of history: movements, developments, causes and effects, and so on. One of our principal goals, as the final chapter shows, is to help historians of all kinds to find ways to link the particulars with the universals.

This book seeks to help increase the effectiveness of research and writing about the history of people and places nearby. To this end we aim to help our readers understand the nature and purposes of nearby history, realize the importance of caring about it, and know how to research and write or tell about it. At times we inform. At other times we advocate, cautiously and, we hope, subtly. And at other times we show step by step the work necessary to accomplish certain goals.

A book with such broad purposes could not have been written, at least by the two of us, without considerable assistance. We have received such extensive advice and gratifying encouragement from so many quarters that we feel our original premise has been richly confirmed: history is a cooperative enterprise in which the work of any individual is immeasurably strengthened by the skills, learning, and insight of others. We must add that shared interest in the past leads to an amazing generosity among historians who give their time and talent to improve their colleagues' work.

We benefited tremendously at the outset of this project from fellowships awarded by the Family and Community History Center of the Newberry Library in Chicago. The National Endowment for the Humanities funded grants that allowed us to spend an extremely productive month working together during the summer of 1979, exploring and discussing ideas, exploiting the collections of the Newberry Library, and learning from many of the people who have been drawn together at that extraordinary research center. Richard Jensen, D'Ann Campbell, Janice Reiff, Arthur Anderson, David Ruchman, Richard H. Brown, and Mark Friedberger were particularly helpful to us. The Newberry fellowships provided an opportunity for truly collaborative work.

Once we had completed a draft of our manuscript, we sent it to a number of people with diverse professional backgrounds, asking for their criticisms and suggestions. Without exception, they read carefully and responded thoughtfully, compelling us to make an extensive revision of the manuscript. For their assistance we acknowledge and thank James M. Denny (Missouri Department of Natural Resources), Thomas Fuller (Public Historical Studies Program, University of California, Santa Barbara), H. Roger Grant (University of Akron), James K. Huhta (Middle Tennessee State University), Julie Roy Jeffrey (Goucher College), George Knepper (University of Akron), Jeanette Lauer (St. Louis Community College), Martin Marty (University of Chicago), Shirley Marty, John V. Miller (University Archives, University of Akron), Gayle Olson (American Justice Institute), Jerrald Pfabe (Concordia College, Nebraska), Charles Piehl (Mankato State University), Robert Schnucker (Northeast Missouri State University and Society for History Education), John Alexander Williams (National Endowment for the Humanities), and William F. Willingham (Lewis and Clark College).

A number of persons gave us such extraordinary assistance that we mention them separately. Gerald Danzer of the University of Illinois, Chicago Circle, made numerous editorial and practical suggestions. Glen Holt of Washington University, Howard S. Miller of the University of Missouri/St. Louis, and Raymond Pisney of the Missouri Historical Society compelled us to sharpen our objectives and refine our approach. Alice and Randall Shrock of Earlham College and the Conner Prairie Pioneer Settlement helped us with bibliographic recommendations and technical advice on questions relating to material culture. Ingrid Winther Scobie of the University of California, San Diego, led us to reconsider various issues and gave us the benefit of her experience in oral history.

The contributions of these people significantly improved the manuscript. Since we did not always follow their advice, however, we hasten to add that we bear final responsibility for our words. We offer the book in the hope that it will contribute to a further growth of interest in the expanding field in which our first readers have all been significant participants.

Three capable and cheerful individuals assisted in production. Ruth Ross, reference librarian at St. Louis Community College at Florissant Valley, did extensive bibliographic searching. Garnette Dorsey and Dorothy Richards, both of the University of Akron History Department, typed various drafts of the manuscript.

Some of our work was done while we were on sabbatical leaves—David Kyvig from the University of Akron in fall 1980 and Myron Marty from St. Louis Community College in fall 1979. We are grateful to both institutions.

Finally, we would like to dedicate this book to our families— grandparents, parents, siblings, spouses, in-laws, children, and others present in person or memory—who have done so much to shape our appreciation and understanding of the nearby world.

DAVID E. KYVIG
MYRON A. MARTY

# NEARBY
# HISTORY

# · 1 ·

# Why Nearby History?

"HISTORY IS MORE OR LESS BUNK," DECLARED HENRY FORD. Like many other people then and now, he did not believe "history" had any significance for his everyday life; the word referred, he thought, only to the stories of colonial settlement and early national development, presidential achievement, and military victory which constituted the bulk of historical literature during his day. "We want to live in the present," he explained, "and the only history that is worth a tinker's dam is the history we make today." It was the experiences, the beliefs and behavior, and the changes in the lives of average people over the generations which interested him. Henry Ford was ignorant, even contemptuous, of traditional "history," but he instinctively knew that what had happened nearby, to himself, his ancestors, his neighbors, and other ordinary people, had shaped their lives. Events and conditions in his family, church, school, workplace, and community had helped form him and his personal world. To Ford, such nearby history was not "bunk"; it was very important.

Ford's inexpensive, mass-produced automobiles profoundly altered twentieth-century life, of course, accounting for everything from the congestion of central cities to the sprawl of suburbia, from the success of fast-food restaurants to the inability of parents to keep track of their teenage children, from energy shortages to pollution excesses. Henry Ford realized how rapidly America was changing and how vital the memories of a disappearing society were to an understanding of the changes. So he spent millions of dollars gathering objects, buildings, and other memorabilia from the preautomotive age: a country store, tools, dolls, the house where he was born, wagons, furniture, Thomas Edison's workshop, radios, vacuum cleaners, a blacksmith shop, cigar store Indians, clocks, and a thousand other

1

A

B

    Photographs of communities can only hint at their individual character and rich diversity. Think of all that it would be interesting and valuable to know about an all-black midwestern town (View A), a congested city early in the twentieth century (View B), a California migrant worker settlement during the Great Depression of the 1930s (View C), and a public housing project built in the 1950s (View D).

C

D

items. Ford was often sloppy in his efforts. He mistook the phony for the real, removed objects from the setting which gave them meaning, and failed to organize his vast collections so that the process of development over time could be appreciated. He believed that he knew just as much as experts on American history, architecture, and technology about how to collect, display, and interpret the commonplace objects in which he was interested. By ignoring professional advice, Ford often fell short of his goals of caring for, learning from, and teaching with his collections. Indeed, some scholars laughed or sneered at Ford's activities. But the millions of visitors who flocked to Dearborn, Michigan, to the Greenfield Village and Henry Ford Museum, vindicated Ford's belief in the importance of the commonplace past. An iron sign at the entrance bears his conclusion: "The farther you look back, the farther you can see ahead."

This book is for everyone who shares—or is even willing to consider sharing—Henry Ford's concern with the past. The authors believe that every person's world has a history which is useful, exciting, and possible to explore. Rather than identify this past as "local," or "community," history as some have done and limit it to a concept of *place*, or call it "family history" and restrict it to a concept of *relationship*, or talk about material culture and confine the discussion to *objects*, we have chosen the term "nearby history" in order to include the entire range of possibilities in a person's immediate environment. Since for various elements of nearby history, the resources, research methods, questions, and insights often overlap, we approach the subject in an inclusive fashion. We also wish to employ "nearby history" to distinguish the new approaches which emphasize analysis, comparison, and the examination of change over time from the rather static, narrow, and nonanalytical historical undertakings of past generations.

The book is intended as a guide to help the interested person, with many resources or with few, explore elements of nearby history: families, houses, farms, neighborhoods, churches, schools, businesses, civic organizations, public buildings, and communities. By referring to the efforts of other individuals and groups, the book points to possibilities for enjoyment, self-awareness, and intelligent decision making. It assumes that beginners and experienced historians alike need to consider issues and methods in order to learn about the past close at hand. It suggests various questions, approaches, and techniques for studying our immediate environment and for preserving its history. It demonstrates the wide variety of ways in which historians have probed the nearby past. Above all, it actively encourages readers to consider the importance of nearby history and to investigate it for themselves.

## The Need for History

We all need to know who we are, how we have become what we are, and how to cope with a variety of situations in order to conduct our own lives successfully. We also need to know what to expect from people and institutions around us. Organizations and communities require the same self-understanding in order to function satisfactorily. For individuals and groups alike, experience produces a self-image and a basis for deciding how to behave, manage problems, and plan ahead. We remember—sometimes accurately, sometimes not—what occurred, the causes of certain responses or changes, and our reactions to different circumstances. These memories, positive and negative, help determine our actions.

Without memory individuals and groups would be forced to start fresh in analyzing each situation and deciding how to respond. Life would become extremely complicated. Even minor decisions would take much time and effort. Of course, no one has the capacity to store every detail or experience. Too much memory is paralyzing, and so everyone remembers selectively and incompletely. Yet, the more extensive and accurate the memories, the greater the ability to decide whether to follow or depart from past practices. Thus the adult is generally more capable of sensible decision making than the toddler. The ability to observe and recall what has taken place in the nearby world constitutes an essential aspect of human intelligence and well-being.

History serves both society and individuals as memory serves the individual alone and has all the same values and flaws. Stretching beyond one lifetime and one locale, history is a collection of remembrances in a variety of forms and serving a variety of purposes. Historian Arthur Link has noted: "The single most important attribute that enabled man to emerge from his primitive savage state was memory. Collective memory, preserved for long ages at first by oral tradition, enabled primitive man to maintain the practices and customs and to develop the institutions necessary to an ongoing social life."

As society became more complex, social memory acquired functions beyond recalling how things happened before. History also became a tool for stimulating group pride and distinctiveness, comparing the experiences of different groups, making plans, and setting expectations. Similarly, the means of transmitting historical knowledge expanded from storytelling to written records, material objects, photographs, and a host of other devices which convey information about the past. And finally, the recognition grew that not just the general story but many individual facets of a society's history deserved examination.

## The Importance of the Nearby Past

Just as many distinct, separate, and equally useful recollections contribute to an individual memory, so, too, do many separate elements compose "history." The national and international political, military, and diplomatic developments that Henry Ford dismissed as "more or less bunk" are a part of human history, but no more so than the activities and environments of the ordinary folk whom Ford celebrated. "There is a history in all men's lives," William Shakespeare observed, and that is equally true for plumbers and presidents, printers and prime ministers. The president will no doubt have wider-ranging influence, but the plumber's grandchildren, neighbors, and clients may be more directly affected by him than by the president. An executive order from Washington may affect the world, while a decision made in a small town may only affect one neighborhood, but the local event may nevertheless have great and lasting influence on a community, a family, or an individual. A good understanding of the past, whether designated memory or history, needs to take into account nearby as well as national and international developments.

"We may picture the family, the local community, the national state, and the supra-national society as a series of concentric circles," wrote H. P. R. Finberg, an English specialist in local history. "Each requires to be studied with constant reference to the one outside it; but the inner rings are not the less perfect circles for being wholly surrounded and enclosed by the outer." The useful image of concentric circles around the individual makes understandable the relationship of one level of history to the others. Obviously, conflict between countries, a national depression, or a community decision on the budget of public schools can affect the family and the individual. Less obviously, personal or family decisions to move, to bear fewer children, or to buy a foreign automobile, especially if they are repeated by others, can radiate influence to the outer circles. Each of the circles surrounding a person affects the others yet also involves a distinctive past deserving of separate consideration.

Just because the inner circles involve fewer people or less well known events does not mean that they are less important to the person at the center. Indeed, your own past and that of people closest to you, family and community, have had a great impact on you. Learning about it enhances your memory and helps you comprehend influences on your life. Your grandparents' decision to leave Europe for America, for example, or their cautious spending habits learned in the Great Depression, have affected your parents and you in turn. Similarly, an organization or a whole community can become aware of why certain practices or patterns developed. The presence of foul-smelling factories in the center of the city at one time may help explain why the wealthy neighborhoods, pleasant parks, and better schools are all to be found on the upwind side of town, and investigation may lead to questions about the advisability of permitting such a residential pattern to continue, now that the factories have moved or changed. Nearby history is thus worth exploring as it serves important needs of the individuals and communities directly involved.

The image of concentric circles suggests that nearby history has other values that we should consider as well. An understanding of national and even international history benefits from increased knowledge of nearby history. The national and international circles contain not one but many communities, just as each community circle contains many families. When we describe national or international history, we must usually identify common threads and general patterns in order for a coherent picture to emerge. The variety and detail of various community and individual experiences necessarily disappear from view, and as a result our sense of what actually happened to ordinary people is often missing. A history of the American Revolution or World War II may give an excellent picture of the general issues and overall pattern of the developing conflict without revealing anything at all about a particular community, family, or individual experience at the time. Furthermore, the attempt to generalize about a widely shared experience, such as the Great Depression, may in the end distort the actual, personal situation for many of those involved. Careful examination of what happened to particular families and communities can clarify and illustrate the broader picture.

During the past few years, historians have begun to appreciate the importance of family and community history, and growing numbers of them have

The life of an individual and family intertwines with that of the surrounding community. The history of one illuminates the other. For example, this family's history provides glimpses of community educational and business practices, the impact of changing technology, and social customs regarding death. Additional research would be required, of course, to obtain a full picture of any one of these matters.

When Cyril was fifteen he began to work in the steel mills. His first job was that of messenger. Soon he worked as a tally boy counting and marking the sheets of steel. When he was twenty-one, he quit the steel business and entered mortuary school in Cincinnati. Cyril's father wanted him to be a mortician.

At Cincinnati Cyril went to school for three months, took his state board exam, and passed. Since the required amount of schooling to receive a license was six months, he supervised other class members and taught them the principles of raising veins and arteries. He received his license on October 20, 1917. License requirements and embalming procedures have greatly changed in the past 70 years. Now one year of mortuary school, two years of college, and one year of internship at a funeral home are required before licensing. Embalming fluid has been greatly improved. The chemicals now used to preserve the body do so for a much longer time.

Cyril established his first funeral home at 127 River Avenue in Memphis. A large store room for caskets and sleeping quarters was in the back. In the daytime some of the caskets were kept on the bed. Cyril and Mary would lift them off the bed to go to sleep at night.

Funerals in the early 1900s weren't held in funeral homes, but in the homes of the deceased. The embalmer would carry his instruments to the home and embalm the deceased at his home. One of the instruments was called a cooling board. This board was made so that it could be folded up and carried under the arm. The cooling board was unfolded and placed on the bed before the person was embalmed. The average funeral director's salary was twelve dollars a week.

Cyril entered into partnership with Andrew Sherlock under the firm name Medzan and Sherlock. One year later Cyril sold his partnership to Sherlock for one dollar because he was angry with him. Cyril lost the house and all of his equipment.

About the time Cyril and Mary's first child, Tom, was born, Cyril established his own funeral home at 336 South Broad Street. While at this address Cyril purchased an ambulance which he ran with the business. In

*1925 the family moved to 222 East Center Street so that they would be located in the center of the city. Just before the move a second child, Rita, was born. While at Center Street Cyril purchased his first hearse. The "hearse" was a 1927 Ford pick-up with a turtle back. The box was carried in the back of the truck. Funeral directors began to wear special outfits: silk hats, striped pants, frocked coats. The mourners wore black.*

*As more and more funerals were being held in the chapels rather than the home, Cyril again changed his residence to Davis Street. This funeral home had two chapels, a show room for caskets, two offices, a morgue, and a garage. The family had living quarters above the funeral home. Everyone had their own room, even after Ed was born in 1928. In 1933 while Mary was pregnant with her fourth child, Cyril moved his family once more. Besides another addition to the family, the children were getting too noisy to remain above the chapels.*

*Source*: Family History Collection, American History Research Center, University of Akron, Akron, Ohio.

become involved in "the new social history." Several developments in the 1950s and 1960s, particularly the black civil rights movement, the growth of awareness of the plight of poor people, and the rise of feminism, led to calls for the study of America "from the bottom up." The nation's history, it is now apparent, cannot fully be understood by looking only at leadership elites and their decisions. The experience of other social groups, particularly anonymous people who form the mass of society, needs to be examined. Slavery cannot be understood by investigating only Abraham Lincoln; one must find out what it meant to the slave. The Great Depression of the 1930s cannot be comprehended by analyzing only Franklin D. Roosevelt; one must consider how the families of unemployed workers lived through it. The Vietnam War cannot be appreciated by viewing it only from the perspective of Lyndon Johnson or Richard Nixon; one must learn what soldiers, draft evaders, and civilians on the home front thought about it. At first many historians doubted that much could be learned about obscure people, organizations, and communities, who left few of the traces—letters, speeches, diaries, newspaper stories—with which scholars were accustomed to working. But once serious interest arose, scholars began to adapt their traditional methods and develop new techniques to explore past society at the grass roots.

A great stroke of good fortune for the new social history was the development of computers as these new questions were being raised. Before computers, it was difficult if not impossible for a historian to keep track of many
facts about all the people in a community. A computer can store endless bits
of information about individuals and communities and can organize them
into meaningful patterns. Large groups can be studied systematically rather
than on the basis of haphazard impressions. For example, information from
the United States Census on the parents, birthplace, previous residence,
education, occupation, family relationships, and wealth of each of a community's hundreds or even thousands of residents can be fed into a computer, and the computer can be programmed to report on mobility patterns
and rates, average family size, amount of education by sex, occupation, and
economic status, and many other useful community characteristics which
may change from time to time as well as from place to place. Although
computers are not necessary for many sorts of interesting and useful nearby
history, historians have been using computers and quantitative techniques
to identify economic, social, political, and growth patterns of families and
communities, thus developing a much fuller and more accurate picture of
American society from the bottom up.

Computers are but one research tool available to the historian of the
nearby world. Depending on the topic or question involved, a variety of
other research methods may be more appropriate and less difficult to master.
Examining photographs, interviewing people, reconstructing old buildings,
sorting out and piecing together a business's financial records, and tracing
neighborhood growth patterns from maps and tax records are only a few of
the ways in which useful and interesting information about the past can be
collected and verified. Research skills developed in doing nearby history can
often be applied in other endeavors as well.

## History for Now

Doing nearby history encourages a way of thinking which can help in
dealing with a great variety of current situations. Uncovering what has
taken place over the years in a family, an organization, or a community
reveals the origins of conditions, the causes of change, and the reasons for
present circumstances. It becomes evident that not just one influence but a
complex of forces affects most developments. Examining how conditions
evolve over a period of time and considering the impact of a wide variety of

factors on that process—in other words, thinking historically—provide enlightenment and perspective. Just as searching one's memory for accurate, pertinent recollections can help an individual reach a wiser decision, so, too, can thinking historically be of use to a person, a business, a family, a church organization, a city planner, or a whole community.

The value of history beyond its traditional importance in a sound general education seems to be gaining recognition. A most significant development in recent years has been the increase in "public history," a term coined to describe the various types of specialized work that people with historical training and skills can do other than teach. Basically, public history involves two kinds of activities: historical resources management and applied research.

Historical resources management is concerned with saving, caring for, and encouraging the use of materials from the past. Archivists seek to locate historically valuable documents, assure their preservation and accessibility, and assist anyone with an interest in using them. Museum curators and historic preservationists engage in similar activities with objects and buildings. Saving historic buildings and adapting them for new purposes is becoming an increasingly important part of conserving the environment, reviving downtowns and neighborhoods, and holding down construction costs. The federal government gives various types of aid to restoration projects, and experts in the field are in increasing demand. Resources management can also involve directing historical societies, editing publications, and other activities which call attention to what remains from the past.

Applied research involves historical investigation to aid in current problem solving or policy planning. Corporations, consulting firms, government agencies, and newspapers are some of the organizations which need to examine past developments in order to function and plan effectively. Whether for marketing and development decisions, public and governmental relations, personnel management, land use planning, assessment of the impact of policies on the physical and social environment, or for other purposes, research of a historical nature, even if not labeled as such, becomes vital. The skills involved in uncovering and analyzing information about particular aspects of the past, comprehending and assessing complex factors which influence directions of growth, and accurately describing processes of development have great utility for public and private institutions alike.

"It is our discipline that asks the question, how did the subject of concern evolve over time into its present condition?" notes historian Robert Kelley. "Other disciplines, as in economics, engineering, political science, and sociology, are concerned with the dynamics of the existing situation. The examples of badly formed policies which would have escaped that condition had some attention been paid to the history of the issue at hand, or of the problem or situation, are endless." Kelley concludes: "Historically-grounded policies, in small and large settings, cannot help but be sounder in conception, and they are likely to be more effective, consistent, and, one hopes, more aligned with human reality. In the long run, they should be less costly to administer. . . ."

The territory of nearby history is, obviously, both a training ground and a principal workplace for public historians. In exploring the past of subjects close at hand, a person learns to identify, collect, organize, and exhibit historical materials, to analyze complex factors, to examine the relationship of the inner concentric circles of nearby situations to the outer circles of national and international development, and to focus research to answer specific questions of importance to the historian or the client. Practicing public historians are often concerned with helping a planning agency, filmmaker, museum, advertiser, real estate developer, business, or other public or private body understand a particular community, neighborhood, or local social group's experiences and needs. This emerging field may well offer the greatest opportunities for historical employment for the next generation, and clearly the individual interested in a career as a historian would do well to explore nearby history.

But beyond the serious importance of examining the past of our immediate world to extend memory, understand the contemporary situation, sharpen social, political, and economic generalizations, or facilitate intelligent policy making, nearby history has a further intangible appeal which may be its most notable quality. The emotional rewards of learning about a past which has plainly and directly affected one's own life cannot be duplicated by any other type of historical inquiry. It can be exciting to understand for the first time why your grandparents treated your parents in a certain way, why your community developed certain traditions, why your corporation adopted specific practices, why your civic organization became involved with particular issues. It can be satisfying to feel oneself part of something larger and more lasting than the moment, something that stretches both backward and forward in time. Despite his disparaging remarks about "history," Henry Ford instinctively sought that emotional lift.

The same feeling can be shared by all who accept the challenge to explore the history of their nearby world.

## Notes

Henry Ford's statement to the *New York Times*, May 20, 1919, is quoted in Keith Sward, *The Legend of Henry Ford* (New York: Holt, Rinehart and Winston, 1948), which discusses the context of the statement, pp. 100–10, as well as the development of Greenfield Village, pp. 259–71.

Henry Ford's historical activities are described in Geoffrey C. Upward, *A Home for Our Heritage* (Dearborn, Mich.: Henry Ford Museum Press, 1979). The other statements quoted in this chapter were made by Arthur Link at a 1967 conference which produced *The Challenge of Local History* (Albany: New York State Education Department, 1968), p. 71; H. P. R. Finberg, "Local History," in Finberg and V. H. T. Skipp, *Local History: Objective and Pursuit* (Newton Abbott: David and Charles, 1967), p. 39; and Robert Kelley, who was quoted in Dianne Martin, "History Goes Public," *History News* 34 (1979): 122–23.

# ·2·

# What Can Be Done Nearby?

EXPLORING NEARBY HISTORY DOES NOT FIRST REQUIRE a long, difficult search for a rare appropriate topic. To the contrary, the initial step involves selecting from a wide range of possibilities. Nearly everyone is surrounded by a vast assortment of people, objects, and institutions, each with a potentially interesting past about which an enormous amount of information exists in one form or another. This chapter seeks to provide help with the all-important task of deciding where to focus one's attention.

## Focusing

Even if an individual wanted to do so, it would be impossible to cope with every aspect of the nearby past simultaneously. Just as every memory cannot be summoned up and used at the same moment, every facet of local history cannot be investigated at once and expected to fall into place. During close examination of a particular event or circumstance, it is hard to maintain a sharp image of the overall community, and vice versa. Thus it is important to take some time at the outset to define an objective.

As well as determining what he or she wishes to know, every investigator must decide how much depth and detail of knowledge is desirable and what effort is worth expending. Individuals obviously possess varied backgrounds, skills, and interests. A beginner cannot be expected to proceed as fast and far as can an experienced historian. The amount of time and other resources available for the acquisition of techniques and the pursuit of inquiries differs widely. Some people may be prepared to tackle the most complex issues, others not. Nor will everyone be satisfied with the same level of answer.

Some historians of the nearby past may want or need to investigate a topic at great length, while others—for equally valid reasons—may decide not to carry it very far. Part of the process of choosing a focus wisely is setting it realistically in terms of one's capacities and interests.

Only after the purpose and scope of an inquiry into the past are clearly in mind can research plans be formulated. Decisions can then be reached as to what information is worth gathering, examining, and analyzing in order to answer a particular question. Obviously some interesting information will not be pertinent, although were a different question asked, it might have great relevance. Therefore, to determine an approach and judge the value of information, a focus is essential.

Historians find their focus in various ways. Sometimes simple curiosity leads to an interest in a totally new topic or one related to previous investigations. "I want to know something about this strange town to which I have just moved," or "Having read a fascinating history of the rise of the sky-scraper in America, I would like to know about the first one built here and its impact on this community." Sometimes a personal need to know sparks interest. "Has this civic organization been sensible and successful over the years in supporting causes which I care about, or would I be wasting my time and money by joining?" Ownership of an object or a building can stimulate an inquiry. "I need to find out the background of this house I inherited and the neighborhood in which it is located so that I can determine whether I should keep it and restore it to its original condition."

Often the focus of an historical investigation is not chosen but assigned in the course of school, political or civic involvement, or employment. "In this course, students will investigate the history of their family during the twentieth century," or "The company needs to know about this town's past growth patterns in order to make intelligent investment and marketing decisions, and it is your job to find out and prepare a report." Such research assignments are likely to increase as the notion of public history spreads and as private and public agencies realize the value of acquiring accurate information about the past. However it is selected, a focus on a particular topic, whether as narrow as the origins of the antique chest in the attic or as broad as the centennial history of a city, helps determine how to proceed.

Some people feel guilty about shifting their focus after they have begun their research. There is no reason why they should. Initial choices are necessarily based on limited knowledge and must naturally be considered tentative. As research goes forward, obstacles, better approaches, and more worthwhile topics often reveal themselves, signaling the need to broaden, narrow, or redirect the investigation. Indeed, this refining process is normally a sign of progress. But without an objective to begin with, it becomes difficult to sort through the vast heap of information about the past.

## Possibilities

Whether you already have decided upon a subject or are trying to choose one, it is most helpful to think about the range of possibilities. Considering different topics helps expand awareness of the opportunities, assists in determining where interests lie, and leads to ideas for using resources already at hand. Thinking about the great variety of possible questions helps in deciding exactly what you wish to know. Also, identifying other questions related to yours may make you aware of other ways of looking at a topic, may help you recognize useful information, and may thus assist you in finding a more complete, satisfying answer. Explanations are seldom closer to the target than the questions asked. By taking time at the start to consider potential questions, you will bring your undertaking into the sharp focus you seek.

Basically, historical questions seek answers which will help fulfill three purposes: description of the past, measurement of change over time, analysis of cause and consequence. Often the goal of inquiry is simply accurate portrayal of an event, personality, set of conditions, or place at some past moment. Such a description may become complex because many interrelated factors are involved. An acute concern with time distinguishes the historian's effort to understand society; the sequence in which various matters unfold and interact is considered crucial to their relationship and individual character. In analyzing causation and effect, the historian must be sensitive to the influence of a wide variety of forces and the impact of timing. If these three fundamental objectives of historical explanation are applied to any topic, appropriate questions for research should suggest themselves.

Keep in mind also that the past is filled with subtle developments as well as obvious ones. Matters which were conspicuous at the moment—the opening of a factory, a local election—may be considered manifest events. Slight alterations in unspectacular aspects of life, many of which were largely unnoticed by contemporaries but which over a long term represent significant change—shifts in family size or structure, economic patterns, or assimilation of minorities into the dominant culture, for instance—may be called latent events. The relationship between manifest and latent events is

Research often begins with a summing up of what one knows, believes, or suspects about a topic. Thereafter it is possible to identify the questions to be answered, the information to be verified, and the relationships to be examined. A student in East Chicago, Indiana, summing up her view of her ethnic community, touches on a number of issues which could be investigated to discover how conditions developed and changed over the course of time.

*The Greek Community of East Chicago, despite its small size of 2,000 people, has made its presence felt in a city of 50,000 inhabitants. There are, for example, at least 8 Greek restaurants there. This business group represents the better established Greek families of East Chicago, the elite in a sense. However, since they are not educated, their style of life does not contrast sharply with that of the community. Yet quite paradoxically, from this pool of wealth springs the inevitable pursuit of the good life: the mod clothes, new cars, socializing with different types of people, in short, Americanizing. This seems to be less true of the parents than their children. Generally speaking, they are a conservative force and speak the language of those who have pulled themselves up by their own bootstraps. There is no such thing as good luck, they insist; one must work and work hard, for "God helps those who help themselves." The Greek immigrants have done their best to demonstrate that God is favoring them. They are employed for the most part, and their incomes provide for a decent living. Exceptions to this generalization are the very recent newcomers from Greece and those who have been beset by costly setbacks. My father, for example, is a restaurant employee, who has been in a precarious economic state ever since his savings were drained by family illnesses for which he was not insured. Fortunately, the majority of Greek immigrants have not experienced such a catastrophe, being employed by the steel mills of Inland and Youngstown which provide them with a family insurance. In terms of work, they are less successful in obtaining good jobs due to the language barrier and their lack of specialized training. After several years in the mills, some manage to get promoted but not before being affected by the heavily polluted air. A substantial number of family acquaintances have been hospitalized, following one or two years of work. The common joke is that since they were never examined by a physician while in Greece, this is a good opportunity for them to receive some medical care.*
*It would seem from their modest annual wages that little could be put aside for future needs; but the Greek immigrants lead a life of austerity and*

*are able to save. There are cases where the saving power is too unrealistic to be credible, were it not for the simple fact that it is true.*

*My personal feeling is that the Greek people of East Chicago are not very secure despite their apparent economic progress. Among those who have prospered is my uncle, who did so when he was already past the age of 60. He worked long hours, and the best years of his life were consumed in his striving for success. The surplus money which he now has can do little to brighten his life, for he is old, conditioned, and unable to adapt to a new and better life. His story is that of the Greek immigrants in general, who defer a decent and comfortable present for some undefined future gratification which will never come to pass. . . .*

*The Greek people socialize among themselves, the women visiting their lady friends, and the men meeting in coffeehouses or other Greek-owned businesses where they play cards. There in some obscure corner they are brought together by a common background to discuss issues ranging from politics to personal problems. They're not a bunch of naive peasants, as one might expect. They read Greek newspapers and are able to follow political developments around the world.*

*Among themselves they feel a sense of support and freedom derived from their adherences to common values. . . . They ask favors of one another much more readily than do Americans. Friendship is giving, and the Greek people understand that very well. . . . The Church gives identity and cohesion to the group who view themselves not only as Christians but Greek-Orthodox-Christians. The Church is not an organ for spiritual and social reform. . . . The Greek family is patriarchal-based with the husband making the important decisions and the wife running the household and raising children. There are cases where the wife works alongside her husband, and this is the trend among the younger couples. . . . Social mobility between the generations is apparently a reality for most Greeks. The climb upward isn't easy or startling. Some have found a handy formula for social advancement through mixed marriages. . . . This demonstrates that many Greek-Americans find the demand of an ethnic community difficult to accommodate. Some are very blunt about it and declare that they find the Greek Community confining, which it is, and want no part of it.*

*Source*: Georgia Kollintzas, "The Greek Community of East Chicago," in *Steel Shavings*, edited by James B. Lane and Ronald D. Cohen (Gary: Indiana University Northwest, 1976), pp. 20–23.

a central consideration for historians. For as historian Bernard Bailyn has remarked, "The essence and drama of history lie precisely in the relationship between latent conditions, which set the boundaries of human existence, and the manifest problems with which people consciously struggle." Sensitivity to both manifest and latent developments in pursuing the objectives of description, measurement of change, and analysis of cause and consequence is fundamental to any inquiry and essential to a strategy for devising the questions you wish to ask.

The following lists, which are far from complete, suggest focuses for inquiry and indicate some possible sorts of questions. A great many other questions can be raised about the nearby past in general or about any individual's particular nearby world. These simply raise some important issues which are common to most communities, usually answerable, and often exciting to explore. Some are straightforward and relatively simple inquiries; others are quite complex and formidable. The list is intended to demonstrate the range of possibilities and to stir thought. It is not meant to suggest that everyone can or ought to tackle each question. You definitely can make additions, deletions, and improvements using your own experiences, imagination, and judgment.

Questions are grouped in institutional or functional categories so that various facets of a general topic can be considered together. This arrangement hints at related issues which may be of interest and divides a potentially enormous catalog into manageable sections. Furthermore, the ordering of various elements of the immediate environment in this fashion allows the dimensions and possibilities of nearby history to be seen more plainly.

### The Family

The family is the most common and for many the most interesting element in the nearby world. Each one has its own history, the details of which are significant to its members and often to others as well. The following questions suggest the wide range of possible family structures, functions, and experiences.

#### Family relationships
Who was considered to be a member of the family?
What considerations were involved in the formation of a family unit,
    whatever form it took?

How did the people meet who eventually formed a couple?

What was the relative social and economic status of each member of the couple? What was the effect of any differences?

How did courtship and the decision to form a family occur?

If a couple later separated, why and how?

What were the respective roles of men and women in the family?

How and by whom were decisions made? Did males and females have different areas of responsibility for decision making?

How do men and women of different generations within the family compare in age at marriage, age at birth of first child, number of pregnancies and live childbirths, and age at birth of last child?

Was the birth of children evenly spaced, planned, or unexpected?

Where were children born?

What role, if any, did family members or outsiders—friends, neighbors, professionals—play in childbirth?

Family portraits can be revealing. They may contain clues to personalities, relationships, economic and social circumstances. Group photographs like this one prompt observers to use a magnifying glass to study the more than eighty individual portraits it contains. The occasion was the fiftieth wedding anniversary of the patriarch and his wife, on whom one's eye naturally falls.

How have child-rearing practices and the roles of mothers and fathers changed over the years?

How were children regarded before they were old enough to take care of themselves or to work?

What expectations regarding work and other responsibilities did each generation have for persons of different sexes and ages?

On what basis and at what age were persons considered to be adults?

How long did fathers and mothers continue to have authority over their sons and daughters?

Why and how did relationships between parents and children change as people aged?

How have separation, divorce, or death affected the family?

What family crises occurred and how were they handled?

Has the family had any dominant figures, superstars, outcasts, or embarrassments? What has been the relative esteem for men and women?

Who cared for sick, aged, or dependent family members?

What were the family's customs in the event of a death?

Where, if anyplace, were family members buried?

Who inherited what?

*Physical characteristics*

What did family members look like?

Were there any recurring physical characteristics (stature, complexion, or distinctive features, for example) that made family members similar in appearance?

What was the general condition of their health?

Did individuals or the family as a whole suffer from any chronic illnesses, mental problems, disabling injuries, or deformities?

Did men and women in the family generally live long lives or die young?

What relationship, if any, did the family maintain with a physician or other health services?

Were "home remedies" commonly used or passed along through the generations?

Did superstitions or old wives' tales play an important part in medical diagnosis and treatment?

*Location and movement*

Where has the family lived?

How and by whom were places of residence determined?

Who first migrated to the United States or to the community in which the family became more permanently located? Who followed?

Did the family move from place to place within the community?

Why were moves undertaken—to change jobs, for health reasons, to escape unsatisfactory conditions, or for other reasons?

How were moves made?

What difficulties did moving cause for various members of the family?

How was the place of origin remembered?

Did friends, boarders, or servants live with the family?

Did married sons or daughters continue to live in their parents' households?

Did elderly persons live in their own homes, with their children, in retirement communities, or in old-age homes?

Did related families live in the same neighborhood or community?


*Family economics*

How did members of the family earn a living?

Specifically, what kinds of work did they do as, for example, machine operators, small-business proprietors, clerks, farmers, secretaries, professional people, or executives?

How did their work change through the years, even though they held the same job?

How were occupational choices made?

What part did an individual's sex play in determining occupation, opportunity, family support, and success?

What were reasons for changing jobs?

Did family members help each other in obtaining jobs or in developing farms or businesses?

What were family members' relations with employers? With unions? With other workers, farmers, or business people?

Did they participate in strikes?

What was the family's general or evolving economic status?

Were all family members expected to bring all or part of their earnings home?

How and by whom were family finances decided and handled?

To what age and extent were sons and daughters supported financially?

What was the general outlook on material possessions?

How did the family cope with hard times?

Did charity or public assistance (welfare) provide part or all of the family's income?

How did the family feel about such measures?

What did family members feel about their economic status, ambitions for advancement, and "keeping up with the Joneses"?

*Daily living*

What were the daily routines of family members?

What were the roles and responsibilities of individual family members?

How was failure to conform to family expectations or values treated?

How did mothers and fathers decide upon and carry out discipline of sons and daughters?

How has the family's diet and clothing changed over the years?

How did changing technology affect the family; that is, when and how did such things as cars, refrigerators, telephones, radios, vacuum cleaners, televisions, microwave ovens, and so forth come into use, and what impact did they have?

What kind of family celebrations and reunions were held?

How were holidays and special occasions observed?

Did the family use alcoholic beverages routinely, on festive occasions, seldom, or not at all?

Did alcohol cause problems?

Who were family members' friends: relatives, neighbors, fellow workers, others of the same gender, ethnic group, or religion?

How were friendships formed and maintained?

In what kinds of social activities did the family engage?

To what churches and voluntary organizations did family members belong? What was the extent of their involvement, and what effects did this have?

How did they participate in the life of the community in which they lived?

What were their attitudes toward people in the community of other faiths, different ethnic or racial backgrounds, or lower and higher economic status?

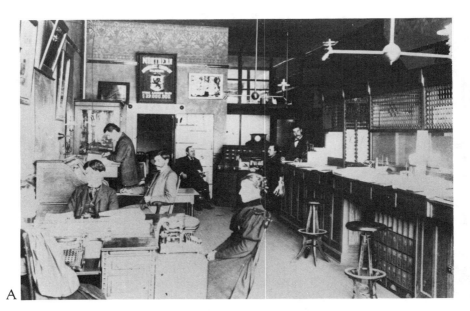

A

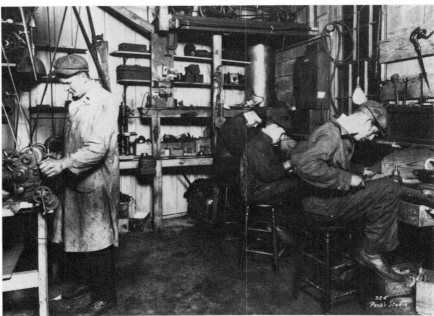

B

What can be learned from these pictures of an office (A), a factory (B), and a farm (C)?
What is indicated about the physical setting, work practices, equipment, and the workers
themselves?

C

*Education*

What sort of educational training took place within the family?

What value did the family place upon formal education?

Did expectations differ for boys and girls?

What level of schooling did family members achieve?

What schools did they attend?

Did they serve apprenticeships, undergo special training in the military, or obtain other nonschool education? If they went to college, what did they study?

What do they remember about their teachers?

What part did their education play in their later vocations and their avocations?

Did lack of education hinder them?

What unusual skills and abilities did they possess?

What attitudes did they have about persons less or better educated than themselves?

What encouragement did they offer to others in the family who sought schooling?

By what criteria—financial, educational, occupational, or social—did the family measure success?

*Military*

What was the nature and extent of military service by family members?

What were their attitudes about it?

What did they do during wartime?

What were their experiences with defense plants, war information and propaganda, rationing and price controls, war bond drives, changes in the community?

How did wars disrupt their lives?

What ties with military or service organizations were maintained once active duty ended?

What use was made of veterans' benefits?

How did attitudes toward wars and the military change through the years?

*Public affairs*

Did family members become involved in community affairs, charitable activities, reform movements, or local government?

How and why did they or did they not participate? Were some activities considered appropriate for only one sex? Why and to what effect?

What were their attitudes toward politics, political parties, and prominent local, state, and national political figures?

What was their political outlook (conservative, moderate, liberal, radical, erratic), and how was it shown in their political actions?

How did political views and actions differ within the family by age, sex, or other characteristics? What were the consequences of differences?

Did they participate in party activities? What party?

Did they benefit from being socially or politically active?

Did each generation follow the same pattern? Why or why not?

### Places of Residence

A house or apartment building can be a part of a family's past, but it can also have a history of its own.

#### Physical features

When was the building built?

Who designed and constructed the building?

What was its architectural style?

What were its dimensions?

How many rooms (and of what size) did it contain?

Did the building have porches or balconies?

Was it one of a kind, similar in style to others in the community, identical to others in the neighborhood constructed at the same time?

Did it ever undergo substantial remodeling or expansion? Why?

How was sleeping, living, and working space arranged?

How has the use of various rooms, porches, and balconies changed over time?

How was the building heated, cooled, and illuminated?

Did the building have fireplaces, indoor plumbing, electricity, or other features?

How was the house or apartment decorated and furnished?

How was the kitchen equipped?

How much property surrounded the building, and how was it used (farm, yard, garden, parking, business)?

What is the history of other structures on the property?

*Ownership and use*

Who lived in the building?

Was it owner occupied or rented?

Was it used for any purposes other than housing?

When and how did ownership of the property change?

Was it purchased outright, with mortgage loans, with government assistance?

How did the owners maintain the property?

Did owners and renters have conflicts?

Did local government agencies ever inspect or condemn the property?

Was it ever seized for nonpayment of taxes or mortgages?

## Neighborhood

A neighborhood can be a cohesive social unit or merely a geographical district. In either case, its history can help explain the presence of particular persons, structures, institutions, and problems; patterns of development; and relationships among those who reside there. The history of each family and residence in the neighborhood can be examined and compared in terms of all the questions already posed. In addition, significant questions may be asked about the neighborhood itself.

*Physical features*

How is the neighborhood defined?

What, if anything, is its central focus?

What are its boundaries, and what distinguishes it from the surrounding urban or rural area?

How and why has the size and shape of the neighborhood changed over the years?

What sorts of structures and open spaces could be found in the neighborhood at various stages in its history?

Was it built up gradually or all at once?

How and why have architectural styles varied or remained the same?

Has the use to which various structures have been put changed significantly?

Where did residents go to work, shop, obtain services, worship, and seek entertainment or recreation?

How did they travel?

What have been the important institutions in the neighborhood (parks, grange halls, churches, taverns, libraries, stores, shopping malls, schools, hospitals, others), and what has been their role in the neighborhood's history?

*Social features*

Who has lived in the neighborhood?

What family or other ties linked various households?

What ethnic, religious, occupational, social groups and economic classes have been represented? In what proportions?

Has this situation changed over time? Why or why not?

Has one group dominated?

Have various groups clashed?

What has caused people to move into and out of the neighborhood?

How and why have events, activities, or problems brought residents of the neighborhood together, if at all?

Have there been neighborhood parties, festivals, parades, or other celebrations?

How have neighborhood news and rumors traveled?

Have disapproved activities been conducted in the neighborhood (such as bootlegging, gambling, begging, vandalism, drug dealing, prostitution, or organized gangs)?

How has the neighborhood reacted?

Who have been the neighborhood's leading figures (a politician, religious leader, businessman, farmer, cop on the beat, school principal, or other)?

Why did they acquire influence, and how did they use it?

Has the neighborhood thought of itself as different from the rest of the community? Why? Or why not?

### Organizations

Institutions and organizations within the communities vary from place to place. They may be educational, religious, cultural, of a business, voluntary, or other nature. Some are quite common and others quite unusual. Their histories can be worthwhile and interesting and can also form an important part of the past of a neighborhood or an entire community. Some historical questions apply to almost all such bodies, while others relate to particular types.

*General characteristics*
When, how, by whom, and why was this institution or organization formed?
How and why did its structure, leadership, support, location, and purpose change over the years?
What were the pivotal events and issues in its past?
What role has the differentiation of sex roles played in its evolution?
What has been its influence in the community?
What have been its relationships with other bodies within and outside the community?
How have members, supporters, and employees of these bodies regarded themselves in relation to the rest of the community?
How has the community regarded them?
How and why have such attitudes changed over time?
If the institution or organization is no longer part of the community, why, when, and how did it decline, disband, or depart?

*Business*
In what sort of activities has this organization engaged throughout its history: agriculture, manufacturing, service, marketing, transportation, finance, or a combination of these?
Who has owned and managed this business over the years?
Were they local people?
Were employees hired locally or brought in? If the latter, from where?
How have business practices changed or remained constant?
What has been the business's history of relations with its employees? With unions? With government?
How has the business responded to changes in the economy (periods of prosperity, inflation, stagnation, or depression), technology, or markets?
How did the business view the community and act toward it?

*Education*
What educational institutions (public, private, parochial, preschools,

schools, colleges and universities, technical institutions, youth associations, and others) have existed in the community?

Who have been the teachers; and what have been their backgrounds, qualifications, methods, and ideas?

What has been the nature of the curriculum and extracurricular programs, buildings and other facilities, financial support, and special problems?

Have separate schools and school districts consolidated? When, why, and to what effect?

What special and separate programs and facilities have existed for non-English-speaking students, ethnic, racial, or religious minorities, migrant workers, handicapped or gifted persons, the wealthy, and other groups?

How has the pattern of school attendance varied?

What has been the history of mandatory attendance requirements?

How have schools been supervised, controlled, and supported?

Have school board elections been struggles over educational policies, financing, or other issues?

What does the physical appearance of a school suggest about the nature of the educational experience?

What have they revealed about community attitudes toward education and the school system?

If institutions of higher education are located in the community, what has been the "town-gown" relationship?

*Culture*

What cultural institutions (museums, libraries, theaters, performance groups, broadcasting stations, publications, and festivals) and styles have attracted local interest and support at various times?

What sorts of performances, exhibits, lectures, and other activities have these institutions held over the years?

Are the efforts of local artists, performers, and writers preferred to those from outside the community, or vice versa?

Have creative individuals born in the community tended to leave or stay?

Have outsiders been attracted to the place? Why or why not?

How have cultural organizations or activities influenced the rest of the community's life?

*Religion*

What religious groups and denominations have been present in the community?

What have been their beliefs and practices?

What has been the nature of their leadership, membership, facilities, and other characteristics over the years?

What splits and unions have occurred? Why?

What activities have religious groups engaged in individually and collectively?

How have they affected the life of the community?

Have particular religious groups sought community support and endorsement on specific issues, such as charity or civil rights drives, liquor restriction, Sunday business bans, abortion, school prayer, or censorship?

Has the general community treated religious groups by discriminating against them, isolating them, or according them leadership roles, or has there been some other response?

*Voluntary associations*

What fraternal, civic, patriotic, charitable, professional, recreational, social, political, or similar organizations have existed in the community?

Who have been members, and how were they selected or admitted?

Have the stated organizational purposes served primarily as excuses for the group to get together for social companionship, political cooperation, or other unofficial reasons?

How has the organization felt and acted toward other groups and the community as a whole?

How has the size, activity, and importance of the group changed over the years?

### Community

The community may, of course, include any and all of the individual elements already mentioned, but it also incorporates features which are shared by many if not all of its parts.

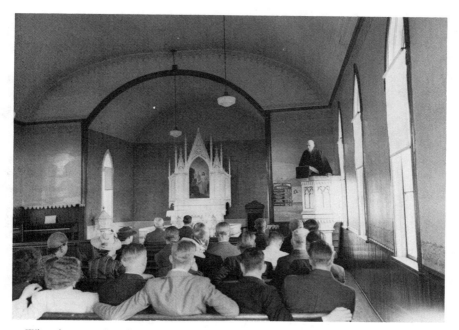

What does visual evidence suggest about this church? Consider the church's interior and its furnishings, the attendance register, and the attire of the minister and the congregation.

*Physical characteristics*

When and why was a community established in this location?

How did it acquire its name?

How has the location and landscape influenced the nature and direction of community growth?

How have transportation systems caused or been shaped by patterns of growth?

What factors have affected the location of commerce; industry; educational, social, and governmental facilities; parks and open space; differing types of neighborhoods; and other community features?

Have the centers of various activities shifted? If so, why?

When did the community obtain electricity, telephones, hardsurfaced roads, parking meters? What changes did this cause?

What architectural styles have been predominant at various times and why?

Have old buildings been regarded as treasures or as obstacles to progress?

The name chosen for a community may reflect the aspirations or identities of its founders, ties to another community, location, or other considerations. Discovering the reason for that name is a good way to begin an inquiry into the community's history.

*Social characteristics*

What has been the pattern of the community's population growth or decline?

What have been the major sources of immigration and the destinations of departing residents?

Has the population been stable, or has there been rapid turnover?

Has the community had significantly more or fewer children, aged, singles, males, or females than the national average at the time? To what effect?

What ethnic, racial, religious, and economic groups have made up the community, and how has the balance altered over the years?

What conflicts have occurred between groups in the community, and how have these been decided?

What events have produced displays of community pride or unity?

Have communitywide patterns of social, religious, cultural, recreational activity existed at any or all times?

Can community moral and social standards at various times be seen in low or high rates or out-of-wedlock childbirth, abortion, white-collar or street crime, prostitution, gambling, littering, child abuse, or other characteristics?

*Economic characteristics*

What has been the basis of the local economy?

How and why has this changed?

If the community has risen (or fallen) as a regional or national economic center, what have been the causes and effects?

How have individuals and groups, financial institutions, and local government influenced growth, stagnation, or decay?

What has been the history of labor unions locally?

How have business development associations, chambers of commerce, and consumer protection organizations arisen?

What have been their activities and effect in the community?

What has been the pattern of unemployment, and how has the community responded?

*Maintenance of order*

How has the community established and enforced its standards?

What has been the nature and rate of prohibited activity?

How has such activity compared with national norms?

Have changes in patterns of lawbreaking been related to changes in other community social or economic conditions or population shifts?

When, how, and why was a police force established? How has the ratio of police to population changed?

Who have been the police?

What techniques have they employed?

How well have they met community needs and demands, and in what public esteem have they been held?

How have police treated juvenile delinquency, prohibition violations, strikes, civil rights and antiwar demonstrations, gambling, white-collar crime, or prostitution?

Who have been the criminals?

How have the courts functioned?

How have judges been chosen and regarded?

Have sentencing patterns varied?

What changes have taken place in penalties and in the nature of penal institutions used by the community?

*Health*

What has been the nature of health problems in the community?

Have there been epidemics or unusual concentrations of particular afflictions?

What have been the community's standards and institutions of health care?

When and how were hospitals, nursing homes, hospices, abortion clinics, and other facilities established?

When did doctors and pharmacists appear to replace home remedies, specialists to replace general practitioners, group practices to replace individuals?

What public health programs developed?

When and how were water, sewer, and waste disposal systems created?

How have private groups and government agencies been involved with health issues, such as poor people's clinics, alcoholism and drug programs, birth control information, and abortions?

When did psychologists and psychiatrists begin to practice locally?

How have diagnosis, treatment, and community attitudes toward mental illness changed?

*Leadership and government*
Who have been the community's leaders?
How have they gained and held their positions?
In what fashion and to what extent do they exercise leadership?
How has gender, race, or some other characteristic entitled individuals or groups to leadership roles or excluded them?
Is effective community leadership exercised through government, business organizations, the media, ethnic, religious, or labor organizations, or some other device?
Under what circumstances and to what extent has local government or an alternative become the instrument for meeting community needs for public services (police and fire protection, utilities, street construction and cleaning, and so forth); parks and recreation facilities; care for the impoverished, troubled, handicapped, aged, or otherwise dependent; and community land use planning and development?
To what extent have local elections addressed and resolved conflicts and reflected community concerns?

### Functional Categories

By dividing the community into many of its component parts and then raising questions about each, we may usefully call attention to many features which have evolved and changed over time. Another way of approaching the study of the community's history involves thinking in terms of *functional categories* applicable to a wide variety of situations. Doing so will not only suggest additional significant questions but will also help link some of the elements already mentioned.

*Environmental setting*
How has the natural situation, the climate and the terrain, influenced the distribution of space and the design of buildings?
How have each of these factors influenced family, neighborhood, and community life?

Sudden community growth has causes and consequences, both of which need to be investigated if the development process is to be understood. In William F. King's short history of California's San Gabriel Valley, the introduction of an adequate and dependable water system, the start of a profitable citrus fruit industry, and the completion of a second railroad into the area, turning a monopoly into an intensely competitive situation, were identified as the causes of population influx and land boom in the 1880s.

*More than any other east valley city, Pomona embraced the boom spirit and thrived upon it. Of course, the town had a considerable head start on most of its neighbors in the struggle to become worthy of the name "city." Pomonans welcomed the prospect of being a large enough city to have "suburbs" like Lordsburg and Palomares.*

*Several promotional pamphlets attracted people to Pomona. . . . Attention centered on the climate, agriculture, homes, land prices and the citizenry's quality. The railroad poster exhibited the more outlandish side of boom publicity. It failed to mention that millions of acres of available government land were located in the desert or mountain regions, or that earthquakes had replaced cyclones as a natural hazard.*

*In the pre-boom days of 1885, Pomona had boasted a population of 2,000. During the peak of the boom, the figure approached 4,000. Some of this later melted away, but real growth in the late eighties topped 80%. Naturally, everything else enlarged to meet the needs of the people. Many years passed before other east valley towns had the capital necessary to form a bank. The Pomona Valley Bank, later the First National, opened in 1886 under the leadership of President Carlton Seaver. The bank erected a small, safe brick building at the corner of Main and Second Streets. One of the first equipment purchases was two sawed-off shotguns. Within a few years the Pomona bank listed deposits of $200,000. There were few phones in the valley then, but Pomona had three of them located in the Palomares Hotel, the bank, and Armour's Drugstore. The company providing the service was the Sunset Telephone and Telegraph Company.*

*During the first stages of growth Pomona enlarged its two-story Central School and later built three new schools. By the end of the decade, ten churches served the people. The outstanding example of boom-year churches was the remodeled Pomona Methodist Church. Now operated by the Seventh Day Adventist denomination, this splendid building, the core of which was the 1877 building, offers a strong example of the building style of that era.*

*Along with the normal events accompanying growth, unusual happenings enlivened Pomona's growth. While the town seemingly welcomed all newcomers, certain exceptions existed. In March of 1886 a branch of the Nonpartisan Anti-Chinese League formed under the leadership of William T. (Tooch) Martin. This was a part of the statewide anti-Asian movement. While some spoke out against the movement, calling it anti-Christian, Martin and a large number of citizens persisted. A boycott on Chinese workers, shops, and goods brought the desired result. Finally the Chinese abandoned their homes and businesses and fled the city. A few relocated in nearby Lordsburg and San Dimas. A by-product of this exercise in prejudice was the incorporation of the Pomona Steam Laundry. In order to compete with the Chinese laundry shops in town, Charles I. Lorbeer and J. B. Clump opened the sizeable plant via an open stock sale.*

The long term as well as the immediate effects of the 1880s boom were important.

*Although the boom inevitably collapsed, the soundness of the agrarian sector of the local economy prevented a true disaster. In fact, the boom marked the birth pangs of southern California as a population center. A large number of towns trace their origin to this period and the growth momentum generated by this influx of residents, while slowing in the nineties, endured so long it became virtually permanent, a standard part of southern California's folklore in the twentieth century.*

*Source*: William F. King, *The Vintage Years: Our Valley before 1945* (Walnut, California: Mt. San Antonio College, Department of Community Services, 1975), pp. 43, 52–53.

How have various community elements shaped the environment?
What has been the impact on the environment, land use, and architectural styles of technological change, alteration of economic activity and conditions, and shifts in values or political power?

*Economic activity*
At the personal, group, and community levels, what has been involved in the creation or acquisition of wealth?
How have economic activities served to integrate and divide?
What economic ideas have been held, and how have they influenced

choices of activity, competition and cooperation, distribution of wealth, decisions on taxation and investment, and other matters?

How has the economy shaped the social, political, and cultural environment?

*Social relations*

What has been the nature of social relationships among various elements in the community?

What conditions of wealth, religion, race, ethnicity, gender, education, and occupation gave individuals and groups greater or lesser status and influence?

What social factors have contributed to tension and conflict, harmony and cooperation?

How stable has the social structure been?

What has caused change?

How are social distinctions important in community life-styles (diet, dress, housing, associations, and activities); religion; values, beliefs, and practices; and political behavior?

*Political affairs*

What political issues and movements have arisen in the community?

How and why have they aroused, divided, or united individuals, neighborhoods, or groups within the community?

How and why have various elements in the community responded to reform proposals; local or national appeals from parties and individual candidates; and specific crises such as depressions, wars, communist scares, public school desegregation, revelations of political abuses?

What have been the patterns of participation and preference in elections?

How have defeated individuals and groups responded and been treated?

*Ideals and values*

What ideas and values have been highly regarded by individuals, families, neighborhoods, particular elements, and the community as a whole?

How have beliefs conflicted—and changed—regarding conduct, property, power, and privilege?

Have the dominant ideas come from local proponents or from outsiders?

How have creative and unconventional persons been regarded?

How have those holding various views promoted their ideas and beliefs?

How have changes in technology, education, or other conditions altered values regarding work, play, religion, society, culture, courtship, sex roles, child rearing, sexual activity, privacy, conformity, or authority?

Armed with a well-chosen focus and specific questions, historians of the nearby world are ready to search for information regarding the past that they seek to understand.

## Notes

Bernard Bailyn is quoted in Michael Kammen, "The Historian's Vocation and the State of the Discipline in the United States," in Kammen, ed., *The Past before Us: Contemporary Historical Writing in the United States* (Ithaca: Cornell University Press, 1980), p. 38.

# ·3·

# Traces and Storytelling

HISTORIANS TELL STORIES. THE STORIES MAY BE COMPLEX, highly analytical, or strongly interpretive and may be told in many different ways, but they are stories nonetheless. In this chapter we examine how they are built, particularly the kinds that historians of the nearby past seek to tell.

The invention of a story begins with the desire to learn, to discover. Indeed, "history" is rooted in a Greek word meaning "to inquire." A spirit of inquiry sends one looking for materials to reconstruct history and shapes the way they are used. But telling a story, more than merely describing the past, means interpreting its significance, which explains why the process involves more than a tale or an anecdote.

Good storytellers are conscious of the meaning of their stories and know why they are told. The reason may be the desire to communicate a lesson; in the case of a church, for example, it might be discovered that the parish was strong and growing when it was in debt and weak and declining when it was solvent. There are obvious hazards, of course, in defining such cause-and-effect relationships, good reminders to us that the lessons of history are not as easy to find as one might think and that, once found, they should not be pushed too far.

Some stories are told to answer questions. What was it like to live in another time or place? Or on a more profound level, What does it mean to be human? How does being a part of this community affect one's humanness? Sometimes stories are means of leaving a record to be passed on or merely a way to satisfy curiosity. Anniversaries or milestones may call for remembrance of past heroes and heroics, and meaning may lie in the spirit and pride such stories build. Whatever their purpose, good storytellers are mindful of the questions of their listeners or readers. They recognize, too, that frequently the telling must arouse a spirit of inquiry in people who might otherwise be indifferent.

Sometimes historians find it difficult to direct their inquiry or even to start it. In such instances it helps to have a first question, an opener. The previous chapter suggested many possibilities, but the most natural and intriguing concerns origins: What conditions gave birth to the town, for example, or who were the founders of the church? Where did the family start in America? When did the community first see itself as a community? Who designed the house? Who began the business? Simple answers to these questions, followed by elaboration, of course, often help storytellers over a formidable barrier—that of putting down the first words. Some people find it useful to start with a question about origins even though they know that both the question and the answer may be drastically reshaped or even discarded as the work progresses. The important thing is to get the story under way.

To keep an inquiry moving, you must know the direction in which you intend to carry it. If you are writing about an institution, for example, you will want to touch on its high and low points, its developing organizational structure, its leaders, or its unique character. Stories about families or communities invite questions about their distinctive features. If you are writing about a business, you are certain to be interested in its successes and failures. If your subject is a building, you will want to know who occupied it, how it was used, when and why it changed hands, and what was unusual about it.

Some of the questions you raise will focus on people. Some will be concerned with time and place. People, time, and place come together in events and ideas and lie at the heart of all good stories. The effective storyteller finds ways of reconstructing events, describing them, explaining them, relating them to ideas, linking them together, and interpreting their meaning. Whether events are tied together chronologically or unfold around a central theme or through some other scheme, the focus of a good story is always on individuals, events, and ideas. Ordinarily they pose issues to be explored and problems to be solved, or they fall together in sequences, which we might call developments, to be analyzed and interpreted. The good storyteller makes description, explanation, analysis, problem solving, and interpretation integral parts of the story. But these parts serve to bring the events and ideas into focus; they are not the focus itself.

A

B

These pictures record milestones in the growth and progress of a church. A small group of people began to worship in a real estate tract office in 1931. Three years later, they moved the building (View A) to a new location and remodeled it (View B). In 1939 they enlarged the structure (View C) while planning for the building of a permanent church building. A partial building was opened in 1949 (not shown) and was used while the money was raised

C

D

to complete it. Completion came in 1955 (View D). A large wing (not shown) was added to the building in 1962. During these three decades of growth, the congregation was dynamic and distinctive. A historian would seek not only to identify the motivations and to describe the character of the congregation during the growth years but also to determine what happened to it during the subsequent decades of stability and decline.

A story may be passed from one person to another before it is written down, as in this case. Details can be lost or altered. The careful historian seeks to verify such stories before accepting them but at the same time recognizes that they are rich with traces. The vivid details of this tale, for instance, provide information about a farm family's diet, money, and way of obtaining news. Would the storytellers have had reason to distort such matters?

*Uncle Martin and my father liked to tell about how Grandmother sold a loaf of bread for five dollars. They had lived out on the prairie for a number of years. Late one afternoon two rough-looking men on horseback rode into the yard. The boys saw them coming and did not like their looks, so they ran into the hay shed that stood out by the road and hid. They peeked out of a hole in the shed and watched. One man got off his horse and went to the house. When Grandmother opened the door, he asked her if she would sell him a loaf of bread. Grandmother told him, "I have no bread but black, dark bread."*

*"Nothing wrong with dark bread!" the man said. "Will you sell me a loaf?" Grandmother went and got one of her big loaves of graham flour bread. She had just taken it out of the oven about an hour before. It was still warm. The man felt of it with his finger and asked, "Will you sell it?"*

*Grandmother put the loaf in a sack and laid it on the table. The man laid down a five dollar bill. Grandmother shook her head and said, "I has no change for money like that."*

*"Lady," he told her, "nobody will ask you for change," and picked up the bread and walked out. They rode off down the trail towards the southwest. The boys watched them go down across the creek and up and over the hill until they were lost from sight on the prairie.*

*A few days later three men rode into the yard. One of them got off his horse and came towards the shed. The boys came out. They could see his big bright star on his coat. He said he was a sheriff from Minnesota and he wondered if they had seen two men on horseback go riding along the trail? They told him that they had seen two men going southwest about two days ago. "We're on their trail," the sheriff told his men. They did not seem to be in any hurry and slowly rode down the trail toward the southwest.*

*The next week when they got their weekly paper it said that Jessie James and his partner had robbed a bank up in Minnesota. A sheriff had chased them all the way across Iowa and then lost their trail down in Missouri.*

*Source*: Guy Johnson, "The Boy on Kiegley's Creek," unpublished manuscript in the possession of the authors.

## Finding Historical Traces

Writers of fiction tell stories, too, but they can draw material from their imaginations. Historians, in contrast, try to work with real events as they happened. Doing so requires the imaginative use of particular abilities.

The most important of these special capabilities has to do with the traces events have left behind. Traces are the remains, tracks, marks, records, remnants, relics, and footprints of events. Historians need to know how to find the traces, how to sort them out, how to establish their authenticity, credibility, and importance, and how to assemble them to reconstruct events. In turn, historians must know how to combine events in a chronological sequence or some other way, to relate them to ideas, and in so doing to build a story that is history.

It is important, therefore, to examine traces systematically and to formulate some rules for evaluating them. Because everything around us bears the mark of past events, the first distinction to be drawn is between historical and nonhistorical traces. There is no absolute or objective distinction between them, for it is the interest of a historian that makes remains historical. Nonhistorical traces are those that historians regard as of no use in probing or reconstructing events of the past. What is historical to one person, therefore, may well seem nonhistorical to another. Or what is nonhistorical at one time might be regarded as historical at another.

The point of the distinction is that it helps historians confront the need to sift and sort the materials they work with. Without the ability and willingness to draw distinctions and make selections, a would-be historian is paralyzed. If *everything* is pertinent to a story, it is almost as if nothing is. Selecting historical traces for their authenticity, reliability, accuracy, credibility, and usefulness in relation to the topic under consideration is the most important task we must face after choosing a topic for research. Dismissing nonhistorical traces allows us to proceed with our work.

Historical traces may be divided into four categories: immaterial, material, written, and representational. Immaterial traces are intangible but clearly apparent remnants from the past, such as institutions, customs, traditions, beliefs, principles, practices, superstitions, legends, and language. The history we study—that is, the past as it has been processed by historians—is itself an immaterial trace. The word "immaterial" carries with it neither a positive nor a negative implication but simply denotes traces that we discern rationally rather than through our sensory perceptions alone.

Material traces, easier to grasp, consist of objects, things, artifacts of the past, products of human doings. In the sense that they are the culmination of a series of activities, they are themselves events. Their sale or exchange is an event which might leave another trace, such as a bill of sale or a title. Some material traces are still in use, even though they may be "antiquated." They range in size from the very small—a jewel, perhaps—to very large. Buildings and landscapes, for example, are material remains of events and sequences of events. So are such things as tools, machinery, vehicles, paintings, sculpture, clothing, and furniture.

Written traces come in many varieties. Some may be handwritten, such as letters, diaries, journals, and manuscripts. Newspapers, books, magazines, and pamphlets are printed traces. Some may be partly printed and partly handwritten, such as immigration papers, birth and marriage certificates, report cards, and business and financial forms. Sometimes written traces are a part of material ones, such as inscriptions on tombstones, engravings on jewelry, and labels on clothing.

The fourth kind of trace is both a real thing, having tangible, sensory presence, and a representation of something else. For want of a better term, we call this a "representational" trace. The best example is a photograph. It is itself a trace, and it captures and preserves other traces. An entire chapter in this book is devoted to consideration of visual documents as historical traces.

Representational traces are also found in ballads, folksongs, and folktales. They are immaterial in one sense, but they are perceived sensorily, capable of being written down or captured on tape or disc recordings. Like photographs, they convey information, ideas, or sentiments; they are of inherent interest and at the same time they represent something else.

There are yet other ways of categorizing traces. Historians must be mindful that some traces are intentional; they were created for the specific purpose of leaving a record. Some people, for example, know that someday their diaries are likely to be read by someone else, which explains why such documents are sometimes tied closed and placed in family archives with a stipulation that says something like : "Not to be opened until ten years after my death or March 31, 2001, whichever comes later." But determining the writer's intentions can be tricky, for some people use daily jottings as cheap therapy, while others regard them as personal historical records. If papers are found with orders that they must be destroyed at their keeper's death, historians face an ethical problem as well as a methodological one.

Some historical traces, mainly material ones, are clearly unpremeditated. Tools, for example, are made to be used, not to establish a record. Most artifacts are mute, existing first of all for their own sake, which does not relate to their later use by historians to establish or reconstruct events. Public records initially serve purposes quite different from those to which historians later put them. A birth certificate, a college diploma, a marriage license, business forms, and a death certificate have specific legal functions. The uses historians make of them—to place persons geographically, to confirm employment records, or to determine turning points in lives—are quite apart from their intended purposes. Presumably, such traces are more reliable factually than are those created to help later historians tell a story. The people who created them had no interest in directing the work of historians or in shaping conclusions.

But the distinction between intentional and unpremeditated traces is often largely artificial. A letter in its original form, especially one that is handwritten, might be regarded as unpremeditated, but if a copy is made and filed, it is intended for later use as the historical trace of an event. (One wonders, incidentally, whether the easy access to photocopiers has made writers more conscious of the possibility that their letters might be preserved, prompting them to write more obviously for the record.) On the other hand, a genealogy may be an intentional transmitter of fact; the compiler may see it as an outline of a family's passage through time. Historians may use it for all kinds of other purposes, such as locating the routes by which a family has moved from place to place, measuring patterns in life spans or determining the stability of nuclear families and the closeness of extended families. The purpose of a church charter, a public record, is to authorize a congregation to hold property as a legal corporate entity or make tax-exempt status possible. A historian examines such a document for clues to the congregation's beliefs, its sense of order, its relations with the denomination of which it is a member, and its leadership at a given point in time.

So it is better to evaluate traces as both intentional and unpremeditated sources of information than to assume that they are one or the other or that one kind is to be preferred over the other in establishing the truth about events. How to establish the authenticity, reliability, veracity, and usefulness of specific kinds of traces is the concern of other chapters in this book.

# MARRIAGE LICENSE.

## STATE OF ARKANSAS.

County of *Randolph*

To any Person Authorized by Law to Solemnize Marriage, Greeting:

*You are hereby commanded to solemnize the rite and publish the bans of Matrimony between Mr.* Charles Plonk *of* Biggers *in the County of* Randolph *and State of* Arkansas *aged* 21 *years, and Miss* Minnie Barhm *of* Biggers *in the County of* Randolph *and State of* Arkansas *aged* 19 *years, according to Law; and do you officially sign and return this License to the parties herein named.*

*Witness my hand and official seal this* 3rd *day of* Dec *19 04*

Ben F. Spikes *County Clerk*
By Ben E. Johnston *D.C.*

## CERTIFICATE OF MARRIAGE.

*State of Arkansas*
*County of* Randolph *§ I* C. D. Jones *do hereby certify that on the* 4th *day of* December 19 04 *I did duly and according to law as commanded in the foregoing License solemnize the rite and publish the bans of Matrimony between the parties therein named.*
*Witness my hand this* 4 *day of* December 19 04
*My Credentials are recorded in Recorder's Office*
*County* Ark *Book* *Page*

C. D. Jones J. P.

NOTE--This License with the Certificate duly executed and officially signed, must be returned to the office whence it is issued within sixty days from the date of License, under penalty of forfeiture of the License.

What factual information can be drawn from this legal document? What does the picture on it suggest about marriage ideals at the turn of the century? Descendants of this couple discovered that the family names of both the bride and the groom appear in census data with variant spellings through the years. What might account for the variations?

# CERTIFICATE OF RECORD.

STATE OF ARKANSAS,

County of *Randolph* I, *Ben F. Spikes*

Clerk of the County Court of said County, certify that the above License

for and Certificate of the Marriage of Mr. *Charles Plunk*

and Miss *Minnie Barton* was filed in my office on the

*6* day of *Dec* 1902 and the same is duly recorded on page

*276* of Book *14* of Marriage Records.

WITNESS my hand and the seal of said Court this *6*

Seal here

day of *Dec* 1904

*Ben F. Spikes* Clerk

by *Ben E. Johnston* D.C.

MARRIAGE CERTIFICATE.

Mr. *Charles Plunk*

TO

Miss *Minnie Barton*

Recorded Book *14* Page *276*

Returned and filed this *6* day of 1902

*Dec*

*Ben F. Spikes* Clerk

## Using Historical Traces

Still, some general guidelines for the use of traces can be summarized here. First, their relationships to events must be clearly established. The best and most useful records are those nearest in time and place to the event. Thus an account by an eyewitness written the day of an event is ordinarily to be preferred to a recollection years later by someone who received it second-hand. Then, too, the questions asked of the evidence should be ones that it can answer. Do not expect a physical object, for example, to reveal its worth, either at the time of its creation or at any later period. External evidence is required to make such determinations. Third, the traces must always relate to events in affirmative and identifiable ways; inferences drawn from the absence of traces are highly questionable. Suppose a family had the tradition of recording its Christmas gatherings with family portraits. Would a gap in the series of portraits indicate that no gathering had occurred? Not necessarily.

Fourth, while traces may be presented in open or unprocessed form, that is, without interpretation, the historian has the responsibility of declaring their authenticity and potential usefulness. As historians must be careful that they do not put evidence to unwarranted uses, so they must carefully protect it from improper uses by others. For example, one might want to include in a publication a facsimile of an interesting letter containing choice bits of information. Suppose, though, that the letter is undated and was written by someone of unascertained identity. The historian must not only advise readers of these facts but must lay out the external evidence that lends credence to or challenges the plausibility and usefulness of the information in the letter. Fifth, because traces do not exist in isolation, they may not be used without regard for their context. Thus in using an item drawn from the minutes of an organization, a historian must take into account the character and completeness of the minutes, the range of issues with which they deal, the recording practices of the secretary, the circumstances of their preservation, and other matters pertaining to the topic under consideration.

Finally, since it is impossible to reconstruct events in precise form—to provide, so to speak, instant replays—historians' inferences about events must always be expressed as probabilities. Although the aim should be, of course, to describe in terms that are completely accurate, historians must content themselves with conclusions comparable to those acceptable in a court of law, that is, findings that seem plausible "beyond a reasonable doubt." In other words, when absolute and incontrovertible proof is lacking, a verdict may be regarded as highly probable if evidence to contradict it does not exist or has been discredited or neutralized. It is appropriate to apply this rule in a consideration of historical traces, for traces are historical evidence. Indeed, most historians use the word "evidence" rather than "traces."

## Acquiring Skills

It is certainly clear by now that those who do the history of communities, towns, neighborhoods, cities, clubs, churches, houses, landscapes, artifacts, and other things in their own locale must be more than historians in the traditional sense. Besides knowing how to tell a story based on real events, they must know how to gather and make the most of a wide variety of traces. Working with documents, many of which they collect and preserve themselves, demands archival skills. But historians must also pick up fieldwork skills such as those used by cultural anthropologists and folklorists. Concerns with terrain, landforms, landscapes, cityscapes, building forms, maps, and measuring devices puts them next to historical and cultural geographers. Locating, extracting (literally and figuratively), analyzing, cataloging, and preserving artifacts requires historians to learn, at least in rudimentary ways, the skills of archaeologists, museologists, and curators. And as historians, they must become conversant in social history, the history of art and architecture, and possibly even psychohistory.

## Sharpening Perceptions

Before we turn in separate chapters to specific kinds of evidence historians look for, let us suggest a first step to be taken by those wishing to become better historians of things nearby. As we noted earlier, historical traces surround us. Yet we may not see them because we are not looking for them. If it is true, as Thoreau remarked, that "you can't say more than you see," it seems useful to suggest ways of expanding the powers of perception—and thus also the trace-gathering powers—in the course of daily living. On one level people can simply heighten their awareness of the natural and cultural environments in which they move; on another, actual practice with real or imaginary tools is needed.

We come to know our natural and cultural environments through our

How many traces of two different communities' distinctive characteristics during the 1930s are contained in these two photographs of Atlanta, May 1938 (View A), and Cleveland, August 1937 (View B)?

senses, as we see, hear, smell, touch, and taste. Psychologists may disagree as to exactly how the sensory processes work, but there seems to be a relationship between perception and our knowledge of the language that describes it. For example, our sense of taste becomes sharper as we learn words for taste. Even the four basic tastes—sweet, sour, salty, and bitter— are apparently learned, since there seem to be no corresponding physiological sensors. The language of taste is actually much larger, including as it does tart, sharp, flinty, tangy, mellow, rich, and bland. When we add texture words such as crisp, fluffy, light, succulent, dry, crunchy, and gooey, our ability to express and to distinguish is enlarged further. Those who would dispute the relationship between language and taste need only to be asked whether their mouth waters when they hear words describing foods they like.

Perhaps the most important sense that historians use is the visual. Learning the language of seeing and putting it to work while walking or driving or flying is a way of expanding powers of perception and therefore a way to improve one's capacity to observe traces effectively. Concentrating on ten terms in the language of vision and looking for places to use them in the environment is a first step: light and shadow; color and texture; lines, shape, and patterns; similarities and contrasts; and movement.

Suppose you set out to use the language of vision in ordinary places to describe things you have never noticed before. You might begin with foundry art—fire hydrants and manhole covers, sturdy sentries of the landscape and guardians of secrets of the underground. Besides noticing their shapes, colors, patterns, and textures, you might also take note of the dates you find on them. And as you do this, think about what you might learn from hydrants and manhole covers about patterns of residential growth in your community. Notice the shapes of the numbers in the dates. And then carry this awareness to other places. Take note, too, of differently formed dates chiseled into cornerstones, perhaps, or painted on the side of a delivery truck declaring "since 1921." Look for clues in these numbers to insights regarding the community's past.

While you are looking at numbers you might look at letters as well, not only for the messages they communicate, but for their shapes and the patterns in which they appear. Your eyes will turn to billboards, of course, giving you a chance to do another exercise. Try to imagine how the landscape would appear without them. You might then look at nonverbal signs, particularly arrows. Notice the orders they give as well as the confusing symbols they sometimes are. Do the same with barriers: fences, walls, roadblocks, guardrails, barrels. What were the purposes of those who erected them? What attitudes do they suggest?

Places to study the language of vision are endless. Look at the texture of buildings, streets, and sidewalks, at public sitting places, at gingerbread or fanciwork on houses, at the geometric interplay of shapes on bridges as you move across them, at the recurrence of forms such as circles and squares, at patterns in grillwork. In all of these things, keep in mind the words in the language of vision, consciously trying to increase your sensitivity to them. And then go a step further by observing how your sense of vision is sharpened or otherwise affected by messages from your other senses—perhaps the blowing wind, the roar of the traffic, the pounding of machines, the splash of a fountain, the stench of a smokestack, or the drifting aroma of a barbecue grill.

And take still another step by picking up a camera and looking at the world through a lens. If nothing else, doing this exercise increases your capacity to concentrate on the narrow piece of the environment you are observing. The camera provides a frame, eliminating for a moment extraneous distractions and reducing your subject from three dimensions to two. If carrying a camera is inconvenient, simply cut a rectangle in the center of a card and use it to frame your subject. Increasing or reducing the distance between your eye and the card has some of the same effect as changing the lens on your camera or repositioning yourself in relation to your subject. Practicing with a camera will have another beneficial effect on your work as a historian, for you will start looking at photographs more intelligently and more critically.

Traces are also found by listening. Being aware of the language of hearing—pitch, volume, and timbre—may be helpful in sharpening your listening skills. More important, though, is the ability to concentrate on the words that reach your ear. A trace-gathering technique of historians is the oral interview, usually conducted with a tape recorder so that the conversation may be reviewed and transcribed later. One can practice interviewing by simulating, perhaps in the privacy of one's automobile, the technique of radio talk-show hosts. The trick is to formulate questions that build on the previous answer and at the same time elicit information you would genuinely want to have. Second-guess the interviewer; listen critically to the responses. Not all such practice, we should add, needs to be done in covert ways. The best way to learn the art of interviewing involves a real tape recorder, a live microphone, and another person.

It is also possible to heighten one's sensitivity to written historical traces. One might, for example, take the simple step of creating personal or family archives by pulling together all papers, records, photo albums, certificates, letters, diaries, income tax and other forms, house plans, scrapbooks, and such things. This project may also prompt you to file in your archives photocopies of the most valuable such items and to place the originals in a safe deposit box along with negatives of your photographs.

You might also consider keeping a daily journal of your activities and thoughts or at least filing a copy of letters you write. Doing so will not only help you preserve a record but will make you conscious of practical distinctions between intentional and unpremeditated traces as well. It may also

In studying the traces found in this picture of a slice of man's world, notice the place of women in it. What would a comparable picture from woman's world in this small town reveal?

help you to realize that while long-distance phone calls may be convenient, they leave no traces for the records; as a result you might even become a better letter writer.

This chapter is a general introduction to traces, events, and storytelling. We believe that doers of local history should begin where their competence and interest are greatest. Consequently, the seven chapters which follow have been written so that they can be used independently or in any sequence that best responds to the user's needs. We will return to the matter of trace gathering and storytelling in chapter 11, where we will use the more formal terms "research" and "writing."

## For Further Information

Because the succeeding chapters contain many references to works that show how to find and use traces and an entire chapter is devoted to research and writing, the list of references here is brief. The book that develops most effectively the idea of traces in the work of historians is G. J. Renier's *History: Its Purpose and Method* (1950; reprint ed., New York: Harper and Row, 1965). Allan Lichtman and Valerie French describe and assess current methods in *Historians and the Living Past: The Theory and Practice of Historical Study* (Arlington Heights, Ill.: AHM, 1978). In *Historians' Fallacies: Toward a Logic of Historical Thought* (New York: Harper and Row, 1970), David Hackett Fischer discusses with wit and insight historians' uses and misuses of traces. A good introduction to ways of heightening one's perceptual abilities is found in George Nelson's *How to See: A Guide to Reading Our Manmade Environment* (Boston: Little, Brown, 1977).

A journal that will be cited frequently in the following pages is *History News*, published since 1946 by the American Association for State and Local History (708 Berry Road, Nashville, Tennessee 37204); the format of the journal was enlarged significantly in January 1980. Each issue contains a removable "technical leaflet" dealing with a specialized topic. Many of these leaflets are cited in later bibliographies.

# ·4·

# Published Documents

A DOCUMENT IS RECORDED INFORMATION IN ANY FORM. Whether the information is handwritten, typed or printed on paper, etched on glass or metal, carved on wood or stone, or impressed on film, audiotape, or computer disk, it speaks of its moment of origin. Documents can often be the most direct and reliable link with an earlier day, preserving eyewitness observations, capturing sights and sounds, or tabulating conditions of the time. Indeed, sometimes the only surviving trace of a past event, individual, or circumstance may be recorded in a letter or diary, office memorandum or ledger, newspaper, photograph, map, or cemetery marker, all of which have different historical uses, values, and limitations that are worthy of consideration.

The utility and reliability of documents vary nearly as much as their form. The circumstances of creation, intended purposes, and preservation all influence historic value. This chapter and the three which follow examine different types of documents. The first sort to be considered is produced in multiple copies and is typically found in scattered locations. The following chapter will deal with one-of-a-kind documents, individually created, which are usually to be found in private hands, office files, or archives. Next, chapter 6 will examine records on audiotape or in written transcripts of interviews with participants in (or eyewitnesses to) past events, so-called oral histories or oral documents. Finally, separate consideration will be given to visual documents—in particular photographs—because of their distinctive values and problems. These four chapters not only indicate the worth of documents in exploring the past but also suggest the sorts of evidence of contemporary life that ought to be preserved for future generations.

Since the act of recording information creates a document, the circumstances in which the act is performed need to be considered first in any evaluation.

> Was it a hasty, spur-of-the-moment act, a routine transaction, or a thoughtful, deliberate process?
>
> Did the recorder possess firsthand knowledge of whatever was being described or simply report what he or she was told?
>
> Was the recorder a neutral party or did he or she have interests which could be positively or negatively affected by what was recorded?
>
> Did the recorder intend the document for his or her own use, for one or more selected individuals, or for a larger audience of one sort or another?
>
> Was the recorder's intention merely to inform, or was it to persuade the reader?
>
> Was the information recorded immediately or only after time had passed, causing memories to change or fade?

Obviously, one's confidence in the accuracy of any document depends upon the answers to these questions. The circumstances of creation are ultimately much more important than the form of the document, but the form provides clues about the circumstances of creation. The form also determines how easy or difficult it can be to extract desired information, whatever the creator's intent.

Some documents are intended for a wide audience and are therefore prepared and distributed in multiple copies; in other words, they are published. This category includes books, magazines, newspapers, pamphlets, government reports, laws and judicial decisions, catalogs, directories, posters, and maps. The very fact that they would initially have been produced in quantity, for distribution, increases the likelihood that some copies have survived and will be available. Local libraries usually make a practice of gathering published materials regarding the area they serve, but churches, businesses, civic and professional organizations, government agencies, and individuals may have collections as well. Indeed, it may prove easier to find publications pertaining to the nearby past than to evaluate them.

The normal way to locate published materials is to consult library catalogs, union lists (compilations of materials in a group of libraries), and specialized reference guides. Most libraries maintain a catalog in which every book in their collection has one card headed by the author's name (last name first), another with the book's title, and often still others with the book's major topics. All of the cards are arranged alphabetically, often in separate author-title and subject files. Newspapers, serials or periodicals, and government publications are sometimes listed separately, sometimes included in the main catalog. Already some libraries have replaced or supplemented their card files with a computer, and more can be expected to do so before long. The computer responds to inquiries typed on a keyboard by displaying information on a screen. In any case, it is fairly easy to locate books devoted to local topics through title or subject listings, either on one's own or with help from a librarian (especially if a computer is involved).

Subject catalogs can simplify and speed a search for information on a particular topic, as can indexes to reference works and other publications, but they vary widely in coverage. Some are extremely thorough and specific; others are limited to proper names, titles, or major topics. Furthermore, catalogers and indexers may have applied different labels to a single topic. "Liquor control" to one person could be "temperance movement" to another and "prohibition" to a third. One city may have been listed in one index as "Richmond, Indiana," and in another as "Indiana—Richmond." It is important to consider all possible listings and alphabetic locations for a topic. If entries do not appear in a catalog or index as expected, it makes sense to browse in the appropriate section of library shelves or to search the table of contents for a promising section of text. Catalogs and indexes are great time savers if they are used with imagination and caution so that material is not overlooked.

## Books and Articles

Nearby history documents which often take the form of books and articles include memoirs, genealogies, travel accounts, biographies, edited letters, speeches, and public records, and histories. An individual's recollections, a traveler's description of things seen and conditions encountered, or a published letter, speech, or official report may reveal many details about the time or topic under investigation. A genealogy, biography, or history may not be as close to the event but may illuminate related matters as well as the object of the inquiry.

There is a natural tendency to assume that information in cold, hard print must be accurate, but such a conclusion must always be resisted until it has been carefully confirmed. What did the author know from personal experience? How did the author acquire and verify other information? Is the information consistent with that provided by other sources? What appears to have been the motivation for publication? Has the work been issued by a publisher with a reputation for care and dependability, or is the firm an unknown quantity? Occasionally documents are published with the intention of deceiving the reader; far more often they contain statements that lack supporting evidence, speculations and opinions passed off as fact, or partial accounts which overlook significant elements. Careful and wary historians of the nearby world will find much help in books and articles.

Of course, no library collects every book ever published. Even the finest local library has probably not obtained every book with useful information about the nearby past. Regrettably, many institutions have not received the steady support they need, and sometimes acquisition of new material has been curtailed or suspended for years at a time. In other instances, certain types of books have been excluded, for instance, genealogies of families who lived in the area. And naturally, if one is interested in a distant community, the local library is likely to have even less to offer.

For all of these reasons, one should search for material in other places. The Library of Congress publishes author-title and subject catalogs of its own vast holdings and union lists of books held by more than 750 American libraries, helpful although far from perfect tools for discovering documents that may exist elsewhere. Also, the many specialized bibliographies may identify useful publications. (See the references at the end of this chapter for various finding aids.) More and more libraries share their catalogs by means of computer networks, making it easier to discover not only the title of a relevant book but also the location of a copy. Many libraries participate in interlibrary loan arrangements, so that the desired book may be borrowed from a distant library, usually for a small fee.

Articles in magazines, scholarly journals, or newspapers are harder to locate. Most libraries lack the resources to prepare catalog cards for individual articles, though sometimes they will do so for selected items of local importance. Various reference books, however, do catalog articles under author, title, or subject headings. Still, these guides are not complete by any means. Their greatest weaknesses lie in their lack of coverage of small publications with a primarily local rather than national focus and circulation. No one searching for articles on the nearby past should conclude that they do not exist simply because they do not appear in the standard periodical guides. Examining the Library of Congress *Union List of Serials* for the

titles of regional, state, local, and topical journals and then looking individually at those not surveyed by guides or indexes is the only way of assuring
total coverage.

## Theses and Dissertations

Documents quite similar in many respects to books and articles and yet
often overlooked are academic theses and dissertations. The research and
writing requirements for advanced degrees in many scholarly fields produce
an enormous amount of careful, detailed investigation of local topics. Business conditions, educational practices, architectural styles, agricultural patterns, social habits, political developments, and many other matters are
treated either historically or in contemporary surveys. The very fact that the
research is so tightly focused on one locale prevents many of these worthwhile pieces of work from becoming books or articles. Even a poorly written
thesis sometimes contains arduously collected information available
nowhere else which may prove extremely useful. Local colleges and universities keep records of all theses and dissertations done by their own students.
Most dissertations are described and indexed in the publications of University Microfilms International. The number of M.A. theses greatly exceeds
the number of Ph.D. dissertations completed, but unfortunately no general
catalog of theses exists. Theses, even more than dissertations, tend to
involve topics close at hand, so one can safely assume that if a thesis has
been completed on the subject of interest, it is most likely to be found in the
collections of local college, university, or public libraries.

## Newspapers

Newspapers, a rich source of information about communities, have been
published in America since the early eighteenth century, although they
have greatly changed in style and content with the passage of time. Even
very small communities have often supported a local paper for at least part of
their existence. For instance, Minnesota's first, the *Minnesota Pioneer*, was
established in 1849. Before the territory was granted statehood nine years
later, seventy-five more papers had been founded. Virtually every significant
settlement in the territory had its own. Many times communities have been
served by papers in foreign languages as well as in English. Furthermore,
ethnic groups, labor unions, corporations, professional societies, civic asso-

ciations, and religious, commercial, and neighborhood organizations have frequently produced their own newspapers and newsletters to transmit information of importance within their special community.

The observant historian will find both general and special newspapers useful not only for reports of specific news events but also for many other traces. The relative attention given to international, national, and local news may provide clues to community concerns. In recent decades newspapers, competing with radio and television, have in many cases turned to more extensive coverage of local activities. Social and sports pages may provide insight into community interests and activities. A careful examination of advertisements offers many clues to readers' tastes, styles of dress, entertainment preferences, and other cultural characteristics. Classified ads may provide insights about housing arrangements, occupational shifts (what skills are in demand and surplus), and other matters. Letters to the editor may offer a crude gauge of public opinion on contemporary issues.

Thorough, accurate, and objective coverage of news significant to their readers may be their proclaimed goal, but most papers fall somewhat short of the ideal. Editors and publishers no longer acknowledge their political preferences as openly as they did before the twentieth century, but in many cases their views continue to influence their treatment of stories. Furthermore, the need for haste in turning out each edition can lead to omission, distortion, or error. Caution and skepticism are at least as important in dealing with newspapers as with any other type of document.

Finding what one wants in a newspaper may seem a formidable task. Thousands of separate newspapers have appeared, and the published union lists of titles are incomplete. A survey of Ohio newspapers conducted in the early 1970s, for instance, located more than 5,000 titles, many of which had escaped notice in previous union lists. Not only are better catalogs being developed, but also the number of titles on microfilm is growing rapidly. Local libraries often have collections of local publications or at least have information as to where they may be found and how microfilm copies can be obtained.

Research is further complicated by the fact that very few newspapers have been indexed. The *New York Times* has an excellent index beginning with its first issue in 1851. A number of other newspapers have partial indexes, some of them compiled as Works Progress Administration (WPA) projects during the Great Depression and thus ending in the early 1940s. These indexes, particularly the *Times* index, may be of use if the indexed paper

Newspaper obituaries can be very useful sources of information about the lives of individuals and, taken collectively, about patterns of association, social and religious practice, and other matters within a community. It is always wise to check the reliability of obituary data against other sources if possible, since the survivors who provide it may be emotionally upset and their memories of the deceased's earlier life may be uncertain. The style and content of obituaries varies with time, place, and family preference, but generally speaking obituaries from the nineteenth and early twentieth centuries, such as the following, are more detailed than those of more recent years.

*The death of Dr. Roswell Rothrock occurred at his home, McClure, Snyder Co., Pa., on Monday, at 5, P.M., March 1, 1897. His death was caused by Bright's disease. He was confined to bed 17 days. During his sickness he suffered great pain. All that medical skill and loving hands could do was done to subdue the pain and stay the ravages of the disease, but all of no avail; the angel of death claimed him and he passed over the River peacefully. The death "taps" have been sounded and he has answered to the last Roll Call of the Great Commander. His remains were interred in the McClure Cemetery on Friday noon, March 5. He was buried, as requested, by the members and ceremonies of Capt. M. Smith's Post, No. 355 G. A. R. and the McClure Lodge I. O. O. F., No. 770. The funeral was very largely attended by loving friends, many of whom came from a distance to pay their last tribute of respect. Rev. W. H. Hilbish and Rev. W. M. Landis officiated at the funeral. Very able and interesting sermons were preached in the English and German language in Christ's Evangelical Lutheran church, from the text, "I have fought a good fight" &c. The deceased attended catechectical lectures held by Rev. Wieand at Samuel's church, was baptized and joined said church in 1873. He afterwards was received into the Christ's Evangelical church at McClure, where he remained a faithful member to date of death.*

*He was born at Adamsburg, Snyder Co., Pa., Oct. 14, 1831. He was the oldest son of Dr. Issac Rothrock, deceased, who was elected a member of the House of Representatives in 1866, representing the district composed of Lycoming, Union and Snyder. The deceased was a soldier in the late Civil war. He was enrolled in company C., 78th regiment, Penna., vol., on the 29th day of August, 1861, and was discharged Nov. 27, 1864. He was captured by the Rebels in Shenandoah Valley, Va., and held prisoner in Libby, Belle Isle, and Andersonville, 14 months. He was a faithful member of Capt. Michael Smith's Post No. 355, G. A. R. He served as commander*

---

*of said Post one term and was surgeon for ten years. He was also a member of the McClure Lodge, No. 770, I. O. O. F., and was R. S. to V. G.*

*Dr. Rothrock was a successful practitioner of medicine for about 45 years. He first began the practice of medicine with his father at Adamsburg and in 1853 first located at Millville, Clarion county, Pa., where he practiced until 1855. He then located at Beavertown, Snyder county, where he practiced until 1860. He then located at New Bethlehem, Clarion county, where he practiced until Aug. 29, 1861, the date of his entering the war. In 1866 he located at Bannerville, Snyder county, where he practiced until the Spring of 1879, when he removed to Middleburg, where he followed his practice until 1885, when he located at McClure, where he continued the practice of medicine up to the time of his last sickness. He was intermarried with Catherine Mohney, August 4, 1853, at New Bethlehem. This union was blessed with 5 children, 3 sons and 2 daughters. The widow, 5 children, and 13 grand children survive to mourn the loss of a kind and loving husband and father.*

*"Can we forget departed friends? Ah, no!*
*Within our hearts their memory buried lies,*
*The thought that where they are we too may go,*
*Will cast a light o'er darkest scenes of woe."*

*Source*: Family History Collection, American History Research Center, University of Akron, Akron, Ohio.

---

carried a story on the topic or event under investigation; the index may provide a date which will pinpoint the issues to look for in nonindexed papers.

For the most part, research on local topics requires searching all the issues for the time period concerned, keeping in mind that there may be delays of days or even longer before an event is reported and that worthwhile information is not confined to the front page but may be scattered through one or more issues. Careful newspaper research can pay rich rewards for the historian. Detailed biographies may be found in the obituary columns. Business pages provide descriptions of new products, factories, and business activities. Reports of the construction or remodeling of local buildings, social activities, labor negotiations, school curriculum reforms, and other important local news will come to light elsewhere.

## Government Documents

Government documents frequently prove to be valuable sources of published information on local conditions and developments, but all too often they are overlooked because the circumstances of authorship and title do not reveal the wealth within. Many federal, state, and local officials and agencies perform activities which involve collecting information, then tabulating and summarizing it in annual reports. A county or municipal planning department in publishing its projection of the community's future might include detailed maps, statistics, photographs, and descriptions of political and economic decisions to account for the area's past growth. At the state or federal level, for instance, an agriculture department concerned with the affairs of farmers might survey each year the types of crops being grown, the acreage planted in each, the prices obtained, the problems of weather or insects encountered county by county as well as statewide. The same report could well have information on the average size of farms, the percentages worked by owners and by tenants, the amount of machinery, the size of families, and the extent of income and indebtedness. Likewise, a treasury department may report on the rate of highway or canal traffic and other economic conditions affecting tax collection, an attorney general's office on the extent and nature of illegal activities being prosecuted, a commerce department on business trends and unemployment levels in various occupations, a department of natural resources on recreational patterns in each of the parks under its jurisdiction. Some of this information may be presented in special reports with clear and descriptive titles, but more often it will appear routinely in agency annual reports. Also, from time to time, city and county councils and state legislative committees conduct hearings or investigations in order to determine whether laws, taxes, or administrative regulations need to be revised; transcripts or reports sometimes contain useful information regarding local conditions.

Libraries often handle government documents differently from other materials, shelving them in a separate section, for instance. More important, ordinary library subject catalogs seldom adequately reflect the range of topics which a single government document may cover. Most libraries do not even catalog such reports by individual titles; instead, they simply list the agency title and a general description, such as "Oregon, Department of State, *Annual Reports of the Secretary of State.*" The historian interested in a nearby topic should consider which federal, state, or local agencies might have been involved in related activities or information gathering and should then examine their publications. Often one librarian is responsible for government documents and can help in locating government surveys and reports concerning local matters.

## Ephemera

In addition to books, serials, newspapers, and government documents, many libraries try to collect miscellaneous other materials, often labeled "ephemera," which contain valuable information about nearby history. Ephemera, having many origins and purposes, vary widely in nature. Local businesses, agencies, and organizations issue brochures and pamphlets describing their background, activities, and accomplishments. Railroads, airlines, and bus companies print routes and timetables. Annual reports to stockholders are often very useful corporate documents. Businesses and educational institutions publish different sorts of catalogs describing their products and services. For various reasons, many different groups distribute handbills, programs, broadsides, or posters.

Libraries collecting ephemera may try to describe it in their card catalogs, but more often they simply keep it in vertical files, folders of assorted materials relating to a topic. Much of this sort of material was intended to be thrown away after its immediate use. It is often undated, and its information may be hard to verify. But a library's vertical files often contain surprising treasures and should not be overlooked.

It should be evident by this point that published documents concerning the nearby past exist in great volume and variety. It should be equally apparent that even the best library catalogs and published finding aids cannot always lead historians to the document sought. What should be obvious, but often is not, is that librarians can frequently provide extraordinary assistance. These professionals are familiar with a wide range of reference works, bibliographies, indexes, and other tools for locating materials. Furthermore, they often have more information about documents pertaining to the nearby area than even the finest reference works or card catalogs. They have assembled the vertical files of ephemera, and they may know of individuals and organizations with private collections. Wise researchers discuss their interests with librarians, ask their advice about sources of information, and pursue their suggestions. No librarian can or should do

Ephemera can provide useful and sometimes unexpected information. This Chicago real estate advertising handout not only shows how working-class houses appeared from the street, but also provides floor plans, details about price and financing, and even indications of the developer's appeals to ethnic groups. Such ads often appeared in newspaper classified advertising sections.

your research for you, but a good one can often speed and enrich your efforts enormously.

A few varieties of published documents deserve particular attention because of their unusual character and exceptional value for nearby history: commercial histories, directories, and maps. Simple and straightforward on their face, these publications have been put to many uses by historians and have revealed far more about a community's past than their creators would have imagined.

## Commercial Histories

Community histories have been written by authors of widely varied background for a great many years, especially in New England and the Midwest. More than 1,000 town and county histories for New England had been published by 1900, and the number increased rapidly thereafter. Similarly, Michigan had close to 200 state, county, and local histories by World War I. Many of these works were compiled by local people interested in their own community's past. A few were prepared by scholars. But in addition, a distinctive type of historical publication began to appear frequently by the late nineteenth century: the commercial history, sometimes of a town, but usually of a county.

Commercial histories were announced in advance by enterprising publishers who would then solicit local residents and businesses to purchase copies of the forthcoming book. Subscribers who paid a certain fee (ten to fifty dollars was common) were assured that space would be devoted to their lives and achievements. An additional fee would ensure that the subscriber's picture or that of his home, place of business, or family was included. In community after community, leading citizens and those who aspired to such status rushed to subscribe. The promoter generally accepted the narratives, biographies, dates, and other material that was submitted with little or no checking, eager to assemble information pleasing to as many subscribers as possible. After the completed work had been delivered, the promoter moved on to another profitable locale.

Commercial histories have often been scorned as "mugbooks" by those with a serious interest in knowing what the past was really like. One critic in 1890 saw county history and atlas promoters as swindlers on a level with salesmen of "lightning rods, fruit trees, and patent medicine." Relentlessly cheerful in their descriptions of local conditions and development, silently

County histories of the late nineteenth and early twentieth century, long on local pride and short on critical observations, nevertheless contain much useful information. Notice how much information is woven into the boasting about developments in towns outside the county's two main population centers.

*One of the respects in which Story is an exceptionally good county has to do with its minor towns. It is a very long time since Story County has had all of its interests concentrated in a single place. There are numerous counties in Iowa in which there is one city of considerable consequence and no other town to be considered at all. But such is not the situation in Story. The advancement of Ames by the cross railroad and the college enabled it to become a rival of Nevada, the county seat, and the rivalries of these two towns made easier the development of other towns. Also the fact that other railroads, when they did come, failed to radiate from a common center, but rather crossed the county in parallel lines, had been a condition favorable to the outside towns. Indeed, it was a real blow to Nevada when within two years of each other in the early '80s the Milwaukee railroad was built through the south part of the county and the Iowa Central through the north part. These roads did not touch Nevada nor contribute anything to it. But, on the contrary, they cut off territory, developed some villages and established new towns. Some of these towns, located as they were in good territory and not too convenient to a larger town, have had the opportunity to grow such as is not vouchsafed to outside towns in many other counties. When all of these matters are considered, it would appear that Story County ought to have some good outside towns and that really the inhabitants of such towns have had the responsibility of making good.*

*Of the outside towns the first place has been fairly won by Story City. It*

*has a population not far from what Nevada and Ames had twenty years ago. But it is much better improved than they were at that time. When the town was laid out, a sentiment of public spirit caused the laying out of exceptionally wide streets; and though the time was when some of these streets were convenient pastures, they are now a conspicuous feature of the town's beauty. Its business district is well built up and its homes give evidence of taste and wealth: it has perhaps the largest department store in the county and it unquestionably has the best public park in the county.*

Source: W. O. Payne, *History of Story County, Iowa*, 2 vols. (Chicago: S. J. Clarke, 1911), 1:450–51.

ignoring people who would or could not pay to be included, commercial histories gave an unbalanced and unreliable view of the local community. Still, they should not be dismissed altogether. These volumes often contain information, drawings, maps, and photographs not otherwise preserved. The biographical sketches give a reasonably good impression of the structure of the local elite as well as of reasons for migration and settlement, dominant tastes, customs, and social conditions, and the community's self-image at the time. No doubt many subscribers felt a responsibility to describe themselves, their families, their businesses, and other matters accurately. Nevertheless, when commercial histories are used, the need to verify information should always be kept in mind, as should the likely underrepresentation of the lower social-economic groups and the neglect of darker moments of the community's past.

## Directories

City directories also had commercial origins, but of a different nature. These alphabetical listings of residents, together with their occupation, home and work addresses, and occasionally additional data, came into being in an era when businesses found communication with each other as well as with customers difficult because of frequent movement and lack of reliable information about the identity and whereabouts of local inhabitants. The business demand for such directories made their publication a profitable sideline for a printer or newspaper. Boston had one as early as 1790, and by the eve of the Civil War more than three-quarters of America's 6,200,000 urban dwellers lived in places covered by directories. Not all of these works were restricted to urban areas; rural counties such as Henry County, Iowa (population 18,701), and Kane County, Illinois (population 30,062), had them by 1860. More specialized business, professional, and social directories generally appeared later.

Directories were often revised annually, and in some cities they even competed. As a result these volumes often provide frequent reports on individuals present in a community. On the other hand, editions were hastily assembled and were never absolutely complete or accurate; revisions often merely updated information, leaving misalphabetized names in the same incorrect order from year to year. People who have studied directories carefully and have compared them to census records report that their origins as business tools are reflected in the fact that they very fully and accurately cover middle- and upper-class residents but offer much scantier treatment of lower economic groups. In the 1840 Boston directory, for example, more than 75 percent of heads of white households were listed but only 40 percent of households headed by blacks. Another scholar found that only 7 percent of Boston white-collar workers listed in the 1880 census were missing from the city directory, but 35 percent of unskilled and semiskilled workers were unlisted. The economic bias of directories needs to be kept in mind.

Directories can be very useful for identifying residents and their occupations as well as for judging the local business community (which advertised in the volumes). Street-by-street listings of residents can reveal the character of a block or neighborhood. Comparison of successive volumes may indicate the rate at which people moved into and out of the community and the occupational patterns of stable residents. Other information can be gained indirectly. The absence of occupation in a listing often means that a person was retired, the omission of home address that he resided in a suburb, and no work address that his occupation lacked a fixed location (perhaps day labor, perhaps a skilled trade such as carpentry, plumbing, or masonry). Alternative explanations are quite possible, and it is wise not to depend exclusively on directories. Comparison of their information with the much fuller but less frequent descriptions in a census return may provide clarification. Many city directories, as well as business, professional, and other specialized directories, continue to be published to the present day.

## Maps

Maps, either published or unpublished, can have great value for the historian. As historian G. J. Renier put it, "Geography is indispensable

TO FIND A NAME YOU SHOULD KNOW HOW IT IS SPELLED.

# MATZENGER'S
# MOBILE DIRECTORY

## FOR THE YEAR 1892.

### ABBREVIATIONS:

| | | |
|---|---|---|
| agt.. ....agent | es.... ... east side | res ..... residence |
| ave.... avenue | ins ....insurance | s.... ... south |
| bds.... boards | lab.... laborer | se.... southeast |
| bkkpr.... bookkeeper | mnfg .... manufacturing | sec.... secretary |
| c .... colored | mnfr.... manufacturer | stbtman.... steamboatman |
| carp.... carpenter | n.... north | ss.... south side |
| clk .... clerk | ne.... northeast | sw.... southwest |
| com, mer... commission merch't | ns.... north side | up st.... up stairs |
| cor.... corner | nw.... northwest | w.... west |
| dom.... domestic | prop.... proprietor | wid.... widow |
| e.... east | rd.... road | ws.... west side |

| AAR | 1 | ACA |
|---|---|---|

Aarnes Annie C. wid Hans, res 122 s Royal

Abbot James L. jr. cotton buyer 104 n Commerce, up stairs, res 850 Government

Abbott John H. painter Dure & Chaudron, res 355 Lipscomb

Abbey Elizabeth, wid Michael, res 909 Church

Abels Andrew J. c, blacksmith Mobile Coal Co. res 609 south Broad

Abels Benjamin, c, porter Mobile Stationery Co. res 218 north Bayou

Abney Simon, c, lab, res 156 Knox

Abrahams James A. resident student City Hospital, res 925 Government

Abrahams William T. mdse broker 109 n Commerce, up stairs, res 925 Government

Abrams Daniel, vegetable peddler, res 323 Davis ave

Abrams Joseph R. policeman, res 205 Marine

Abrams Walter J. machinist L&NRR shops, res 205 Marine

Academy and Convent of the Visitation, (B. V. M.) Summerville, 3¾ miles, in charge of the Nuns of the Visitation

1

This page from a Mobile directory begins the alphabetical listing of residents; it follows the street-by-street listing. Blacks were singled out in many northern as well as southern directories. Occupations with commercial significance were more clearly identified than others.

because an event that is not situated in space is as difficult to incorporate in a story as one that is not situated in time." Often remembered in connection with the history of exploration or that of diplomatic and military affairs, maps can also be of considerable use to local historians. Maps visually indicate influential landscape elements and the spatial relationships of natural and man-made features. They provide traces of items which have long since disappeared. Individually and collectively, they also record growth patterns and other historical developments. Fortunately for historians of the nearby past, maps exist in great profusion and variety.

The earliest explorers of every portion of what would become the United States drew maps. By the end of the colonial period, there were thousands of American maps, ranging from crude sketches based on cursory examination, reports of other travelers, and conjecture to accurate and detailed surveys of limited areas based on careful fieldwork and other research. Individual map sheets of locations, regions, and states were common, but the first American atlases did not appear until almost 1800. Not until the nineteenth century was there systematic standard national mapping. The Congress in 1807 authorized a survey of the nation's coastline to aid navigation and finally in 1879 mandated a topographical survey of publicly owned lands, at first in the Far West and eventually nationwide. The U.S. Geological Survey has published large-scale topographic maps for much of the country, with some areas covered more than once, showing landforms, towns, roads, and railroads. The twentieth-century introduction of aerial photography allowed federal agencies to complete an accurate survey of about 85 percent of the national landscape between 1934 and 1943.

Localities have been mapped over the years by a variety of agencies in different formats and for many reasons. Governmental units and land developers produced plats, flat projections, to show land subdivision and record individual property ownership for taxation and sales promotion. Rail and bus companies distributed sketches of their routes, just as oil companies issued road maps, to encourage travel. Businesses, convention bureaus, parks and recreation departments, churches, and planning agencies all published specialized maps to serve their own purposes.

Commercial motives led to the creation of a variety of maps very useful for the nearby historian. County maps and atlases were produced in much the same way as commercial histories. Subscriptions were solicited, and for a fee a picture of one's home or business was used as a border illustration. Since this enterprise proved lucrative to publishers and the space available on a sheet map was limited, cartographers understandably shifted to the atlas

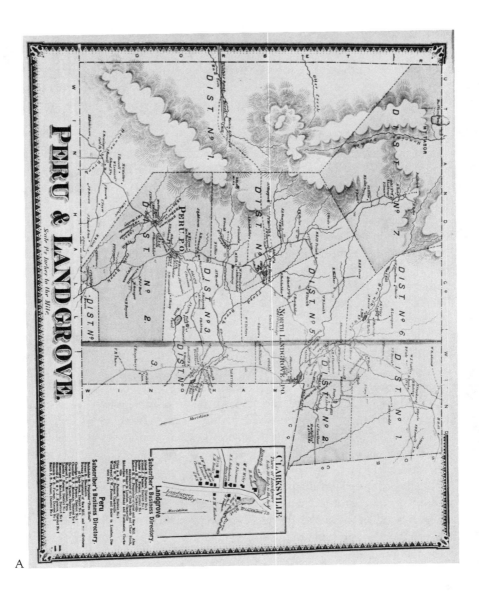

A

This township sheet from the 1869 Bennington County, Vermont, atlas (View A) with the "Clarksville" inset enlarged (View B) shows quite clearly the physical features, major structures, and residents' names.

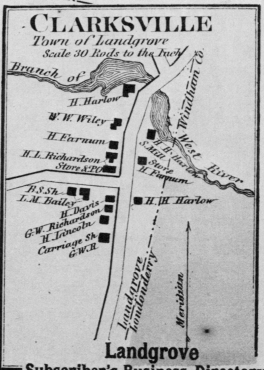

# CLARKSVILLE

*Town of Landgrove*
*Scale 30 Rods to the Inch*

## Landgrove
## Subscriber's Business Directory.

Abbott E..Farmer, District No 2
Abbott J..Farmer, District No 1
Bolster J. H..Farmer, District No 1
Farnam H..Merchant, Clarksville
Harlow H. H..Proprietor of Grist and Saw Mill. Also
    manufacturer of Cloth Boards and Chair Stock,
    and dealer in Lumber, Clarksville
Richardson H. L..Merchant and Postmaster, Clarks-
    ville
Utley A. & H..Farmers, District No 3
Wiley W. W..Farmer. Clarksville
Woodward C. W..Farmer and dealer in Lumber, Dis-
    trict No 2

## Peru
## Subscriber's Business Directory.

Batchelder E..Proprietor "Peru Hotel"
Bryant R..Blacksmith
Burnap E..Proprietor of Saw Mill, and manufacturer
    of Chair Stock, District No 6
Cooledge C. H..Farmer, District No 5
Chandler E. P..Mechanic, District No 4
Davis Geo. K..Farmer, District No 2
Hapgood L. B..Merchant, Peru
Lincoln J..Farmer, District No 4
Messenger E..Mechanic, District No 2
Simonds J. H. & A. J..Farmers, District No 2
Simonds W. B..Farmer, District No 2
Smith F, B..Farmer, District No 5

format, which allowed greater space. County atlases ordinarily had a separate plat for each township and sometimes even for smaller areas. Each plat showed roads, railroads, property lines, and names of property owners, usually compiled quickly from existing county maps and records. Subscribers could, for a fee of course, have pictures of their properties, their families, or themselves and biographies included; these were prepared from a few days sketching in the township and from standard questionnaires. Publishers found atlases inexpensive to prepare and produce by lithography, and they proved quite profitable, especially in heavily populated areas. The mid-Atlantic and north Atlantic region, especially Pennsylvania and New York, first attracted county mappers, but the Midwest became their area of greatest activity and success. By the end of the nineteenth century, some Corn Belt counties had ten atlases, whereas half of all U.S. counties, especially those in the South and West, had none. Since more than 4,000 county atlases were produced, considerable variety in format and accuracy is to be expected, but for the most part county atlases are very informative.

A special variety of commercial map, popular from the 1840s to the 1920s, was the panoramic, or bird's-eye, view of an urban area, a drawing of a city as if seen at an oblique angle from a height of 2,000 to 3,000 feet. Assembly involved preparing a street plan in perspective, then having artists walk through town sketching buildings, trees, and other landscape features. The famous printmakers Currier and Ives prepared panoramas of a few large cities, but most such maps were produced by a half-dozen midwestern artists who concentrated on small communities of the East and Midwest. Civic pride and promotion spurred the production of panoramas, which became popular wall hangings. Although permanent features were accurately rendered, they were not always drawn to scale. Mapmakers catered to local pride by showing streets crowded with people and carriages, smoke billowing from factories, harbors filled, and railroads busy. Also, panoramas sometimes showed areas planned for development but not yet actually built. Nevertheless, used carefully, bird's-eye maps can be extremely worthwhile, particularly for their depiction of buildings. The largest collection of American panoramic maps, more than 1,100, is held by the Library of Congress, which can provide copies of most for purchase.

Other commercial motives led to the development of the even more detailed and far more common fire insurance maps. The maps were developed in the mid-nineteenth century in response to a growing need for information on the potential fire risks of individual commercial, residential, and industrial structures. At first, fire insurance underwriters of rating bureaus inspected buildings, but as the business grew and companies proliferated, this procedure proved neither feasible nor economical, and insurers turned to mapping. By 1900, the Sanborn Map and Publishing Company of New York dominated the business, and by 1924 it had mapped 11,000 towns. Sanborn maps provided great detail for central city areas, showing building materials as well as structural features. Frequently revised, their dating of building construction, alteration, or destruction is fairly precise.

On the other hand, because of their limited purpose, these maps lack information on the use of land without buildings, specific details on homogeneous residential areas, or buildings used for multiple purposes which posed no special fire risks. After World War II insurance companies became less dependent on maps, and they gradually ceased to be produced. A fairly complete collection, more than 700,000 sheets on more than 12,000 communities produced by Sanborn and others between 1852 and

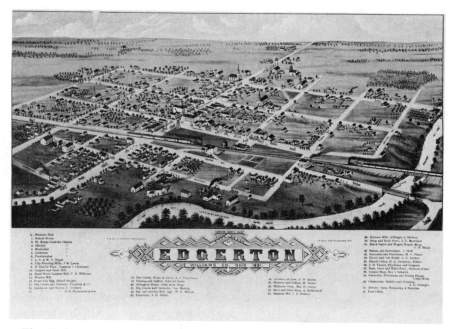

This bird's-eye view of the northwest Ohio village of Edgerton in 1881 is typical of panoramic maps. Note the fine detail, the bustling streets, and the two trains steaming into town on a single track.

1961, is available at the Library of Congress, Geography and Map Division, and many may be available locally. Sanborn maps may also be obtained from the Sanborn Map Company, 629 Fifth Avenue, Pelham, New York 10803.

Maps must be used carefully, since they vary so widely in purpose, method and care of construction, and accuracy. They should be checked against accurate modern maps and reliable noncartographic traces. Establishing their date is crucial and often difficult, because sheets were often reissued with later dates but without new features on the actual landscape having been added. It is important to try to determine how complete a map might be, what details might have been overlooked. Considering the scale and purpose of the map, as well as the mapmaker's bias, eye for detail, or interest in certain features, is useful.

Singly or in sequence, maps can be very informative about the history of a community. For example, settlers from different countries initially divided up land in different ways. The Spanish and Mexican governments granted large blocks of land to influential developers or groups of settlers. In dry areas, further division was linked to water, with strips of land 100–220 feet wide extending away from streams for distances of ten to fifteen miles to the next watershed. In land of marginal quality, gaps or overlaps between grants were considered unimportant. In modern California and the Southwest, large-scale residential development has often been easiest on previously undivided old land grants. The French also laid out long, narrow strips at right angles to waterways, with areas ten times as long as they were wide followed by a second rank of strips. This system was cheap and easy to survey, provided a variety of soil and vegetation on each property, gave easy access to transportation, and allowed residents to live close to neighbors along waterways or inland roads. The French used this system not only in Canada, but wherever they settled, along the Mississippi and elsewhere.

The English, in contrast, preferred to divide land into more regular blocks. Six-mile-square townships granted to groups which then parceled out town and farm lots to members were the norm in New England. Early southern settlement was more irregular, as poor land was often bypassed. A rectangular grid, or checkerboard system, used by William Penn in planning Philadelphia, was adopted in the development of New York City, and was later applied to the Northwest Territory. Land was surveyed along north-south, east-west lines, then systematically divided into townships, one-mile-square sections, and 160-acre quarter sections. This simple, orderly pattern became the standard for most of the American Midwest, determin-

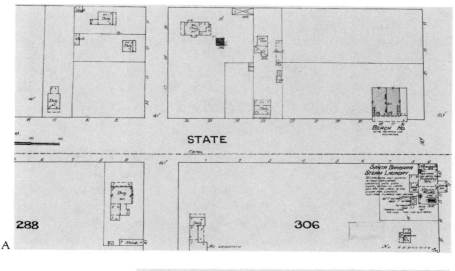

A

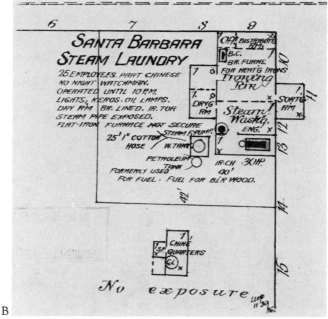

B

This section of an 1886 Sanborn map of Santa Barbara, California (View A), and the enlargement of the small inset area in View B reflect the detailed and often unexpected information such maps contained. Two years after this map was issued, the Santa Barbara Steam Laundry had been renamed the American Laundry, and an added notation described it as "moderately tidy."

ing the course of roads and, some claim, insuring the isolation of most American farm families.

Towns, too, have been laid out in different patterns. New England towns, not expected to grow very large, were laid out informally around an open space, or common. William Penn's grid for Philadelphia, featuring rectangular blocks, straight streets, right-angle intersections, systematic naming of streets, and a central public square, was widely copied. Its rational and efficient use of space as well as its potential for easy expansion appealed to New Englanders moving west to establish Cleveland, Chicago, and a thousand other towns. Other city plans, such as Savannah's ward modules (each with open squares, sites for community facilities, building lots, and narrow local streets, all surrounded by broad avenues), Washington's spacious symmetry (broad avenues radiating from circles and important public building sites, generous provisions for open space, and considerable distance between principal facilities), and Detroit's reconstruction following a devastating 1805 fire (a triangular street pattern without a focal point, as in Washington) not only were seldom copied but were eventually abandoned as these cities grew. An unusual plan raises interesting questions about the ideas of the town's founders.

Maps provide traces of city growth. They reveal whether towns were originally laid out along a river, trail, or railroad or around the site for the county courthouse (if the courthouse square is not at the center of the original town, the county seat may have moved there sometime later, or something else, the railroad depot perhaps, may have been more important to the town fathers). Maps can suggest how the city's development was shaped by geographical features—the waterways and hills of Pittsburgh, Cincinnati, San Francisco, or Seattle, for instance. The names of streets, churches, and schools can indicate original ethnic enclaves, even if the Irish, Chinese, Greeks, or Poles have long since dispersed. Interruptions in regular street patterns, or switches in directions and designs of streets or grids, may show the limits of original settlement, as in Atlanta or in Hays, Kansas, or where two developing communities came together, as in Milwaukee, Denver, or Indianapolis.

Thoughtful and imaginative consideration of maps can stimulate many ideas and questions about a community's past. Maps are like other documents in that they are usually available in considerable numbers and variety for anyone who cares to search for them. Although they provide much information, they cannot provide all the answers themselves. Those interested in knowing as much as they can about the nearby past should consult and compare a variety of traces, not only the several types of published documents mentioned in this chapter, but also unpublished documents and other sources yet to be discussed.

## Notes

G. J. Renier's comment appears in *History: Its Purpose and Method* (1950; reprint ed., New York: Harper and Row, 1965), p. 116.

## For Further Information

An extremely useful introduction to materials for nearby history published before July 1970, is Frank Freidel, ed., *Harvard Guide to American History* (Cambridge, Mass.: Harvard University Press, 1974). This mammoth compilation lists local histories by state, biographies, books and articles on many specific topics, and many bibliographic tools.

Several specialized bibliographies have particular value: individual state volumes in Clifford L. Lord, ed., *Localized History Series* (New York: Bureau of Publications, Teachers College, Columbia University, 1964–71); C. S. Peterson, *Bibliography of County Histories of the 3,111 Counties in the Forty-eight States* (Baltimore: Clarence Peterson, 1946); and Marion J. Kaminkow, ed., *United States Local Histories in the Library of Congress*, 5 vols. (Baltimore: Magna Carta, 1975).

Titles of books relating to specific localities may be discovered in Robert R. Hubach, *Early Midwestern Travel Narratives: An Annotated Bibliography, 1634–1850* (Detroit: Wayne State University Press, 1961); Louis Kaplan, *A Bibliography of American Autobiographies* [to 1945] (Madison: University of Wisconsin Press, 1961); and William Matthews, *American Diaries: An Annotated Bibliography of Diaries Written Prior to the Year 1861* (Boston: J. S. Conner, 1959). Matthews's later work, *American Diaries in Manuscript, 1580–1954: A Descriptive Bibliography* (Athens: University of Georgia Press, 1974), should not be overlooked.

A starting place for learning more about local publications is G. Thomas Tanselle, *Guide to the Study of United States Imprints* (Cambridge, Mass.: Harvard University Press, 1971).

Finding articles can be harder than locating books, but several reference works ease the search. *The Reader's Guide to Periodical Literature* surveys many twentieth-century popular magazines, while *Poole's Index to Periodical Literature* does the same for nineteenth-century material. Guides to more scholarly journals, at least for the twentieth century, are the *Social Sciences Index* and the *Humanities Index*, and since 1964 *America: History and Life* has provided unrivaled coverage of state and national historical journals.

Locating dissertations is made easier by Warren F. Kuehl, ed., *Dissertations in History*, 2 vols. (Lexington: University of Kentucky Press, 1965–72), which lists the titles of all works submitted for the Ph.D. in history at American and Canadian universities from the first in 1873 until 1970; it contains a subject index. *Dissertation Abstracts*, issued several times a year by University Microfilms, lists titles and provides summaries of works in all scholarly fields, but not every university allows its students' work to be included. Harvard University is the most notable omission from the *Abstracts*. *The Comprehensive Dissertation Index* is a very useful general finding aid for University Microfilms holdings, and the company has also begun publishing special bibliographies of dissertations pertaining to individual states. These state bibliographies can be obtained free of charge from University Microfilms International, 300 North Zeeb Rd., Ann Arbor, Michigan 48106, or by calling 800-521-0600.

Newspaper guides are quite inadequate. *American Newspapers, 1821–1936: A Union List of Files Available in the United States and Canada* (New York: H. W. Wilson, 1937) and *Newspapers in Microform: United States, 1948–1972* (Washington, D.C.: Library of Congress, 1973) should be regarded as only starting places for a search. One excellent specialized guide is Karl J. R. Arndt and May E. Olson, *German-American Newspapers and Periodicals, 1732–1955*, 2nd ed. (New York: Johnson Reprint, 1965), and their successor volume, *The German Language Press of the Americas* [1732–1968] (Munich: Verlag Dokumentation, 1976).

It is necessary to consult a number of guides in order to cover the great variety of government publications. For federal and state documents, one should look at the United States Government Printing Office, *Checklist of United States Public Documents, 1789–1909* and *Catalogue of Public Documents of the United States, 1893–1940*; William W. Buchanan and Edna A. Kanely, eds., *Cumulative Subject Index to the Monthly Catalog of United States Government Publications, 1900–1971* (Washington, D.C.: Carrollton Press, 1973); and thereafter the *Monthly Catalog of United States Government Publications* (Washington, D.C.: U.S. Government Printing Office). Also see the Congressional Information Service, *U.S. Serial Set Index* (Washington, D.C., 1975–79), for federal publications during the period 1787–1969. For the period since 1970, consult each year's Congressional Information Service, *Annual Index to Congressional Publications and Public Laws*.

Individual states often produce similar guides. R. R. Bowker, ed., *State Publications: A Provisional List of the Official Publications of the Several States of the United States from Their Organization*, is an incomplete but very useful compilation for the period before 1900, which William S. Jenkins, ed., *Collected Public Documents of the States: A Check List*, carries forward to 1947. The Library of Congress produces an ongoing *Monthly Checklist of State Publications*, covering only publications which it receives, which is useful for locating more current material. There are few finding aids for local government publications, the best being J. G. Hodgson, ed., *Official Publications of American Counties: A Union List* (1937), and A. D. Manvel, ed., *Checklist of Basic Municipal Documents* (Washington, D.C.: U.S. Bureau of the Census, 1948).

Two critical but informative examinations of commercial histories are [Bates Harrington], *How 'Tis Done: A Thorough Ventilation of the Numerous Schemes Conducted by Wandering Canvassers together with the Various Advertising Dodges for the Swindling of the Public* (Syracuse: W. I. Patterson, 1890), and Betty and Raymond Spahn, "Wesley Raymond Brink, History Huckster," *Journal of the Illinois State Historical Society* 58 (1965): 117–38. For commercial projects involving maps, see John R. Hebert, "Panoramic Maps of American Cities," *Special Libraries* 63 (1972): 554–62.

A helpful guide to early city directories is Dorothea N. Spear, *Bibliography of American Directories through 1860* (Worcester, Mass.: American Antiquarian Society, 1961). An excellent discussion of the use of city directories for historical research can be found in an appendix to Peter R. Knights, *The Plain People of Boston, 1830–1860: A Study in City Growth* (New York: Oxford University Press, 1971). Some of the values and defects in later directories as well as other sources are discussed in Stephan Thernstrom, *The Other Bostonians: Poverty and Progress in the American Metropolis, 1880–1970* (Cambridge, Mass.: Harvard University Press, 1973), pp. 265–88.

Index maps showing available federal topographic and aerial photographic maps are available free from the Map Information Office, U.S. Geological Survey, Washington, D.C. 20242. Aids for finding other maps include James C. Wheat and Christian F. Brun, *Maps and Charts Published in America before 1800: A Bibliography* (New Haven: Yale University Press, 1969); Clara E. LeGear, *United States Atlases: A List of National, State, County, City, and Regional Atlases in the Library of Congress*, 2 vols. (Washington, D.C.: Library of Congress, 1950–53); *Checklist of Printed Maps of the Middle West to 1900*, 11 vols. (Boston: G. K. Hall, 1981); Richard Stephenson, *Land Ownership Maps: A Checklist of Nineteenth-Century United States County Maps in the Library of Congress* (Washington, D.C.: Library of Congress, 1967); Ralph E. Ehrenberg, *Geographical Exploration and Mapping in the Nineteenth Century: A Survey of the Records in the National Archives*, National Archives Research Information Paper No. 66 (Washington, D.C., 1973); John R. Herbert, *Panoramic Maps of Anglo-American Cities: A Checklist of Maps in the Collections of the Library of Congress, Geography and Map Division* (Washington, D.C.: Library of Congress, 1974); Charles E. Taylor and Richard E. Spurr, *Aerial Photographs in the National Archives*, National Archives Special List No. 25, (Washington, D.C., 1973); Norman J. W. Thrower, "The County Atlas of the United States," *Surveying and Mapping* 21 (1961): 365–73; Walter W. Ristow, "U.S. Fire Insurance Maps, 1852–1968," *Surveying and Mapping* 30 (1970): 19–41; *Fire Insurance Maps in the Library of Congress: Plans of North American Cities and Towns Produced by the Sanborn Map Company* (Washington, D.C.: Library of Congress, 1981); and Douglas R. McManis, *Historical Geography of the United States: A Bibliography—Excluding Alaska and Hawaii* (Ypsilanti: Eastern Michigan University Press, 1965).

An introduction to the use of maps in nearby history can be obtained from Grady Clay, *Close-Up: How to Read the American City* (New York: Praeger, 1972); Karl B. Raitz and John Fraser Hart, *Cultural Geography on Topographic Maps* (New York: Wiley, 1975), a series of representative maps with explanations of what can be learned from each; and Thomas J. Schlereth, "Part Cityscapes: Uses of Cartography in Urban History," in *Artifacts and the American Past* (Nashville: American Association for State and Local History, 1980), pp. 66–86.

Many varieties of useful maps are described in Ralph E. Ehrenberg, "Cartographic Records in the National Archives," *National Genealogical Society Quarterly* 64 (1976): 83–111.

David Greenhood, *Mapping* (Chicago: University of Chicago Press, 1964) provides an introduction to the techniques of mapmaking. An excellent general history of American mapmaking can be found in Seymour I. Schwartz and Ralph E. Ehrenberg, *The Mapping of America* (New York: Abrams, 1980).

The influence of geography on history is explored in John Fraser Hart, *The Look of the Land* (Englewood Cliffs, N.J.: Prentice-Hall, 1975); Constance Perin, *Everything in Its Place: Social Order and Land Use in America* (Princeton: Princeton University Press, 1977); W. Gordon East, *The Geography behind History* (New York: Norton, 1967); and Norman J. W. Thrower, *Maps and Man: An Examination of Cartography in Relation to Culture and Civilization* (Englewood Cliffs, N.J.: Prentice-Hall, 1972).

American historical geography on the local level is discussed and profusely illustrated by John W. Reps, *The Making of Urban America: A History of City Planning in the United States* (Princeton: Princeton University Press, 1965), *Town Planning in Frontier America* (Princeton: Princeton University Press, 1969), and *Cities of the American West* (Princeton: Princeton University Press, 1979); David Ward, *Cities and Immigrants: A Geography of Change in Nineteenth-Century America* (New York: Oxford University Press, 1971); and Edward T. Price, "The Central Courthouse Square in the American County Seat," *Geographical Review* 58 (1968): 29–60. Examples of efforts to analyze community development in geographical terms can be found in Walter M. Whitehill, *Boston: A Topographical History*, 2nd ed. (Cambridge, Mass.: Harvard University Press, 1968); Reyner Banham, *Los Angeles: The Architecture of Four Ecologies* (New York: Harper and Row, 1971); Peirce F. Lewis, *New Orleans: The Making of an Urban Landscape* (Cambridge, Mass.: Ballinger, 1976); and Carl Condit, *The Railroad and the City: A Technological and Urbanistic History of Cincinnati* (Columbus: Ohio State University Press, 1977).

The names given to towns and other places on the map are often of interest to the historian. Of use in analyzing them is the introduction to George R. Stewart, *American Place-Names: A Concise and Selective Dictionary for the Continental United States of America* (New York: Oxford University Press, 1970), and by the same author, *Names on the Land: A Historical Account of Place-Naming in the United States*, 2nd ed. (Boston: Houghton Mifflin, 1967).

# ·5·

# Unpublished Documents

DOCUMENTS WHICH HAVE NOT BEEN PUBLISHED BUT EXIST instead in single or few copies represent a vast and vital source of nearby history traces. Such materials may remain in the hands of their creators or recipients in homes, businesses, schools, community organizations, or government offices, or they may have been moved to an archives or manuscript collection at a library, historical society, or elsewhere. They may even have been microfilmed for preservation or for the convenience of users. Use of unpublished sources poses problems unlike those involved in working with published ones, although both must be evaluated for their accuracy and value. But finding the particular unpublished record needed can present a much greater challenge than locating widely duplicated materials, and even when it has been brought to light, uncovering desired information in a collection of letters or official files remains a larger task than examining a book, newspaper, or published report. At the same time, the rewards of the search can include the wonderful excitement of discovering something unique which unlocks a mystery about the past. Knowing about archives and manuscript collections in general and a few special types of records in particular can be helpful in appreciating the worth of unpublished documents for nearby history.

## Archives and Manuscript Collections

Unpublished documents typically are found in one of two settings. They may exist as part of an ongoing records-keeping system, where the routine maintenance of ledgers, correspondence files, wills, journals, and other sorts of records created or received by an organization or institution is carried out

87

in pursuance of legal obligations or for the effective transaction of business. Such bodies of records, maintained because of their continuing legal, administrative, or historical value after their original purpose has been fulfilled, are considered to be archives. Documents of historical worth which are not part of an archives but which have been preserved individually, collected according to a plan, or accumulated by persons or families are referred to as papers or manuscript collections. The difference between archives and manuscript collections is frequently overlooked, especially as both types are often found in the same repository. "Archives" is commonly used as a general label for all unpublished documents. But the distinction is important to keep in mind both in locating pertinent documents and in making judgments about the merits of information obtained.

Archives are maintained and organized according to a routine by an agency for whom the keeping of records is an aspect of carrying out duties. A county government's archives might contain complaints received, hearings held, contracts approved, and laws adopted. Court records include a wealth of testimony and evidence offered in all manner of cases. Differences of opinion or conflicts of interest in local matters of all sorts have a way of eventually presenting themselves to a judge or jury. A church's archives might contain membership, financial, and social action files, while a business's might have accounts, correspondence, personnel reports, and advertising files. An organization or institution keeps materials to preserve a record of its activities and policies, its customers, clients, or membership, decisions made, problems brought to its attention, and the like on the assumption that the information may be needed later. In any case, the records would have been created shortly after the event or conditions described. The creator of the records normally considers its best interests to be served by maintaining them as completely and accurately as possible so that they may be relied upon subsequently. However, the records creator has a particular purpose in mind and will not bother to gather information unrelated to that purpose, even if it might involve the same person, property, or activity.

An institution's records will be arranged in a form and filing system appropriate to the use their creator has for them. A large organization, for example, will create and maintain files in different offices and departments, according to need, rather than assemble all information on a particular subject in a central location. Information about a church member might be found in the minister's correspondence files, the treasurer's journal of contributions received, the Sunday school committee's minutes, and elsewhere. Several agencies of a county government might maintain records relating to a house or neighborhood, among them the real estate appraiser, the building inspector, the board of health, the public works or street and sewer department, the planning and zoning board, the sheriff, the treasurer or tax collector, and possibly others.

Knowing something about how and why records are kept can be very useful when one looks for unpublished information. Traces of the very recent past may be contained in records which are still used for an ongoing government, business, or civic activity and thus remain in office files. Otherwise the records may be in the institution's own archives, or perhaps they have been turned over to a government, university, or private archives. In either of the last two instances, only the documents thought to have enduring legal, administrative, or historical value are likely to have been preserved, while routine or duplicated material will usually have been discarded. Archivists give considerable thought to the appraisal of records, wishing to use available resources to save only those most likely to have lasting value. Usually less than 5 percent of a business or government agency's files is deemed worth saving. In any case, the documents will most likely still be arranged in the fashion established by the office or department where they were created. Archivists believe that records should be maintained in their original order whenever possible. Rearranging large groups of records not only is very expensive and time consuming but also destroys the picture of how the records-creating agency operated.

Careful thought about who might have kept records having to do with the topic under investigation is the first step in successful archival research. At the same time, thinking about who might have created and preserved a record leads to the question of why and how it would have been kept, which leads in turn to a consideration of how reliable and complete it might be. The county treasurer's tax records may list the names of the owners of a particular house throughout its history, while the real estate appraiser's files may contain less frequent but more detailed descriptions of its value and condition prepared after eyewitness examination. The records of the art museum might indicate who in the community donated money and perhaps even the nature of their tastes and preferences, but information in the museum's files on benefactors' wealth is likely to be secondhand, incomplete, and undependable. Sometimes files are passed from one office to another, and in the process records may be weeded out and even altered.

Thus in several respects the *provenance* of records—the facts of their origin and subsequent custody—is very important to consider in searching for records and then evaluating them.

Manuscripts, or personal papers, as they are sometimes called, can be more difficult to locate and assess as traces of the past simply because their own history can be so much more erratic than that of archives. Whereas archives are accumulated routinely, manuscripts by definition are collected, thus preserved haphazardly, incompletely, and in no particular order. Individuals and families do not exist to record their own activities. One person may keep every letter he or she ever wrote or received, every photograph ever acquired, and a diary for every day of his or her life, while next door someone kept only documents considered important or flattering, and across the street no one kept a scrap. Furthermore, libraries and manuscript repositories have probably collected only a fraction of what may have been created originally, usually the records of the famous, the powerful, the wealthy.

If papers are found, whether in the family attic, the local library, or elsewhere, they are still difficult to judge. In the days before telephone, typewriter, photocopier, and jet travel, letters were used to convey ideas and emotions in intimate detail. Now, when face-to-face meeting and oral communication are much easier, letters may contain less information, perhaps only that needed to confirm or distribute a record to a secondary audience. Do papers represent everything a person wrote or knew about some subject, what he or she chose to leave behind so that the matter would be remembered in a particular manner, or merely the fragments found by someone else? Papers may be arranged by a collector rather than by the creator or may be found in no order whatsoever. All the standard questions regarding the origins and dependability of documents apply to manuscripts. Again, any information about provenance can be very enlightening.

## Finding and Using Unpublished Records

The search for archives and manuscripts having to do with the nearby past should naturally begin at the source: the family, the business, the civic institution, or government agency directly involved. Families may have kept a variety of records: correspondence from distant relatives, between couples separated because of war, work, or schooling, or from a mother or father to their scattered children; personal and business financial records;

diaries; photographs; copies of wills, deeds, credit and job applications; Bibles with information about births, marriages, and deaths written on the flyleaf; school report cards and yearbooks; newspaper clippings; scrapbooks; even trophies, ribbons, or awards in other forms. Within these records may be information covering a long span of years concerning the behavior and motives of individuals, activities and relationships within families, the nature of family residences and possessions, neighborhood and community institutions and events, and many other topics.

Businesses may have files on customers and employees as well as accounts, inventories, minutes of meetings of the board of directors, correspondence, research and development files, and production, financial, and advertising records. These may show how the company operated, how products were developed and marketed, how workers and labor disputes were treated. Such records may also reveal how local economic circumstances and consumer tastes changed.

Community organizations such as churches, labor unions, political parties, service clubs, and philanthropic or fraternal groups may retain membership lists, minutes of meetings, reports of speeches and activities, and financial records. Such records will reflect the behavior and concerns of particular groups. They may also indicate patterns of social relationships within the neighborhood or community, lines of local authority and decision making, and the identity of the local elite.

County and municipal government records are likely to include legislative minutes; executive reports; highway, engineering, welfare, health, and planning department records; treasurer's accounts and tax lists; election records and voter lists; wills; deeds; school district records; police and court records; and records of poor farms, orphanages, and homes for the elderly and physically or mentally dependent. These records reveal a great deal about individuals, groups, and conditions within the community, the evolution of issues and public policies, the characteristics and uses of buildings and property, the development of transportation systems, and other local phenomena.

Finally, state, regional, and national bodies have records reflecting not only their own activities but also information they have gathered regarding the affairs of local communities. A state or federal census or a corporate marketing survey could provide descriptions of the local population and conditions. The files of a government agency or national association might contain information regarding a project undertaken locally.

A search for unpublished documents sometimes turns up a surprising amount of material. There may be long-forgotten records within a home. Employers, corporations, churches, labor unions, and civic bodies are often very cooperative when the purpose of research is explained clearly and positively, and their files may prove extremely useful. Most local government records are public by law, though polite requests rather than demands usually produce a more cooperative response from clerks and officials.

Records no longer in the possession of the creator may still exist, having been deposited in an archives or manuscript repository. Government agencies, businesses, and other ongoing agencies are usually aware of their own arrangements along these lines and will share this information. In any case, it is wise to inquire about the holdings of nearby libraries, historical societies, universities, and the like.

Various published guides to archives and manuscript collections aid researchers in locating the materials they seek. The National Historical Publications and Records Commission (NHPRC) has provided brief summaries of the holdings of more than 3,200 repositories, arranged geographically, in its *Directory of Archives and Manuscript Repositories in the United States* (Washington, D.C., 1978) and intends to update this basic reference work regularly. Significant individual collections are described in the Library of Congress's elaborately indexed *National Union Catalog of Manuscript Collections*, additional volumes of which are issued periodically. Neither NUCMC ("nukmuk," as it is called) nor the NHPRC *Directory* guarantees complete coverage, since some repositories fail to report their holdings and since small collections are seldom mentioned, but these two volumes are the best general guides available.

A more specialized guide, but one which is national in coverage and may be of particular value is Andrea Hinding, ed., *Women's History Sources: A Guide to Archives and Manuscript Collections in the United States*, 2 vols. (New York: Bowker, 1979). Thousands of collections having to do with women, arranged by city and state, are briefly described and well indexed.

More information about holdings of individual repositories is often available in the guides that they themselves publish to their collections. Significant series of records maintained by various federal agencies, bureaus, and departments are described in *Guide to the National Archives of the United States* (Washington, D.C.: National Archives and Record Service, 1974). State and local institutions with a geographically confined collection may produce guides, as may denominational church archives and repositories with topical collections, such as the business-oriented Eleutherian Mills Historical Library of Wilmington, Delaware, and the Immigration History Research Center at the University of Minnesota. News of recently acquired material appears regularly in historical society publications, scholarly journals, and the *American Archivist*. Nevertheless, it is important to keep in mind that few guides or other publications can adequately describe the holdings of an archives or manuscript collection.

The very nature of any archives or large manuscript collection makes its full description in guides or catalogs difficult. Even after unimportant and duplicate items have been eliminated, the remaining documents judged to have enduring value may cover countless topics and may run to several or even several hundred cubic feet (a standard unit by which archivists measure the volume of records). A single cubic foot of archival material may contain three thousand pages of documents. The National Archives building in Washington, one of more than a dozen repositories for records of the federal government, alone contains nearly one million cubic feet of records.

It is impossible for archivists to catalog each individual item in a large collection as librarians catalog books. In most cases, archivists must settle for general descriptions of records series, documents or file units arranged in accordance with a filing system or maintained together because they relate to a particular form, or because of some other relationship arising from their creation, receipt, or use. A typical record series description might be as follows: "Executive secretary's correspondence, 1916–1928, arranged alphabetically by correspondent, 6 cubic feet" or "Annual reports, 1887–1903, 1911, 1915–1954, 2 cubic feet." Knowing which agency, office, or individual might have created or kept records pertaining to the subject in which one is interested comes in handy here.

The archivist responsible for a body of records can be very helpful to a researcher and usually knows far more about them than could possibly be included in a NUCMC entry, a repository guide, or even a finding aid to a body of records, called a register or inventory. The archivist may have acquired the records for the institution, put them in order and written the finding aid, or worked with other researchers using them. The wise researcher, suspecting or hoping that a repository may have relevant materials, goes directly to the archivist, describes the project, and asks what materials might be of use. The archivist can point out the records series which may contain information, sometimes knows what specific files may prove most helpful, and often can suggest other documents in the same repository or elsewhere which may bear examination. Some archivists are willing to identify other researchers who have explored the same records and who might be helpful contacts.

If the repository in which a researcher is interested lies at some distance, it is wise to write in advance of a visit to inquire about records relevant to the project. Generally archivists will respond with a description of what is available. Often they will answer questions or will photocopy small amounts of material. Archivists should not be expected to do extensive research, but they can be extremely helpful and should be regarded as partners in historical inquiry, concerned about preserving and expanding knowledge of the past.

In addition to aiding researchers, archivists bear responsibilities for the care and protection of materials in their charge. Donors of manuscripts and organizations transferring archives often set terms for the use of records, usually in order to protect the privacy of living individuals or to maintain the confidentiality of information for a certain length of time. Archivists may sometimes regret such restrictions and at other times may even encourage them to protect a donor's legitimate interests, but in any case they pledge to abide by rules imposed when the records are acquired. Also, archivists have the duty to see that records are not lost or damaged so that they will be available for the use of future generations of researchers. Because of these responsibilities, archivists must impose certain requirements on researchers. These regulations are not intended to inhibit or frustrate research but rather to fulfill important archival obligations to gather and care for historically valuable materials.

In the first place, repositories usually require that a prospective researcher speak with an archivist before using archives or manuscripts. The purpose is for the archivist to determine what materials the researcher wants to see, to find out whether the researcher has enough background knowledge to benefit from being allowed to examine unpublished documents, to indicate any restrictions on the use of particular records (perhaps the researcher may not mention names or quote directly or perhaps may not examine certain materials until some future date), and to explain the institution's research rules. It is normal for the visitor to be required to show personal identification and to sign a research application agreeing to abide by the rules.

Once access has been granted, all archives insist that files of material be left in their original order and that no marks be made upon documents. (Some researchers have the urge to "correct" documents which seem in error, but that must never be done. Passing on the information to the archivist is the appropriate procedure.) Some archives expect researchers to work only with pencils to protect documents from accidental but ineradicable ink marks. Most repositories require researchers to use archival materials in a reading room, not allowing them into storage facilities or permitting them to remove documents from the designated area. As a further security precaution, some institutions do not allow briefcases, purses, or other personal belongings to be brought into the reading room. If photocopying is allowed, it must normally be done under supervision or by a member of the archival staff. Some of these precautions may seem unreasonable, but in a number of cases, unfortunately, valuable records have been damaged or have disappeared. Most archival and manuscript material is unique; once it has been lost it can never be replaced. The minor inconvenience of some repository regulations is a small price to pay to ensure continued access to the vast amount of information which exists in unpublished documents.

The value of archival material for nearby history may perhaps best be demonstrated by a close look at a few types of documents of almost universal availability which contain important information about families and communities. The variety of archival sources is so vast that it is impossible to say what any one researcher may or may not find in a careful search. But some materials are so widespread, have been used so often, and have proved so helpful that they deserve specific mention.

## Census Records

The United States Constitution mandated the creation of unquestionably the most widely used unpublished source of nearby history information. The founding fathers stipulated that, to ensure the proper apportionment among the states of seats in the House of Representatives, a federal population census must be conducted every ten years. The first federal census in 1790 and the five following enumerations recorded the names and addresses of heads of families together with the number of free white males and females in broad age categories and the number of slaves in the household. With the 1850 census, eager to gain a fuller picture of the American population, the Census Bureau began to ask more questions. For the first time the name of every person was recorded, together with address; age; sex; color (white, black, or mulatto). It was asked whether the person was deaf and dumb, blind, insane, or idiotic; about the value of real estate owned; the nature of the person's profession, occupation, or trade (for men over fifteen); place of birth; whether the person had been married within the year; whether school had been attended within the year; whether the person was unable to read and write (if over twenty); whether the person was a pauper or convict. Other questions were added in later censuses: in 1860, the value of personal property the person owned; in 1870, whether father and mother were foreign born; in 1880, the person's relationship to the head of the household; marital status; months for which the person had been unemployed during the year; whether the person had been sick or temporarily disabled and if so how; whether the person was maimed, crippled, or bedridden; and the birthplace of the person's parents. Later even more questions were added. Summaries of the information for cities, counties, and states as well as the nation as a whole were published, but more important, the manuscript census, the sheets on which enumerators recorded information as they went from door to door, was preserved.

The federal census became an effort to take a snapshot of the American people once every decade, to determine not only who they were and where they lived but also the nature of their health, wealth, work, and family

This typical page from a manuscript census shows how poor handwriting and misspelling could cause census data to be misleading or unusable.

background. Numerous colonial or state censuses had been carried out prior to 1790, recording names of household heads and occasionally other information gathered for some special purpose, but these were often incomplete and in several cases actually involved estimates rather than enumerations. The federal census proved so worthwhile that nearly a dozen states and even a few cities conducted their own enumerations, often at mid-decade, asking the same questions (and in some cases even more) of residents.

The federal census expanded to include special enumerations of agriculture and manufacturing, which, like those of the population, improved after 1840. The agricultural census gathered data on farmers and farm workers as well as extensive economic information for each farm, including the amount of land owned, animals raised, and crops grown. The census of manufactures collected statistics about manufacturing establishments, capital invested, nature, quantity, and value of raw materials and products, power sources, machinery, structures, number of persons employed, and labor costs.

The published volumes of the *Federal Census of Population, Agriculture and Manufacturing* provide, especially for 1850 and after, an unparalleled, comprehensive overview of every American community's social and economic characteristics. Beginning with 1910 for cities with population of more than 500,000 and expanding by 1970 to include all cities of 50,000 or more, census tract data have been tabulated and published. Census tracts are arbitrary divisions of communities into relatively homogeneous areas of a few thousand population which correspond to neighborhoods. Tract data reveal the character of small sections of a city.

The manuscript records, for the years they are available, allow even closer examination of individual families, neighborhoods, farms, and businesses. Since the census takers usually covered their district systematically, house by house, street by street, and always listed addresses, it is possible to compile a picture of a block or neighborhood. Ethnic, racial, occupation, and wealth patterns can be identified. High concentrations of blacks or foreign born, young or old, and male or female residents can be clues to the special character of a neighborhood, as can the presence of unusual numbers of lodgers or households with the same family name.

No census was ever absolutely complete or accurate. Enumerators were under oath to do their best, but the people they interviewed sometimes withheld or misreported information because of suspicion, embarrassment, fear of taxation, or simple lack of knowledge. People either did not re-

Census records can help the historian begin to develop a picture of a community or a neighborhood at some point in the past, as this description of a south-side Pittsburgh neighborhood in 1880 demonstrates.

*[The neighborhood] lies between Eighteenth and Twentieth streets, from the Monongahela River to East Carson Street. A curve of the river broadens the valley here, at the site of East Birmingham, and Carson, Sidney, and Wharton streets were widened accordingly, with narrow alleys added between them. Small, neat houses lined both streets and alleys, fronting squarely on the sidewalk; they were rectangular, two-story boxes exhibiting to the public eye a door and two long, narrow front windows. The 1880 census referred to such structures as examples of good housing for workers. Behind those doors lived generations of glassblowers, puddlers, laborers, and their wives, widows, and children. Nearby were the factories and stores in which they worked, and the churches and taverns where they spent leisure time.*

*The first and most detailed picture of the area appears in the 1880 manuscript schedule census. Jarrett, Duvall, and Plank, enumerators, recorded the inhabitants of each dwelling, their ages, places of birth, literacy, and employment or lack of it. In the 286 houses of these twelve blocks lived 1,777 people—902 men and women and 875 children. Forty-four percent of the adults but less than 3 percent of their children were foreign born, indicating that these immigrants were well settled by 1880. Almost 60 percent of them had come from some part of the German Empire, although German immigrants made up only one-third of the total population of Pittsburgh at this time. In this part of the Twenty-sixth Ward were 238 Germans, 64 Irish, 69 English, Welsh, and Scotch, and a few French and Swiss. One-fourth of the first-generation Americans were of German descent, making this area one of the predominantly German sections of the city.*

The neighborhood was near the center of the city's glass industry, and the census information regarding individual's employment provided clues to the nature of the industry:

*Of the 583 working men, women, and boys in the area in 1880, the largest single group, 169, were glassworkers . . . Fifty-one of the area glassworkers were between eleven and seventeen years of age. Only three boys in this age group were listed by the census as apprentices, but all hoped to learn the skills which might enable them to earn good wages as adults. Most boys performed indispensable small jobs such as 'carrying-in' and 'cleaning-off,' earning between fifty and sixty cents a day. High unemployment rates, even among the more skilled workers, indicated that the glasshouse boys must have been doing more than their share of the family breadwinning. Of working boys seventeen and under, 11 percent were out of work between one and three months; 15 percent between four and six months. But young men between the ages of eighteen and twenty-nine were laid off at the rate of 14 percent for one to three months, 30 percent for four to six months, and 7 percent for more than six months. By comparison, workers over thirty reported an even higher rate of unemployment, with 30 percent not working between one and three months and 28 percent out of work between four and six months. Only six glassworkers in the area were over fifty years old. As one employer stated in his census return, 'when a man reaches 55 years of age he seems to lose his skill as a workman and has to take a subordinate place.'*

*Source*: Josephine McIlvain, "Twelve Blocks: A Study of One Segment of Pittsburgh's South Side, 1880–1915," *Western Pennsylvania Historical Magazine* 60 (October 1977): 352–353, 356–357.

member or would not admit their exact ages, as shown by the phenomenon of "age heaping," the clustering of reported ages around years ending in 5 and 0 rather than a more even spread. When residents could not be found at home, enumerators turned to neighbors and accepted secondhand information. Additional errors could be introduced as a result of differing definitions of occupations or economic value, the census taker's bad handwriting, or personal ideas about how to spell particular sounds. Various enumerators might spell a family name in different ways; for instance, in the 1790 census there were at least 100 persons with each of the following names: Burns, Bearn, Bearnes, Bern, Berns, Berhans, Burn, Burne, Burnes, Byrn, Byrnes, and Byrns.

Inevitably the census would miss people, most frequently minorities and the very poor. But since enumerators were sometimes paid by the number of entries, there might also be overreporting. Censuses were usually supposed to be taken as of June 1, but they could be delayed by weeks or even months; with people constantly moving, individuals could easily be missed and totals distorted. Historian Sam Bass Warner has concluded on the basis of careful studies of Boston that census totals cannot be depended upon to be more accurate than ± 6 percent, while Eric E. Lampard believes that economic statistics may have errors of ± 10 percent. Individual entries may, of course, contain even greater errors or be missing altogether. The researcher who approaches every document with care and attempts to check information against other sources will discover incorrect and missing information in census records but will also find much of value.

The federal census is readily accessible up to a point. The published compilations for states, counties, towns, and census tracts are widely available. The manuscript returns, arranged by state and county, have been microfilmed for each census through 1910 (with the unfortunate exception of 1890, for which almost all of the returns were destroyed by fire in 1921). The search for individual names in the manuscript returns is made much easier by soundex indexes, state-by-state alphabetical lists of names by phonetic spelling of the surname, followed by the given names of heads of households. Many local libraries and historical or genealogical societies have copies of the census microfilm for at least the local area, and it is all available for purchase from the National Archives, Washington, D.C. 20408. Currently the manuscript census is kept closed for seventy-two years after an enumeration from regard for the privacy of people listed therein. Information on individuals from the 1920 and later manuscript censuses can be obtained only by the person described, the next of kin, or an authorized legal representative. (See appendix A for forms.) State censuses, where available, often extend into the 1920s and have no restrictions on their use.

## Federal Records

Lesser known and more specialized federal records can also be quite valuable sources of community and family information. The federal postal system, for example, necessarily took note of the creation and growth of every American town. The Records of Appointments of Postmasters, 1815–1929, contain information on the dates when post offices were established or discontinued as well as changes in town names, significant events in community affairs. Reports of Site Locations, 1867–1946, submitted by postmasters, contain geographical information on communities, including rivers, railroads, and landmarks; they may be especially useful for people investigating small towns. The National Archives, Washington, D.C. 20408, will reply to inquiries about these and other records.

During World War I, all resident males between eighteen and forty-five years of age were required to register for the military draft. Some 24 million

Every World War I draft registrant provided current personal information. Many later changed residence and occupation, of course, although few gained the notoriety and fortune that this young man achieved by doing so.

registrants, almost every male born between 1873 and 1900, gave information on their birth date, race, citizenship, occupation, employer, nearest relative, and physical characteristics. These draft registration cards are stored at the Federal Records Center, East Point, Georgia 30344, and have been microfilmed. Staff archivists will search for an individual registration card if given a name, birth date, and location (at least the county and preferably a street address, especially for larger cities); if the card is found, a modest bill will be sent, and on receipt of payment, a photocopy of the card will be mailed. Since the cards are arranged and filmed by draft board, county, and state, they can be used to study the population of a community as well as to learn about individuals. Although these records contain only the names of males of a certain age, they represent the largest unrestricted body of nationwide information on individuals for the years after 1910.

Other federal records can be useful in research on individuals, if not communities. For military volunteers, 1775–1902, the National Archives holds records which show the person's term of service, rank, and unit, and often his age, birthplace, and place of enlistment. A search will be conducted for an individual record if the person's full name, the war in which he served, and the state from which he enlisted can be provided. If the record is found, copies will be provided and the inquirer billed. Applications for military pensions and service records of those in the regular army may contain even more information. Access to these and other military records is discussed in the pamphlet *Military Service Records in the National Archives of the United States*, available on request from the National Archives, Washington, D.C. 20408. A form for requesting military records can be found in appendix A.

The National Archives also has passenger lists and indexes from the Customs Bureau and its successor, the Immigration and Naturalization Service, for most ships arriving at Atlantic and Gulf Coast ports since 1820. Similar West Coast lists were destroyed by fire. These lists normally contain the name, age, and occupation of each passenger, the country from which he or she came and to which he or she was going, and in later years information on literacy, U.S. relatives, and the name of the person who paid for the passage. Archivists will search the customs and immigration lists more than fifty years old if the name of the passenger, the port of embarkation or entry, the name of the ship, and the date of arrival can be provided. (A request form is included in appendix A). With any part of this information, one may be able to determine the rest from the *Morton Allan Directory of European Passenger Steamship Arrivals* (New York, 1931) for New York arrivals, 1890–1930, and Philadelphia, Baltimore, and Boston arrivals, 1904–1926. The Immigration and Naturalization Service also has records of people naturalized as citizens after September 25, 1906, including date and place of arrival in the United States and names of spouses and children.

Not every difficult-to-solve historical question involves a time centuries past. The Social Security Administration, established in 1935 in the midst of the New Deal, is not a particularly old federal agency. It has yet to turn over its records to the National Archives. Social Security files contain information as to where enrolled persons worked and what income they received year by year. On request (the form is in appendix A), the Social Security Administration will provide this information. Privacy laws require, however, that the request must be signed by the individual involved or by a legal representative. Although this stricture limits access to Social Security records, they may be a useful means of documenting a personal history or buttressing the slipping memory of a cooperative relative or acquaintance.

## Local Records

State and local archives, as mentioned earlier, can be rich sources of information on communities and the people within them. For instance, in some areas the city or county assessor's files not only provide valuable economic data but also list names, addresses, and occupations of residents, arranged by streets. Thus, such records may be used to obtain a picture of occupational and wealth patterns of neighborhoods, even for periods much earlier than federal census returns would allow. Municipal and state courts as well as federal district courts held naturalization proceedings prior to September 26, 1906, and their records can provide information on community immigration patterns as well as on individuals.

Vital records—birth, death, marriage, and divorce records—are among the most useful documents kept by state or local governments. They can provide names, birth dates, and places, names and birthplaces of parents, length of residence in the United States, and other information, and for death certificates, time, place, and cause of death, and burial site. Prior to the early twentieth century, many states did not centralize vital records, and they may have been kept by a county or city official, usually the clerk of courts. The U.S. Government Printing Office, Washington, D.C. 20402, publishes three booklets which can help in locating vital records in individual states: *Where to Write for Birth and Death Records*, *Where to Write for*

In addition to documenting the age, marital status, and death date of Susan Duly, this tombstone suggests by its elaborate design the economic status of her family.

*Marriage Records,* and *Where to Write for Divorce Records.* It is important to remember, however, that even vital records contain errors. Birth, marriage, and death certificates all ask for parents' names, but that information is more likely to be correct when a baby's parents are in a position to give their own names than when an elderly person with long-deceased parents dies. Death certificates are filled out during times of stress and often by persons not in a good position to know. Vital records deserve the same skepticism one brings to any other untested document.

Cemeteries can supplement vital records as well as substitute for them during periods before the latter were kept. It may be difficult to think of a cemetery as an archives or a tombstone as a document, but the marker may have information carved upon it that appears nowhere else. Not only the inscriptions showing name and birth and death date but also epitaphs, symbolic carvings, and the size and style of a headstone may be instructive. Adjacent headstones may mark relatives. In addition, many cemeteries keep written records, copies of obituaries, and interment maps and indexes. A family, church, or community cemetery may reveal details about its sponsoring group. Of course, many people could not afford cemetery markers, and wood and even stone do wear away. Some groups have systematically copied cemetery inscriptions to preserve their information. Such copies can sometimes be found with the local historical or genealogical society or in a nearby library.

Deeds and other property records kept by county officials can be extremely useful for identifying patterns of land division and urban growth, tracing property ownership, and describing changes in the use of real estate. Building and zoning codes, which became widespread in the 1920s, provide further information on land use. They may also provide clues as to the status and treatment of various ethnic and economic groups or businesses within the community.

Wills and related probate records can prove to be very rich sources of information. Even people who die without a will sometimes leave property which a court must administer. Probate records inventory, often with detailed descriptions, a person's property and indicate to whom it is left. Heirs usually include relatives who might appear in other records and sometimes friends and favored organizations otherwise hard to identify. Estate inventories can provide clues to a family's life-style and economic situation and, considered cumulatively, a neighborhood or community pattern. Historians

Wills provide a public record of a deceased person's intentions for the distribution of his or her property. As such they can provide a view of economic status, personal tastes, and life-style. In addition, wills can offer clues about an individual's relationships with family and friends, as in this brief will made in Tennessee in 1822.

*In the name of God, amen, I, John Cox, in the County of Carroll, and State of Tennessee, being weak in body, but of perfect mind and memory, knowing the uncertainty of this life, do make and ordain this my last will and testament. First, I recommend my soul to Almighty God who gave it, and my body to the grave, to be interred in Christian-like manner. As to my worldly estate, which it has pleased God to bless me with, I do will in manner and form as follows, vis; I will that my beloved wife, Purity Cox, have all my estate, during all of her natural life. I do also will that my executors do sell my wagon, hindgear, rifle, gun and ball, horse and grey mare, and with the profits arising from the sale of the above and the money I have on hand, I will that they purchase land for the benefit of my beloved wife, Purity Cox, during all her natural life, at her death the said land to be equally divided between my beloved sons, William and James Cox.*

*I do also will that my beloved daughter, Sally Cox, have one good bed, one cow and calf, one side saddle and one flax wheel. I also will my beloved daughter, Rhoda Barnhart, have twenty-five dollars; I also will that my son-in-law, Peter Culp, have ONE DOLLAR. I also will that at the death of my beloved wife, Purity Cox, that my negro girl Mary, and all the balance of my property not here to fore willed, be equally divided between my daughter, Sally Cox and Sally Culp, and Nancy McMackin, my niece. I do here by make and ordain this my last will and testament revoking all others by me made as witness my hand and seal this fourth day of February in the year of our Lord, One thousand eight hundred and twenty-two.*

*Source*: Family History Collection, American History Research Center, University of Akron, Akron, Ohio.

can easily obtain access to probate records, since they are open to public inspection so that all potential heirs can see that they are receiving their rightful shares of an estate. Laws vary from state to state, but a probate court or some similar county office maintains and indexes such records.

State and local public records might ordinarily be found only in the files of the creating agency or its archives. However, the Genealogical Society of

Utah, an agency of the Church of Jesus Christ of Latter-day Saints, has made such records much more accessible. Since Mormons feel a religious obligation to identify their ancestors, they have sponsored an enormous effort to microfilm and collect documents which may be of use in genealogical research. The Genealogical Society has collected land, immigration, naturalization, probate, vital, and other public records; church and cemetery records; and many other types of records from foreign countries as well as the entire United States. Far more than a million rolls of microfilm are available for use at the society's library in Salt Lake City or through more than 200 branches connected with the Latter-day Saints. Inquiries should be addressed to the Genealogical Society of Utah, 50 East North Temple Square, Salt Lake City, Utah 84111.

Many private as well as public unpublished documents are worthwhile for nearby history. One set which can be useful for many communities is found in the Baker Library of the Graduate School of Business Administration at Harvard University, Boston, Massachusetts 02163: the 2,580 volumes of R. G. Dun and Company credit reports for the years before 1890. Beginning in 1841, the Mercantile Agency, which became R. G. Dun and Company in 1851 and later Dun and Bradstreet, collected information on American businesses in order to rate their suitability for credit. Because the Dun agency wished to continue selling credit reports, it worked hard to provide accurate data. The 2,000 or more local correspondents of the company would file reports at least once a year on the activities, financial improvement or decline, and other noteworthy features of area businessmen. Many reports included information on former residences, marital status, family and ethnic background, business experience and prospects, and personal characteristics, supposedly all factors useful in judging credit worthiness. Although bigger and wealthier businesses were more likely to apply for credit and were therefore more likely to be investigated, self-employed artisans and owners of small retail and service shops, seldom treated in the federal census of manufacturers, may be found in the records of R. G. Dun. The credit reports can help fill out the details of nineteenth-century individual or community business history.

This brief survey can only suggest a little of the contents of archives and manuscript collections. The possibilities are as numerous as the creators of records. During the Great Depression of the 1930s, the Works Progress Administration conducted surveys of local, state, and private records which turned up thousands of series of records in county courthouses and elsewhere. The WPA records surveys can still be helpful in identifying and locating materials for use in nearby history. Since that time universities, social agencies, and other organizations as well as government offices have collected more and more data about individual communities. Keep in mind that if the records first regarded as a source prove to be nonexistent, inadequate, or of doubtful accuracy, there may well be other archives or manuscripts which contain part or all of the information desired. Regional branches of the National Archives, listed in appendix F, and state archives, historical societies, and preservation offices, listed in appendix G, provide starting points for a search. Determined historians of the nearby world, whatever their topics, will pay careful attention to a wide range of unpublished documents.

## For Further Information

Philip C. Brooks, *Research in Archives: The Use of Unpublished Primary Sources* (Chicago: University of Chicago Press, 1969), is a clear and helpful introduction. Also useful are O. Lawrence Burnette, Jr., *Beneath the Footnote: A Guide to the Use and Preservation of American Historical Sources* (Madison: State Historical Society of Wisconsin, 1969); Kenneth W. Duckett, *Modern Manuscripts: A Practical Guide for their Management, Care, and Use* (Nashville: American Association for State and Local History, 1975); and H. G. Jones, *Local Government Records: An Introduction to Their Management, Preservation, and Use* (Nashville: American Association for State and Local History, 1980).

Several guides written to assist genealogists contain information on archival and manuscript materials that can be of value to any nearby historian. Among the best are Gilbert H. Doane, *Searching for Your Ancestors*, 4th ed. (Minneapolis: University of Minnesota Press, 1973; paperback, New York: Bantam, 1974); Val D. Greenwood, *The Researcher's Guide to American Genealogy* (Baltimore: Genealogical Publishing, 1977); Jeane Eddy Westin, *Finding Your Roots* (New York: St. Matin's, 1977); Charles L. Blockson, *Black Genealogy* (Englewood Cliffs, N.J.: Prentice-Hall, 1977); Dan Rottenberg, *Finding Our Fathers: A Guidebook to Jewish Genealogy* (New York: Random House, 1977); and Arthur Kurzweil, *From Generation to Generation: How to Trace Your Jewish Genealogy and Personal History* (New York: Morrow, 1980).

A book that relates individual family research to questions and approaches of broader applicability is David E. Kyvig and Myron A. Marty, *Your Family History: A Handbook for Research and Writing* (Arlington Heights, Ill.: AHM, 1978).

Many ideas on how federal records can be of use in local research appear in Jerome Finster, ed., *The National Archives and Urban Research* (Athens: Ohio University Press, 1974).

The use of census records for community history is discussed in Sam Bass Warner, Jr., "A

Local Historian's Guide to Social Statistics," in *Streetcar Suburbs: The Process of Growth in Boston, 1870–1900* (Cambridge, Mass.: Harvard University Press, 1962), pp. 169–78. More on the subject can be found in Edward K. Muller, "Town Populations in the Early United States Censuses: An Aid to Research," *Historical Methods Newsletter* 4 (1971): 2–8; Robert G. Barrows, "The Manuscript Federal Census: Source for a 'New' Local History," *Indiana Magazine of History* 69 (1973): 181–92; and Lutz Berkner, "The Use and Misuse of Census Data for the Historical Analysis of Family Structure," *Journal of Interdisciplinary History* 4 (1975): 721–38. On the census of manufacturers, see Margaret Walsh, "The Census as an Accurate Source of Information: The Value of Mid-Nineteenth Century Manufacturing Returns," *Historical Methods Newsletter* 3 (1970): 3–13, and "The Value of Mid-Nineteenth Century Manufacturing Returns: The Printed Census and the Manuscript Compilations Compared," *Historical Methods Newsletter* 4 (1971): 43–51.

A guide to state and territorial censuses taken after 1790 is Henry J. Dubester, *State Censuses: An Annotated Bibliography* (1944; reprinted., Westport, Conn.: Greenwood, 1976).

Discussions of more specialized records include James H. Madison, "The Credit Reports of R. G. Dun and Co. as Historical Sources," *Historical Methods Newsletter* 8 (1975): 128–31; Richard K. Lieberman, "A Measure for the Quality of Life: Housing," *Historical Methods Newsletter* 11 (1978): 129–34; and Larry R. Gerlach and Michael L. Nicholls, "The Mormon Genealogical Society and Research Opportunities in Early American History," *William and Mary Quarterly* 32 (1976): 625–29.

Historians faced with masses of material culled from census returns, local archives, and other sources may wish to learn how to assess it quantitatively and perhaps how to store, retrieve, manipulate, and analyze it using a computer. These are sophisticated techniques, but they are not beyond the capacity of most individuals willing to invest a little time to acquire basic statistical and computer skills. It is of course helpful to have access to a computer through one's school, business, or agency. But many useful statistical analyses do not require a computer. To gain a sense of what is involved and how to begin, consult Hubert M. Blalock, Jr., *Social Statistics*, 2nd ed. (New York: McGraw-Hill, 1972); Charles M. Dollar and Richard J. Jensen, *Historian's Guide to Statistics: Quantitative Analysis and Historical Research* (New York: Holt, Rinehart and Winston, 1971); Edward Shorter, *The Historian and the Computer: A Practical Guide* (Englewood Cliffs, N.J.: Prentice-Hall, 1971); and Roderick Floud, *An Introduction to Quantitative Methods for Historians* (Princeton: Princeton University Press, 1973). For examples of the application of these techniques to nearby history, refer to the many recent works cited in chapter 12, especially those having to do with mobility and assimilation.

# ·6·

# Oral Documents

IT MAY APPEAR UNUSUAL TO REFER TO SOMETHING AS AN "oral document," but only until one recalls that "document" derives from the Latin *docere*, "to teach." Not everything that teaches by words is written down, at least not in its original form. With this in mind, we turn our attention to traces of another kind, those carried in the memories of participants in and eyewitnesses to events of the past. If the information and insights in those memories can be reached, they are potentially of immeasurable historical value.

Reaching into human memories is particularly important for historians of communities, institutions, and families, for the history they are dealing with was most likely made by men and women who had neither the time nor the inclination to leave an extensive written record of their doings. Nearby historians are practitioners of "the new social history," that is, the history of the nonelite, of men and women in ordinary walks of life. Some individuals among them stood out from others, of course, and they should receive the attention they deserve, but local historians should not ignore the opportunity to draw composite sketches of the anonymous folks who have through the years played important but unheralded and so far unrecorded parts in the communities, institutions, and families to which they belonged.

Sometimes participants and eyewitnesses to history can be induced to write down the information and insights in which historians are interested. Persons asking for written responses to questions should observe two very important rules. First, the questions should be as specific as possible. Avoid asking questions like: What was Uncle Bill like? Ask rather: What did he do for a living? How did he prefer to spend his free time? What was the nature of his relationship with his parents? Do not ask questions requiring lengthy and involved answers.

Second, make responding to your questions as simple as possible. Leave space after your questions for the answers to be written in. Include a stamped return envelope. Courtesy and appreciation must always be shown. People are more likely to supply information if they are assured that they are providing genuine assistance. Tell them why the information is being sought.

A better way to reach into the memories of history's participants and eyewitnesses is to ask them questions person to person. When conversations embodying the questions and answers are recorded on tape for later use, oral history is being practiced. It is possible, of course, to record interviews over the phone, but the interviewer must tell the responding person that the conversation is being taped.

The decision to devote an entire chapter to the use of oral documents, or oral history, as it is more commonly called, is meant neither to enshroud it in mystery nor to elevate it to a place of superiority among research methods. Oral history is simply a way of recording information gained from persons who have firsthand knowledge of historical events, thus adding to the sum total of knowledge about them. The quest for new knowledge, incidentally, distinguishes the oral historian from the producer of broadcast documentaries. The former seeks, by interviewing, to elicit previously unrecorded traces of the past and to convert them into a form—aural to begin with, but possibly also written—that will make them useful to historians. Quite often the person who will use the information garnered is also the one conducting the interview, but this is not always the case.

Oral history is neither a new nor a rarely used research tool. Historians have relied for centuries on eyewitness and participant accounts that they and others have created by asking questions and writing down the answers. But the method was institutionalized with the founding by Allan Nevins of the Columbia Oral History Project in 1940. It took its first big step toward popular use in 1948 when the wire recorder was introduced, making possible verbatim transcripts of interviews. Tape recorders, both audio and more recently video, and especially cassette tape recorders, have helped to generate an oral history movement. (It should be noted, however, that interviews do not always have to be tape recorded. Interviewers can simply take notes by hand, as reporters for newspapers do.)

Recorded or transcribed reminiscences can preserve descriptions of housing, living arrangements, and other details of ordinary life which may not otherwise survive. This transcription of an interview with a grandfather provides a good example.

*I got a job mining coal for the Reitz Coal Co. in Central City, Pa. (about seven miles south of Windber), and the family rented a home here for about two years just before World War I. This home was owned by the coal company and was built to rent to their employees. One building housed two families (a duplex). There was no basement. Each family had two rooms downstairs, a kitchen and living room, and two bedrooms upstairs, an adjoining front and back porch. There was no central heating, running water, or inside plumbing. Coal stoves in the kitchens were used for cooking, baking, and heating. In the winter the house heating was supplemented by a fancy iron heating stove in the living room. Heat came to the upstairs bedrooms through a hole in the ceiling directly above this stove. The hole was covered by an iron filigreed cover that let the heat up but protected one from falling through the hole from upstairs. Water was supplied from outside hand-operated water pumps located at intervals along the street. Buckets of water were pumped, then kept sitting inside the kitchen door for household use. Rent of the house was about eight dollars per month. Toilets called "closets" were a separate small building in the back yard. An old catalog was usually used for toilet paper. One took a bath in a portable galvanized tub with water heated atop the coal stove. This was done usually in the kitchen. Privacy was gotten by the rest of the family keeping out of the room while one took a bath. A coal miner required a bath each day he worked in the mines, as he came home blackened by the coal dust. The rest of the family members got a bath once a week on Saturday.*

*Source*: Family History Collection, American History Research Center, University of Akron, Akron, Ohio.

## Using Oral History Effectively

How can oral history be used most effectively? From the various manuals on the market, one gains the impression that, reduced to its basics, oral history is nothing more than the application of common sense to the pursuit of information. For how could people with any sense at all

- appear unannounced for an interview at the doorstep of someone about whom they know practically nothing
- bring to the interview equipment they do not know how to operate or that they have not checked before coming
- begin an interview without setting the respondent at ease and with no idea of what they want to accomplish
- ask poorly framed questions
- allow the interview to drift or, quite the opposite, force it to fit into a preconceived format
- fail to listen to answers to questions
- interrupt the respondent's comments and dominate the conversation
- try to interview two or three people simultaneously with the television blaring in the background
- keep the interview going until the respondent collapses from exhaustion or loses interest
- fail to take notes during the interview, recording dates, names— especially how to spell them, and other matters that might need clarification later
- fail to seek the respondent's permission to use the information produced in the interview
- fail to identify on the tape and in writing the respondent, the interviewer, and the subject of the interview
- use the information gained without verifying it for accuracy?

Still, mistakes of the kind that no one would expect to make do occur, and anyone who has worked in oral history could no doubt add to our list.

Before we offer specific suggestions for doing oral history properly and effectively, two general comments may be helpful. First, it is important to remember that circumstances alter practices. Persons working alone—say, on a family history—will approach interviewing of persons with whom they are acquainted in a manner quite different from that used by teams of interviewers working collaboratively in projects with clear and well-defined purposes. In the former instance, the interviewers probably aim to collect reminiscences and to evoke interpretations of facts already known. Knowing that new information may turn up when interviews roam off course, such interviewers are not particularly intent upon keeping to preestablished sets of questions.

In group projects—for instance, a neighborhood history—in which cadres of interviewers set out to elicit information from persons they have never met before and may never meet again, it is desirable to give each interviewer precisely worded questions arranged in a specific order and instructions to use the questions as provided. In such circumstances the interview is part of a larger survey, and questions left unanswered by some of the population surveyed will diminish the value of the entire project.

Circumstances also alter the type and extent of training given to interviewers. Personable and engaging conversationalists working on their own projects can probably do an effective job of interviewing without too much training. A quick reading of the suggestions in this chapter should be sufficient to start them off. They will learn quickly from experience, and the price paid for mistakes will not be too high. On the other hand, interviewing does not come naturally to some people, and training and practice are helpful to them. Again, when interviewing is done as part of a project— one, say, that is attempting to determine migration patterns or to record the experiences of persons who participated in a specific event, systematic training is almost always necessary. Whether the interviewers are volunteers or paid workers makes little difference. The nature of the project and the personality of the interviewer determine the extent of training required.

The second general comment is that oral history is only a means to an end, not an end in itself. It is but one part of a process aimed at gathering, assimilating, and interpreting information. Some of the most enthusiastic advocates and practitioners in the oral history movement occasionally give the impression that the interview itself is of paramount importance. This is understandable, since it can be exciting fun. Furthermore, because the persons interviewed are often elderly, interviewers develop a sense that time is running out. Libraries and archives will always be there, but people die. Someone has said that doing oral history is like climbing a down escalator—there is no time to rest. Enthusiasm for oral history is fine, but what really counts is the potential of oral history for accomplishment, for a contribution to the historical record.

## Guidelines for Interviewing

Whether they are working alone or in a larger project, historians will want to make their interviews as good as possible. These guidelines should be helpful.

Before the interview:

1. Call or write the respondent well before the time you would like to conduct the interview. Explain your plans and purposes, solicit the person's interest in your project, and set a time for an interview. Keep notes on your first conversation. In a larger project it may be desirable to follow the initial contact with a letter describing how the individual interviews fit as parts into the whole and listing four or five major topics to be covered. Your advance contacts will probably set the respondent to thinking about your interests, and you are likely to secure a better interview. More than courtesy is involved in laying the groundwork for interviews.

2. Gather as much background information about the respondent as you can and familiarize yourself thoroughly with the relationship between the respondent and the project you are working on.

3. Outline the main points of interest for your interview. To avoid being trapped in a rigid format, it is best not to write out specific questions but to jot down short phrases around which you can readily build questions. This use of notes will give the conversation a touch of spontaneity and will help set both the interviewer and the respondent at ease. If you choose to write out questions, be prepared to abandon them if the interview takes unexpected but productive turns.

4. If you plan to use a tape recorder, become thoroughly acquainted with its operation, especially the microphone, volume controls, and tape-changing procedures. Practice with someone before going to the interview. If you feel comfortable in the presence of a microphone, so will the person being interviewed. Practice also control of the tape so that you are adept at reserving a minute or so of blank tape before the recording of the interview starts; you will want to use this reserved portion of the tape to record information about the interview. Prepare a kit of materials that you will want to take with you to the interview: your notes and interview outline, pens and pencils, a notebook, an extension cord, and extra tapes.

To start the interview:

1. Situate yourself and the respondent in comfortable positions. The

recorder should be placed within your reach but where the respondent will not be too conscious of it. Try to avoid distractions, interruptions, and background noises from radios, television sets, or traffic.

2. Let the recorder run for a few minutes as you chat about matters not directly related to the interview. Listen to a minute or two of what you have recorded. This should relax both you and the respondent while you make sure that the recording is picking up at proper level. You might be surprised to discover that the respondent is hearing his or her voice for the first time, and you may have to offer assurance that there is nothing unpleasant or unnatural about the sound.

3. If you can do so without making your respondent nervous, begin the interview with identifying information: name the interviewer, the respondent, the date, the place, and the subject of the interview. A conversational style will provide a nice transition between the informal conversation and the interview which follows, establishing the basis for an easy flow between questions and answers.

4. Be sure to check the time and to know the length of your tape so that you will not have to look constantly to see how much recording time remains. Interviews should not normally be scheduled to last more than an hour or at most ninety minutes.

During the interview:

1. Remind yourself that the interview is not intended to show off your knowledge—though you must appear knowledgeable to the respondent—but to elicit from the respondent clear responses to your questions. Above all, do not dominate the conversation with displays of knowledge.

2. Avoid asking questions that can be answered with a simple yes or no. Useful leads include: "What led up to . . . ?" "Tell me about . . . " "What did you feel when . . . ?" and "I would like to hear about . . ."

3. Ask only one question at a time; that is, avoid running questions together or protracting them so that the respondent is confused regarding which one to answer.

4. Keep your questions brief and to the point.

5. Start with noncontroversial matters, saving more delicate ones until good rapport has been established.
6. Listen.
7. Don't let periods of silence fluster you; the respondent needs time to think.
8. Don't worry excessively about a question that seems to be clumsily worded. A little fumbling by the interviewer may help to put the respondent at ease.
9. Do not interrupt a good story simply because another question has occurred to you or because the respondent has wandered from the planned framework of questions. If you do, valuable remembrances might escape. Try to find gentle ways and the appropriate time for pulling the conversation back on the track.
10. To help the respondent describe persons, ask about their appearance, then about their personality, character, and activities.
11. Remember that persons being interviewed are likely to give more interesting and more vigorous responses to questions or statements that imply uncertainty on your part than to ones that suggest that you are merely seeking agreement. A phrase like "I'm not sure I understand" or "this can be confusing to someone who wasn't there" may elicit useful information.
12. Try to establish where the respondent was at the time of the events being described as well as his or her role in them. Determine whether the respondent was a participant or a passive witness.
13. Use the interview to verify information gained from other sources. Do not take issue with accounts given by the respondent even if you believe another version to be more accurate. Be content to elicit as much information as possible, possibly by offering alternative versions: "Some people say . . . " or "I have heard . . ." You can decide later which version of a story is accurate.
14. Try to avoid off-the-record comments; try instead to get the respondent to speak in terms that permit the statement to be part of the record. Sensitive material can be protected by closing the tape for an agreed-upon period of years, that is, by sealing it so that researchers will not have access to it until the material in question is less sensitive. It is better to have such material recorded and waiting for later use than to let it escape entirely.
15. Do not interrupt the respondent unless the story strays too far from

its course. Interruptions, when necessary, should begin with phrases like "let's go back to where you . . ."' or "a moment ago you were telling me about . . ."

16. Avoid turning the machine off and on unless the respondent becomes unduly agitated or uncommunicative. Having some irrelevant material on the tape is better than losing the flow of the conversation by switching the recorder off and on again.

17. Be alert to points in the interview when special factual information is brought out. Take note of this information by writing it down. Asking the respondent to spell names is not at all inappropriate. Accuracy is more important than an uninterrupted interview.

18. Use photographs, clippings, or other documents to encourage the respondent to talk about persons or events that are of particular interest to you and about which his or her memory might need some jostling. Asking respondents to dig out photographs and other memory-prompting materials before the interview may be a way of inviting them to think about the topics you want to discuss. If possible, make copies of these documents and include them with the tape when you deposit it in the archives.

19. At the end of the interview, repeat the identifying information: the interviewer, the respondent, the date, the place, and the subject of the interview.

After the interview:

1. Secure the *written* permission of the respondent to use the tape and transcription.

2. Record the identifying information in writing on a card to be placed in an interview file. On the same card should be a summary of the major topics discussed, along with the time in the interview when discussion begins. This time-topic index, which requires the use of a stopwatch, makes the tape useful to researchers before a typed transcript becomes available. Such an index is important even when the researcher is also the interviewer.

3. Store the tape in a place where it can be preserved without damage, which means low humidity and temperature that avoids extremes of heat and cold.

This brief excerpt from a family history shows how a picture used to elicit information during research can be incorporated into a finished product.

*This is a family portrait with all six sons, around 1941. The ages of the sons are paired in groups of two from three years to seventeen years. This was not a coincidence or some sort of family planning. Hermena wanted a daughter and had been told that if you had a son and then got pregnant soon after that birth, the next baby would be a girl. She tried this three times without success.*

*The car in the background was a neighbor's Buick; however, the family now had a 1932 Chevy. Papa had rebuilt their 1916 Model T continuously until it would not run, even with a miracle. They eventually bought a 1932 used Chevy with the money Papa had managed to save in the three-four years while working for WPA and hiring himself out for farm work.*

*The family was still living on a rented farm, but their clothes are not tattered or patched as they had been three-four years earlier. They had electricity via a "wind charger," a propeller-driven generator, which charged the battery and could light one bulb, taking the place of the kerosine lamp, and run their newly acquired radio. Their diet had improved, with meat much more frequent. The crops had improved and the profits were small but more steady. About a year after the picture Papa gave up farming and moved to the city to work as a carpenter full time, a less risky "business."*

*Source*: Pamela Bohlmann, untitled essay for family histories project (St. Louis, 1977).

A 1941 family portrait, posed in front of a neighbor's parked car.

## Some Open Issues in Oral History

Experts in oral history are not all of the same mind about a number of questions they face, some of which must be discussed briefly here.

*How important is it for tapes to be transcribed?* Transcriptions are the best means for making the content of tapes available and useful to researchers, but the labor involved is very time consuming and therefore very costly. It takes as much as five hours, and possibly even longer, to transcribe a one-hour interview. The consensus seems to be that transcriptions should be made if possible, but that it is better to continue interviewing than to spend most of one's time and money on transcriptions. The time-topic index described above serves as a good interim device for making the tapes useful. Despite this consensus, however, we strongly urge beginners in oral history to transcribe diligently in order to hear and understand the interview. This exercise will make novices conscious of things they missed and the reasons for the omissions. Transcriptions are self-training exercises. Almost always they prompt the interviewer to return for a second interview, which is likely to be much more informative than the first.

*Should transcriptions be literal, or is editing permitted?* The general view is that it is permissible to delete verbal clutter, such as false starts, "you know," "uh-huh," and the verbal reactions of the interviewer that are designed merely to keep the respondent talking. More extensive editing is frowned upon by many oral historians and is not tolerated at all by some. As a practical matter, the extent of editing is dictated by the nature and quality of the respondent's narrative.

*Should transcriptions be shown to respondents, giving them a chance to change what they said on the tape?* Most oral historians agree that if the interviews are likely to be published or quoted extensively, or if they form an integral part of a published work, respondents must be accorded the privilege of reviewing and even revising the transcripts so that they show not merely what people said but what they wanted to say. Giving the respondents this prerogative discourages some oral historians from making transcriptions. In their writing, they quote directly from the tape.

*Should the tapes be cassettes or of the reel-to-reel type?* The argument for the former rests on the fact that they are more convenient by far; but reel-to-reel tapes are thicker, more dependable, less likely to become entangled in the machine, cheaper per foot, and generally better for recording. Some persons believe that reel-to-reel tapes will last longer and are therefore preferable.

One of the New Deal's many programs to put people to work during the 1930s depression was the WPA Federal Writers' Project. Among its other activities, the project sent historians, sociologists, journalists, and others to interview people throughout the country about their lives and customs. In that era, before the time of the tape recorder, responses to interview questions had to be written up from notes or from memory by the interviewer. Many of these early oral histories were then placed in the Library of Congress, where they remain. Best known among the interviews with ordinary people who had been largely overlooked by historians were many with aged blacks old enough to remember slave life, but other ethnic minorities were also represented. For instance, a series of interviews with the Italians and Cubans of Ybor City, Florida, provided much information about that community's past and present.

*I was born in the town of Santo Stefano di Quisquina, Sicily, on May 12th, 1860, and am now 75 years of age. My father was a farm peasant working the soil for a land owner. Since my early years I toiled at the farm with my father.*

*I was married at the age of 22 years, and then leased a tract of land which I worked planting wheat, horse feed, potatoes and vegetables. After we had been married a year, my wife gave birth to a child, a baby boy, who died when he was a year old. In the year 1885 my wife again gave birth to another son who died soon after.*

*In this same year I decided to come to New Orleans where many Italians were living at that time. The trip was long and tedious, lasting 30 days. I was afterwards introduced to Mr. Vaccaro who was the owner of the steamship line in which I had sailed to America with my wife. We soon became fast friends, and he proposed to me that I work for him at his Produce Company in New Orleans. He handled bananas chiefly which he brought from Honduras. There I was employed as foreman, which position I held for some two years.*

*Several friends described Tampa to me with such glowing colors that I soon became enthused, and decided to come here and try my fortune. Accordingly, in 1887, leaving my wife in New Orleans, I took the train to Mobile. At Mobile I took the boat that brought me here. We disembarked at the Lafayette Street bridge. I was then 27 years of age.*

*I had expected to see a flourishing city, but my expectations were too high, for what I saw before me almost brought me to tears. There was nothing; what one may truthfully say, nothing. Franklin was a long sandy street. There were very few houses, and these were far apart with tall pine* trees surrounding them. The Hillsborough County Court House was a small wooden building. Some men were just beginning to work on the foundation of the Tampa Bay Hotel.

Ybor City was not connected to Tampa as it is today. There was a wilderness between the two cities, and a distance of more than one mile between the two places. All of Ybor City was not worth one cent to me. In different places of Ybor City a tall species of grass grew, proper of swampy places. This grass grew from 5 to 6 feet high. I was completely disillusioned with what I saw. There was a stagnant water hole where the society of the Centro Espanol (Spanish Club) is today located. A small wooden bridge spanned this pond. I remember that I was afraid to cross that bridge, and especially so at night, because of the alligators that lived there. They would often crawl into the bridge and bask there in the sun all day long.

The factory of Martinez Ybor had some twenty cigar-makers; Sanchez y Haya had some fifteen; while Pendas had about ten. I worked for a time at the factory of Modesto Monet as stripper [a stripper removes the center stem from the tobacco leaf], and made 35c for my first day's work. Of course, I was then only learning the cigar business, and could not expect to make more. When I became more skilled in my work as a stripper, I would make from $1.00 to $1.25 a day.

While still at this work, I gradually began learning the cigar-makers' trade as I saw that they were making a much more comfortable income. When I had become somewhat proficient as a cigar-maker, I was earning from $14.00 to $15.00 a week.

When I had been in Tampa some two or three years I sent for my wife who was still living in New Orleans. When she arrived in Tampa she burst out crying at what she saw: wilderness, swamps, alligators, mosquitoes, and open closets. The only thing she would say when she arrived was: "Why have you brought me to such a place?"

Here we had two more sons, and one died. We had in all four children, of whom three died. We only had one child left whom we were able to raise.

At about this time Mr. Martinez Ybor (the cigar manufacturer) was offering homes for sale at a very low price. I, therefore, went to him and purchased a home at the corner of 18th Street and 8th Avenue for the price of $725. I still have this house, although considerably remodeled. I paid $100 cash, and the balance I paid off in monthly terms. I was able to do this with the help of my wife, who worked also at the cigar factory. We worked in several factories, sometimes in West Tampa, and sometimes in Ybor City, wherever working conditions were better. . . .

> *There is not much hope in Ybor City. The cigar factories are on a continuous decline. The factory of Corral & Wodiska had 1500 persons working, today it has only some 150 or 200 persons. . . . The Trust has also purchased many factories here and have removed them to the Northern cities. The people of Ybor City are orphans, not only of father and mother, but of everything in life. They cannot find work at the cigar factories because of the machines. . . .*
>
> *Under present conditions the people of Ybor City have no other alternative but to leave for New York City. Here they get only 50c a week for the maintenance of a whole family, and the single person is not given any relief whatever. In New York City they are given a home, groceries, coal to warm themselves in winter, and electric lights.*
>
> *Source*: Federal Writers' Project Records, Library of Congress Manuscripts Division, Washington, D.C.

We suspect, though, that most oral historians will choose the convenience of cassette tapes rather than the durability and quality of the reel-to-reel tapes.

*Should the tapes be kept after transcriptions have been made?* Practices here are often dictated by economic considerations. Oral history on a large scale is expensive, and reuse of the tapes is often necessary. The middle-ground position seems to be that representative portions, at least, should be preserved so that the researchers can hear the voices of the respondents and discern the tone of the conversation. Portions dealing with critical issues should also be preserved. The trend is toward maintaining complete tapes after transcription.

*How should ethical and legal issues relating to use be handled?* Persons using oral history must be mindful that they are working with a research method that sometimes raises ethical and legal questions, which include, perhaps most importantly, those dealing with the right to privacy. At stake are not only the rights of the person being interviewed, who may not wish to reveal certain things, but those of third parties as well. Every precaution must be taken to guard against violation of privacy. While release forms such as the sample in appendix B can be used as a way of preparing for possible questions and the potential consequences of misuse of the interviews, they are no substitute for sensitivity and good judgment. Release forms attempt to ensure only that tapes and transcripts may be used in specified ways by qualified researchers, not that the documents will necessarily be open to all who might be curious about their contents. Legal questions are not likely to arise in the work of most nonprofessional historians of the nearby past, and if they do arise, the issues are likely to be too specific for general comments offered here to be useful.

## Oral History and Folklore

Local history is "naturally and inescapably linked with the study of folklore," as the preeminent folklorist Richard Dorson has asserted, and one of the great attractions of research in local history is "the opportunity to record folk traditions and employ them for the enrichment of the historical narrative." Oral folk history is an adaptation of oral history as described above to the circumstances in which it is used.

The folklorist, Dorson points out, does not *interview*; he *collects* folklore from informants (the folk variant of respondent) in ways that are least disruptive to the situation in which the folk share their lore. And folklorists are interested in much more than lore. They collect, as one guide points out, tales (jokes, tall tales, tales of supernatural, legends, marvelous or fairy tales), songs, (ballads, lyrics, ditties, spirituals), instrumental music, dances, play (drama, games, verbal games), riddles, speech (proverbial, vocabulary, grammar), beliefs (regarding human life, plants, animals, and weather, medicine, and witchcraft), customs (daily, occasional, seasonal, annual, or relating to the life cycle), and material culture (art, craft, cookery, and architecture). This collectors' list amounts to a functional description of folklore, which is perhaps the best kind to give, since practitioners are at odds on formal definitions. The *Standard Dictionary of Folklore, Mythology, and Legend* shows the differences of opinion by supplying twenty-one brief definitions.

The authors of this collectors' guide, MacEdward Leach and Henry Glassie, define folklore further by distinguishing between folklore and popular lore, between folk traditions and "the ephemeral products of mass culture." Folklore, they say, "has internal strengths and beauties given it by generations of carriers and molders," qualities that "distinguish it from comparable materials found at other levels of culture." Although folk things are traditional, old-fashioned, and local in character, the best sign that something is really "folk" is evidence that it may be found at different times and in different places. Variations of folk things, folklorists point out, indicate a long life in the oral tradition.

Historians of the nearby past who use oral history as a research tool do not become folklorists merely by collecting rather than interviewing or by paying attention to folksy aspects of the people with whom they work. Yet, being mindful of the concerns of folklorists may help historians do a better job of gathering material for the story they want to tell.

Nor, for that matter, does reading a chapter on oral history make one an oral historian. As with most kinds of historical research, there is only one way to learn oral history, and that is by doing it.


## Notes

Quotations in this chapter can be found in Richard M. Dorson, *American Folklore and the Historian* (Chicago: University of Chicago Press, 1971), p. 146; Dorson, "The Oral Historian and the Folklorist," *Proceedings of the Sixth National Colloquium on Oral History*, Bloomington, Indiana, October 8–10, 1971, p. 42; MacEdward Leach and Henry Glassie, *A Guide for Collectors of Oral Tradition and Folk Cultural Material in Pennsylvania* (Harrisburg: Pennsylvania Historical and Museum Commission, 1968), pp. 7–8.


## For Further Information

The possibilities for successful though widely different uses of oral history as a research method have been demonstrated in such works as William H. Chafe, *Civilities and Civil Rights: Greensboro, North Carolina, and the Black Struggle for Freedom* (New York: Oxford University Press, 1980); Dorothy Gallagher, *Hannah's Daughters: Six Generations of an American Family* (New York: Crowell, 1976); T. Harry Williams, *Huey Long* (New York: Knopf, 1969); Studs Terkel, *Hard Times: An Oral History of the Great Depression* (New York: Pantheon, 1970); Theodore Rosengarten, *All God's Dangers: The Life of Nate Shaw* (New York: Knopf, 1974); Tamara Hareven and Randolph Langenbach, *Amoskeag: Life and Work in an American Factory-City* (New York: Pantheon, 1978); Peter Friedlander, *The Emergence of a UAW Local, 1936–1939: A Study in Class and Culture* (Pittsburgh: University of Pittsburgh Press, 1978); Renee Schulte, *The Young Nixon: An Oral Inquiry* (Fullerton: California State University, 1978); Tom E. Terrill and Jerrold Hirsch, eds., *Such as Us: Southern Voices of the Thirties* (New York: Norton, 1979); Kathy Kahn, *Hillbilly Women* (New York: Avon, 1972); Laurel Schackelford and Bill Weinberg, eds., *Our Appalachia: An Oral History* (New York: Hill and Wang, 1979); and Joan Morrison and Charlotte Fox Zabuskey, eds., *American Mosaic: The Immigrant Experience in the Words of Those Who Lived It* (New York: Dutton, 1980). The various editions of *Foxfire* have also relied on oral history. *First-Person America* (New York: Knopf, 1980), a collection of interviews conducted in the Federal Writers Project of the 1930s, edited by Ann Banks, shows that oral history has been in use for a long time.

Guides to the practice of oral history are numerous; perhaps the best of them is Willa K. Baum, *Oral History for the Local Historical Society*, 2nd ed., rev. (Nashville: American Association for State and Local History, 1974); also by Baum is *Transcribing and Editing Oral History* (Nashville: American Association for State and Local History, 1977). Other works are: Ramon I. Harris, Joseph H. Cash, Herbert T. Hoover, and Stephen R. Ward, *The Practice of Oral History: A Handbook* (Glen Rock, N.J.: Microfilming Corporation of America, 1975); James Hoopes, *Oral History: An Introduction for Students* (Chapel Hill: University of North Carolina Press, 1979); Edward D. Ives, *The Tape-Recorded Interview: A Manual for Workers in Folklore and Oral History* (Knoxville: University of Tennessee Press, 1980; John A. Neuenschwander, *Oral History as a Teaching Approach* (Washington, D.C.: National Education Association, 1976); Gary Shumway and William D. Hartley, *An Oral History Primer* (Salt Lake City: Primer Publications, 1973); and Barbara Allen and Lynwood Montell, *From Memory to History* (Nashville: American Association for State and Local History, 1981). A handbook that pays more attention to preparation of transcripts from the tape than most others is Cullom Davis, Kathryn Back, and Kay MacLean, *Oral History: From Tape to Type* (Chicago: American Library Association, 1977). Also noteworthy is Ingrid Winther Scobie, "Family and Community History through Oral History," *Public Historian* 1 (1979): 29–39.

The Oral History Association publishes the *Oral History Review* (annually since 1973), the *Oral History Newsletter* (since 1967; issues through 1978 are available on microfilm from Microfilming Corporation of America, 1620 Hawkins Ave., P.O. Box 1, Sanford, North Carolina 27730), and *Proceedings* of its colloquia (1967–1971). The address of the association is P.O. Box 13734, North Texas State University, Denton, Texas 76203. The *International Journal of Oral History* began publishing in 1980; its address is 520 Riverside Ave., Westport, Connecticut 06880.

A book that deals with oral history programs, which consist of more than interviewing, is William W. Moss, *Oral History Program Manual* (New York: Praeger, 1974); it deals with practical questions as well as ethical and legal ones, particularly as they relate to property rights. The best discussion of oral history as history is found in Paul Thompson's *The Voice of the Past: Oral History* (Oxford: Oxford University Press, 1978).

The number of books available on American folklore is considerable. Guides for doing folklore include Jan Harold Brunvand, *The Study of American Folklore: An Introduction* (New York: Norton, 1968) and *Folklore: A Study and Research Guide* (New York: St. Martin's, 1976). Also Kenneth S. Goldstein, *A Guide for Field Workers in Folklore* (1964; reprinted., Detroit: Gale Research Company, 1974); Elaine S. Katz, *Folklore for the Time of Your Life* (Birmingham, Ala.: Oxmoor House, 1978); MacEdward Leach and Henry Glassie, *A Guide for Collectors of Oral Traditions and Folk Cultural Material in Pennsylvania* (Harrisburg: Pennsylvania Historical and Museum Commission, 1968); and Warren E. Roberts, "Fieldwork: Recording Material Culture," in Richard M. Dorson, ed., *Folklore and Folklife: An Introduction* (Chicago: University of Chicago Press, 1972).

A good general introduction to folklore is found in Richard M. Dorson, *American Folklore* (Chicago: University of Chicago Press, 1959). Another is a collection of essays edited by Alan Dundes, *The Study of Folklore* (Englewood Cliffs, N.H.: Prentice-Hall, 1965). More closely related to the concerns of this chapter are Richard M. Dorson, *American Folklore and the Historian* (Chicago: University of Chicago Press, 1971), and "The Oral Historian and the Folklorist," *Proceedings* of the Sixth National Colloquia on Oral History, Indiana University, October 8–10, 1971; and Henry Glassie, *Pattern in the Material Folk Culture of the Eastern United States* (Philadelphia: University of Pennsylvania Press, 1968). Three works that show the wide range of folklore concerns are Kenneth L. Ames, *Beyond Necessity: Art in the Folk Tradition* (Wilmington, Del.: Winterthur Museum, Norton, 1977); William Lynwood Montell, *The Saga of Coe Ridge: A Study in Oral History* (Knoxville: University of Tennessee Press, 1970), and Michael Owen Jones, *The Hand-Made Object and Its Maker* (Berkeley: University of California Press, 1975).

# ·7·

# Visual Documents

PHOTOGRAPHS, DRAWINGS, PAINTINGS, AND MOVIES PLAY natural and essential parts in the work of nearby historians. These and other visual documents offer good testaments to changes through the years—in the skyline, the landscape, or the texture of a neighborhood, for example, or in the appearance of individuals. By freezing time momentarily, they offer fixed moments for extended scrutiny. They reveal customs, preferences, and styles and permit us to observe celebrations of past holidays and special occasions; to watch people at work, at play, and at home; to see how they courted, married, raised children and moved them through the rites of passage, and coped with stress, disruption, hardship, and the changing seasons of their lives. We can see a society discovering, building, and moving; a society at war and in peace. Such documents offer evidence of communities taking shape, institutions forming and growing, agencies serving and struggling, and businesses prospering and declining.

Because of their enormous possibilities, it is important that visual documents be used well, which requires, first of all, a clear understanding of what they are. Their nature depends on how their creators make them. Once they are made, they are independent documents, existing on their own. But they are also susceptible to various uses by their viewers. Just as visual documents that represent the same subject but were produced by different creators are quite different, so a single document may be seen differently by the persons who look at it. Meaning partially depends, too, on how the document is presented for viewing.

Because the discussion to follow can be more clear and direct, with fewer qualifications and digressions, if it is restricted to the form of visual document likely to be used most extensively by historians of the nearby world,

128

this chapter concentrates on photography. But statements that apply to photographs may be adapted to other visual documents as well. So references to "photograph" and "photographer" also pertain to "painting" and "painter" (or to any other visual art form and its creator). Remember, though, that a photograph is not "like" a painting, and attempts to compare them should be cautious.

## Still Photographs: Mediated Documents

Historians of the nearby past are likely to be interpreters of photographs as well as photographers, for photographs are used in reconstructing a story and in telling it. Sometimes a photograph is mainly a bearer of information, evidence of an event. It may reveal who was there, what people wore, and the setting in which the event occurred. If the picture shows a family occasion, perhaps a wedding, it depicts a social rite. But the taking of a picture is, in such instances, a ritual itself. Sometimes the decision to take a picture confers importance on an event that would otherwise be lacking. While a photograph may appear to be a thin slice of a moment in history, a real piece of the past, it may also inspire a feeling of unreality as one studies it intently. The commonplace becomes the mystifying.

Some photographs are works of art—not only those of Eugene Atget, Alfred Stieglitz, Edward Steichen, Edward Weston, and Henri Cartier-Bresson, but also of unpublished and unexhibited photographers whose work may be awaiting discovery. Photos may be artistic bearers of messages, like the work of Roy Stryker, Dorothea Lange, and others, depicting the hardship brought by the depression in the 1930s. They may be attempts to capture one art form through another, as in the picture of a piece of sculpture; in such an instance the photograph might simply be an illustration. An advertiser may use a photograph to entice, a realtor to display, an archaeologist to record, a journalist to report, and a reformer to prod social consciences.

Whatever else it might be, however, a photograph is a mediated document. Cameras and films are media, tools in the hands of the photographer. The relationship between the media and the user is a unique one, for the media function to a large extent mechanically. The camera is thus both something more and something less to the photographer than the brush to the painter. The film is something more and something less than clay to the sculptor. Cameras can be used in ways that do not even require the presence

Two St. Louis historians faced the task of verifying the sparse documentation that arrived with a photograph collection deposited in an archives where one of them worked as cataloguer. The photographs depicted incidents that occurred during a strike by the International Ladies Garment Workers in 1933–1935—a strike involving more than two thousand women dressmakers in forty-eight shops in the St. Louis garment district. One of the historians describes the way they approached their task:

*Writer and photographer Susan Sontag suggests that the use of a photograph may help make it possible to get to the complexity of an event, because it records an event that is different for the photographer, subject, and viewer. But, she argues, a photograph is only a fragment, "and with the passage of time, its moorings become unstuck."*

*What we attempted to do in this project was to stick some old photographs back into their moorings by showing photographs of a dramatic event to some of the people who had taken part in it, stirring their memories of the occasion. The results were startling. When retired St. Louis garment workers, all over the age of sixty, saw for the first time scenes of labor activity in which they had engaged as young women, they recalled not only those events, but how they felt about them at the time. By connecting the years between past and present, the photographs helped the women re-experience their half-remembered emotions of fear and conflict, excitement and satisfaction.*

Bertha Lichtenburg looked at [one] of the Preisler photographs and chided us for not recognizing a scab who was somewhat the worse off for trying to cross the picket lines. "Six of us would get around her," Lichtenburg remembered, as she looked at the strike-breaker, "and she wouldn't go nowhere with us pushing her. And we'd get [her] around the corner of the building, and we'd get her up against the wall and tell her she should join the union!"

Jessie Sulkowski looked at another Preisler photograph (page 130) and exclaimed, "That's me and my sister in that picture!" Jessie told of how she walked the picket lines and of being blackballed by the industry for her strike activities. Then she brought out studio-made photographs of herself in the chorus line of the local ILGWU pageant, *Pins and Needles*, which had been in her scrapbook for forty years.

*Source*: Katharine T. Corbett, "St. Louis Garment Workers: . . . Photographs and Memories," *Gateway Heritage*, Summer 1981, pp. 22-23.

of the photographer at the instant when pictures are taken, and photographs often reveal things that the photographer did not see when taking the picture. Indeed, professional as well as amateur photographers are eager to have their exposed film processed so that they can "see what they got."

## Reading Photographs

There is a difference between looking at a photograph and reading it. Looking comes first. By looking, ignoring the photographer, people take from the picture what they want. The look forms an impression. If you pass up the chance for an impression, it may never come your way again.

Reading a photograph ordinarily means to put words with it. A few photographers help their readers by providing captions. Others, like Henri Cartier-Bresson, fiercely resist captioning or explaining photographs. They argue that pictures should stand on their own, without words. But we maintain that reading photographs, giving them "verbal scrutiny," as novelist-photographer Wright Morris calls it, gives them their image, and it is the image that has meaning for the reader.

Reading a photograph is done best by systematically addressing questions to it. A good way to begin is to form a *consciousness of the photographer*. What did the photographer see when he took the picture? What is in the picture that he possibly did not see? What were his purposes? What were his biases? Why did he pose people as he did? Why did he shoot from the vantage point the picture indicates? How did the circumstances in which the picture was taken limit the photographer's choices?

Then might follow a look at the frame of the picture. The eye would have seen the subject of the picture differently, for it could not have drawn an arbitrary boundary around a section of the field of vision. What was omitted from the picture that the eye would have seen? What effect does the framing have on one's sense of having been there? How would one's reaction to the picture change if the picture were to be cropped—that is, to have its frame reduced further?

Paying heed to the effects of framing leads naturally to a look at the *place* of the photograph. Was it taken indoors? If so, what effect did the indoor setting have on the picture? Was it contrived or artificial? What clues does the picture provide to the cultural landscape? To the natural landscape? If the camera could have caught sounds and odors, how would the image of the photograph have been enhanced?

By freezing the scene for the instant that the camera's shutter is open, the photograph directs the reader's attention to questions of *time*. How does the photograph reveal the time of the day or year? What preceded the taking of the picture? What followed it? How does the picture reveal the stopping of time? What is caught in motion? What does the picture reveal of the times in which it was taken?

It is helpful also to pay special attention to the *details* of the picture and the artifacts in it—the lace on a dress, for example, or the bric-a-brac on the mantel. What do the parts contribute to the whole? How does the picture enable you to interpret the details in it? How do the details help in drawing conclusions about the time and place of the event portrayed in the picture? What is revealed about the occupations, social class, tastes, beliefs, or values of the persons shown? What conclusions can be drawn about the culture of which the setting in the picture is a part?

A little practice enables one to notice the *technical aspects* of a picture. The greater the focal length of a lens (beginning at 85mm or so and in the extreme at 200mm and beyond), the more noticeable is the flattening effect on the picture. (The focal length is the distance from the center of the lens

What do pictures of the family home reveal about economic circumstances, other residents, the surrounding neighborhood, or other matters? What do you make of the curious arrangement and poses in this picture? What do you suppose was the photographer's intent when he took it?

to the film.) As distances are compressed with the longer lenses, it becomes impossible accurately to distinguish spacing between background, subject, and foreground.

A wide-angle lens (35mm or less) distorts in other ways. The shorter the focal length, the more rounded the objects and persons in the picture seem to become; the nearer the camera is to the subject, the more this apparent rounding is exaggerated. Blurred parts of a picture indicate either very fast motion or the use of a slow shutter speed. Because users of older cameras had little control over shutter speed, old pictures are more likely to show such blurring than more recent ones. A fuzzy background behind the focal point of a picture is a sign that the photographer used a wide-aperture setting (low f-stop), either to accomplish a special effect or because scarcity of light dictated such a setting. Flash or strobe lighting tends to give photographs an undesirable harshness. The amount of contrast depends on the light in the scene, the kind of paper the processor used in development, the lens, and the type of film used. Sharpness is determined by the size of the camera and the film exposed, shutter speed, f-stop, and, as suggested above, the point on which the photographer focused. Also to be observed is the distance between the photographer and the subject, which possibly gives a hint as to the degree to which the photographer encroached on the situation.

Attention must be given to *historical considerations* surrounding a photograph, for the technology of photography has changed through the years. A daguerreotype, for example, presents distinctive qualities, as do prints from wet-plate negatives, Kodak snapshots, and pictures taken with contemporary 35mm single-lens reflex cameras. Through experience in working with photographs one develops an eye for the various distinctions.

One should read also the *artistic aspects* of photographs, even of snapshots—those innocent snips from the past that are often characterized by haphazard arrangement of the subject matter and amputation of heads and feet of the persons in them. Look for expressions of the language of vision referred to in chapter 3: light and shadow; color and texture; lines, shape, and pattern; similarities and contrasts; and movement. Look also for the things that photographer Andreas Feininger (in *Photographic Seeing*) lists as photogenic qualities: simplicity; order, and clarity; outlines that are hard, sharp, and concise; surface textures; subject coloration; live subjects and objects in motion; spontaneity; the unusual; and repetition of similar or identical forms. A soft-focus pictorialist, by the way, would undoubtedly

Snapshot portraits like this one of a Nebraska farmer and his wife offer insights into their circumstances and character, as well as a glimpse of their seldom-used parlor. In what respects do the people and the place fit together? What does the picture lead one to want to know about the subjects?

have a different set of photogenic interests, so it is essential to keep the photographer's intention in mind when assessing a photograph.

Pay attention also to the unphotogenic qualities and techniques Feininger lists: insipidity and lack of subject interest; too great a distance between the camera and the subject; overabundance of subject matter; a cluttered or meaningless background or foreground; too much subject contrast; wrongly placed or harsh shadows; overlighting; and posing and faking.

This listing of photogenic and unphotogenic qualities opens the way for a look specifically at the *people* in photographs. It may not be wise to attempt to base psychoanalysis of individuals or groups on photographs, but observations of the kind a psychoanalyst might make are useful for historians. Pay attention, for example, to the manner in which the subjects present themselves in their poses and facial expressions—and then ask who chose the pose or the expression, the subject or the photographer. Notice, too, whether people in a picture are touching one another or how they have arranged themselves in relation to others in the picture or in a series of

A formal portrait like this one prompts the viewer to ask what it reveals about the subjects and what it conceals. The lighting is unusual for such a portrait. Why would a photographer arrange the subjects and the lighting as he did? What is the likely relationship between the three persons pictured?

pictures of the same group taken through the years. Consider also the kinds of emotions projected by persons in the picture, perhaps matching what you see against a list of terms a psychoanalyst compiled in his photoanalyses: shy, compliant, aloof, proud, fearful, mad, suspicious, introspective, superior, confused, happy, anxious, angry, weak, pained, suffering, bright, curious, sexy, distant, blank, bored, rigid, arrogant, content, lonely, trusting, strong, crazy, involved, frustrated, attractive, docile, bemused, correct, friendly, hurt, spontaneous, satisfied, depressed. Your analysis of the people in a picture will lead you to ask such things as whether a group mood is apparent or if there is a dominant figure apparent in the group.

A historian reading a photograph must ask questions that determine whether or not (and why) the photograph is good for historical purposes. Does it present an accurate record? Does it say something significant about the subject or the photographer? Does it provide knowledge and insight into the culture of which it is a trace? Are the time and place of the photograph clear?

It should be noted, of course, that reading photographs in the manner suggested here may become too rational a process, that the parts of the picture should not be emphasized to the exclusion of the whole, and that the reading suggestions should be used with discretion.

## Photographs in Historical Research

Photographs are useful to historians in two forms: first, as traces representing events from the past and as artifacts in their own right, and second, as records of information gathered in fieldwork. The line between the two forms is neither clear nor inevitable, but it is helpful to be aware that an old picture of an old house differs from a contemporary picture of the same house taken for comparison. A variation in the latter form is created when one takes a picture of an old picture to ensure its preservation or for some other purpose.

Whatever the form of the photograph, certain principles apply to its use in historical research. First, photographs must be treated according to the same standards, particularly where accuracy is concerned, that are applied to other documents or artifacts when they are identified, authenticated, described, evaluated, and interpreted. Second, because there are definite limits to the extent to which photographs can speak for themselves, extrinsic data must be used with them. Notes on the backs of the pictures or in albums in which they are mounted often provide some such information, but unfortunately it is sometimes misleading or just plain wrong, and it must always be verified before it is relied upon. Conversations with persons shown in the pictures provide more information (using photographs as points of reference in oral interviews was discussed in the preceding chapter). Third, pictures should not be included in a story merely because they are nice or interesting. They must relate to the story being told, offering some evidence that completes or clarifies it. Fourth, photographs used in telling the story must be captioned, but neither too extensively nor too skimpily. Wright Morris notes, "It is better that the photograph have no commentary at all than that it appear to be necessary to the picture," but he adds, "Words can be as intrusive in their absence as in their presence." And fifth, the technical

Close study of photographs often yields surprises. In this one, a reflection in the window behind the subjects shows photographer Ben Shahn shooting a picture while the subjects watch. While his wife poses in the street as a decoy, he is using a right-angle finder on his camera to take the picture you see.

reproduction of the photographs used in a published or filmed history should be the very best possible. Just as care is given to honing sentences into precise form and to fitting them neatly into purposive paragraphs, so care should also be given to the presentation of photographs used.

## The Limits of Photographs

While capitalizing on the rich possibilities photographs offer, historians cannot ignore the limitations, some of which become apparent in a review of the medium's history. Although photography goes back to the 1830s, the earliest daguerreotype pictures, for all their beautiful details, were always mirror images and could be produced only one time on a metal plate. Furthermore, because exposures had to be lengthy, subjects had to pose rigidly to avoid creating a blur by moving. Although photography achieved almost instant popularity, with thousands of persons acquiring cameras, picture taking remained beyond the reach of amateurs.

By the 1850s the wet-plate process had replaced daguerreotypes, making

Saloons have often been neighborhood gathering places. At times, they have served as social centers, welfare agencies, and political headquarters. Saloon histories, often neglected, deserve the attention often given to churches, schools, and businesses.

possible unlimited numbers of prints from glass-plate negatives. But because enlargements from the plates were impossible, the only way to create large pictures was to use large plates, which made photographic equipment cumbersome. Furthermore, wet-plate negatives could not accurately represent distinctions between colors, all but a few of which printed as black; nor could they distinguish between clouds and the sky, which meant that weather conditions could not be portrayed adequately. The need for bright light coupled with the fixed shutter speed of cameras made pictures in dark places and of things in motion impossible.

George Eastman's success in simplifying the technology of photography in the 1880s allowed for a dramatic increase in the number of persons who could take pictures. The Kodak, with its preloaded flexible film, made possible the snapshot, the amateur photographer's work of art and the symbol of popularized photography. Further advances in technology made photography increasingly a hobby of the masses.

Another limit is imposed by the fact that photographs never represent more than a small part of larger scenes. Because they deal in single rather than repeated moments, it is impossible for them to convey a sense of the routine that is so much a part of life. And because crucial moments ordinarily elude photographers' attention, they are often recreated strictly for the benefit of the camera. The contrived character of such moments is ordinarily apparent in the photographs that record them, depending on the skill of the photographer. Until the development of flash photography, scenes set indoors could not be recorded by the camera at all.

The use of photographs by historians is further complicated by a number of seemingly contradictory circumstances. On the one hand, there is such an abundance of photographs available—whether in family archives, corporate archives, public archives, or institutional archives—that historians must make hard choices to use the right ones in their research. On the other hand, this abundance of material is collected unsystematically, preserved indifferently, and identified and cataloged scarcely at all. While there is an abundance in quantity, not as many significant photographs of good quality have been preserved and filed as historians would like or could use. The majority of family albums are all but useless for want of identification of the persons in the pictures or because the photographs have deteriorated.

One more limit to the uses of photography in historical research is just now being experienced—painfully and with dismay. The pain and dismay

Finding this picture in a family collection makes one wonder whether handicapped and retarded persons get their share of space in such places. On the reverse side, this picture is dated April 18, 1892. In a different handwriting is this statement: "A boy your great-grandmother took care of in an institution." But because the owner of the picture cannot determine when this notation was written (although it is in her mother-in-law's handwriting), and because she cannot verify the statement, its accuracy is questionable.

will surely increase when more and more people who would use the color photographs taken in the past several decades discover that the prints and slides before them have lost their original colors, if they retain any images at all. The massive transition from black and white to color photography was encouraged by the popular appeal of beautiful pictures *for now*. The materials and processes used have left the colors unstable. Although technological changes may soon improve color stability, those who wish to ensure the leaving of a record or the preservation of visual remembrances of events must insist upon doing so in black and white.

## Care and Preservation of Photographs

Historians have a responsibility to provide for the care and preservation of photographs that come to their attention or into their possession, as well as those taken in the course of their work. It is perhaps unnecessary to comment here on the use of photographs already housed in established archives, for the archives will probably have rules governing such things as access and reproduction rights. Yet researchers sometimes find that photographs are not as well cared for as they might be, and a properly placed suggestion to the curator may make a difference in what is available to later researchers.

Persons doing their own photography or having direct responsibility for care and preservation of photographs find themselves confronting many difficult tasks. These tasks are too complex and far ranging to consider in detail here, and those who are deeply committed to photography as a tool of research and storytelling will seek specialized information on what to do and how to do it. Persons who do not have the time or desire to immerse themselves in the ins and outs of photography are well advised to defer as much as possible to professionals who offer services of the sort they need. These comments are intended to help you deal knowledgeably with such professionals.

Photographs are vulnerable to destruction by fungi, moisture, residual chemicals, molds, fumes, insects, and human mishandling—to say nothing of the inherent capacity of paper and dye for natural deterioration. Some basic steps can be taken to ensure their preservation as valuable historical resources.

A first step is deciding whether a given photograph is worth preserving. This requires identification and assessment of its historical significance, as determined through the reading process discussed earlier. Once it is concluded that the photograph should be preserved, the identification must be recorded in writing and stored with it, or at least the photograph should be coded so that it can readily be associated with the written identification. If each photograph is properly stored in a separate acid-free envelope, the identifying information might be written on the envelope. Care must then be taken, of course, to ensure that the photograph and the envelope are not separated or mixed up with other photographs and envelopes.

Late-model photocopying machines are able to make relatively clear plain-paper copies of photographs. Writing information directly on the photocopies serves two purposes: the information is readily accessible for use with the originals, and the photocopies may also be used independently, thus preventing wear and tear on the historically valuable photographs until they are needed for specific purposes.

One rule of identification must never be violated: do not write on the face or the reverse side of a photograph with a ballpoint or felt-tip pen, since the pressure may damage the photograph and the ink may bleed through. A soft lead pencil may be used for writing on the back or the margin, but the impression should be wiped with a soft cloth so that excess graphite does not remain to make smudges.

In storing prints, keep in mind all the sources of damage. As Margery S. Long has observed, photographs "are made of potentially unstable materials that tarnish, fade, stain, discolor, grow fungus and are attacked by insects and gases. If they are in color, the dyes may fade, change color or bleed, destroying the color balance. The supporting material may become deteriorated and affect the images on them. Even the enclosures intended to protect them may contribute to their undoing." Thus, photos must be protected against light, moisture, contamination, pollutants in the atmosphere, insects, and human handling. Optimal conditions for a photo archive are therefore similar to those for archives of any type: darkness, humidity below 50 percent, and temperature kept below 70 degrees; in addition, folders and storage boxes should be free of acid-based material and of substances that give off harmful fumes, dusts, and gases.

There are some very specific rules that are too frequently violated by household archivists, at great cost to photographs they may cherish. Never bundle prints together with rubber bands; rubber bands dry out and stick to prints. Never fasten prints to anything with paper clips, since most paper clips rust. Never allow prints to be touched for any purpose by cellophane tape—and never attempt to repair them with it, since cellophane tape breaks down and leaves a sticky residue. Never mount photographs with rubber cement, which contains sulfur and will eventually fade or stain a print. Wheat paste, available from firms that specialize in technical supplies for libraries and archives, is by far the best adhesive to use for mounting photographs—and they should be mounted only on acid-free paper.

Negatives should always be stored separately from the photographs. Although negatives of 35mm film fit nicely in commercially available plastic holders that will hold as many as thirty-six negatives from which proof sheets (contact prints) can readily be made, these holders can seriously damage them or reduce their life expectancy (despite the claims of their manufacturers). Acid-free envelopes or Mylar sleeves should be used instead. The proof sheets are useful in filing pictures in a way that makes them most accessible. To provide maximum protection against the total loss of a collection of pictures by fire or other catastrophe, it is a good idea to keep photographs and negatives in separate locations.

## Copying Photographs

Sometimes historians would like to use photographs that cannot be removed from their mountings without damage and for which no negative exists. Such photographs can be copied simply by taking pictures of them— simply, that is, if you have the right equipment and observe some basic guidelines. Perhaps this is a good place to mention that the basic equipment of the nearby historian-photographer probably starts with a 35mm single-lens reflex camera. The normal lens, probably about 50–55mm, will not allow one close enough to a print to copy it, but a "macro" lens will; so will the use of extension rings which fit between the camera and the lens. If the camera lens cannot be removed, it can be adapted for closeup work by the addition of thin lenses that fit on the basic lens like filters. Using closeup fittings of this sort in various combinations enables one to place the camera at just the right distance from the photograph to make an acceptable copy of it.

The use of a tripod or copy stand to hold the camera perfectly still is essential. If one plans to do a great deal of copying, a stand with controlled artificial light should be used. Specifications for such stands and lighting are available in the books dealing with technical aspects of photography mentioned at the end of this chapter. Natural lighting may be used, but one must be careful to guard against glare. It may be necessary to place glass over the print to hold it flat, but this could interfere with the clarity of the copy. Sometimes when the image is dark it is necessary to shoot through a hole in a black cloth or paper to avoid reflection. Anchoring the corners with small pieces of masking tape is preferable if the picture can be held flat by this means without damage.

The camera's shutter should be released by means of a short cable or the self-timer, if the camera has one, to prevent jiggling and thus blurring the picture. Sharper pictures are likely to result when a small lens aperture (for example, $f$ 11 rather than $f$ 2.8) is used. It is a good idea to take three shots of each picture—one at what seems to be the best exposure and one each at the $f$-stops just above and below this one.

Once equipment is set up for copying, all kinds of possibilities appear. While it is a good idea to take one picture of the entire original, for the record and for study, the photographer may shoot parts of the original as well, reframing them, bringing out detail or eliminating extraneous material. Stains on prints and documents can be minimized or eliminated by using a darker filter of the same color as the stain.

Patience, care, and experimentation make possible the production of excellent copies of original photographs. In fact, the copies often turn out to be better photographs, from a technical point of view, than the originals.

## Movies

Our concern so far has been with still photography. Much of what we have said, apart from some of the technical considerations, applies also to the use of motion pictures. Historians of the nearby past should not overlook as potential sources of information home movies, films produced by local businesses and industries, locally produced inserts for newsreels once played in theaters, promotional shorts packaged by such groups as the local chamber of commerce, and footage shot by local television stations. Like photographs, movies reveal changes in fashion, the landscape, family composition and relationships, community leadership, business practices, recreational styles, and opinions as to what is worth capturing on film. Running old movies is a favorite pastime, and the very causes of laughter they provoke are likely to be the points of interest for nearby historians. A warning about movies: old nitrate-based film may explode, especially if maintained in sealed storage. Immediate transfer to modern safety film is essential.

A photograph is a special kind of document, a special kind of artifact. Using photographs in historical research requires some knowledge of technical matters, many of which we have considered in this chapter. But the mystical element in photography is as important as the technical. Historical research and writing have not used photographs well if the mystifying merely becomes commonplace.

## Notes

Works mentioned or quoted in this chapter are: Andreas Feininger, *Photographic Seeing* (Englewood Cliffs, N.J.: Prentice-Hall, 1973); Wright Morris, "Photographs, Images, and Words," *American Scholar*, Summer 1979, pp. 457–469; Margery S. Long, quoted in Robert A. Weinstein and Larry Booth, *The Collection, Use, and Care of Historical Photographs* (Nashville: American Association for State and Local History, 1977), p. 124; and Robert U. Akeret (Thomas Humber, ed.), *Photoanalysis: How to Interpret the Hidden Psychological Meaning of Personal and Public Photographs* (New York: Peter H. Wyden, 1973); a very critical review of this book by Richard Chalfen appeared in *Studies in the Anthropology of Visual Communication* 1, no. 1 (1974): 57–60.

## For Further Information

For general works on visual literacy, see Donis Dondis, *A Primer of Visual Literacy* (Cambridge, Mass.: MIT Press, 1973); Stewart Kranz and Robert Fisher, *The Design Continuum: An Approach to Understanding Visual Forms* (New York: Reinhold Publishing, 1966) and *Understanding Visual Forms: Fundamentals of Two- and Three-Dimensional Design* (New York: Van Nostrand Reinhold, 1976). Related books include Rudolph Arnheim, *Visual Thinking* (Berkeley: University of California Press, 1969); Estelle Jussim, *Visual Communication and the Graphic Arts: Photographic Technologies of the Nineteenth Century* (New York: Bowker, 1974)—particularly the first and last chapters; and William Ivins, *Prints and Visual Communications* (1953; New York: DaCapo Press, 1969).

On reading photographs, in addition to Feininger's work cited above, see: Jonathan Bayer. *Reading Photographs: Understanding the Aesthetics of Photography* (New York: Pantheon, 1977); James T. Brooke, *A Viewer's Guide to Looking at Photographs* (Wilmette, Ill.: Aurelia, 1977); Thomas L. Davies, *Shoots: A Guide to Your Family's Photographic Heritage* (Danbury, N.H.: Addison House, 1977); Jonathan Green, ed., *Snapshot: Aperture* 19, no. 1 (1974); Karin Becker Ohrn, "Re-viewing Photographs: Unexplored Resources for Communication Research," *Journal of Communication Inquiry* 2 (winter 1977): 31–39; Marsha Peters and Bernard Mergen, "Doing the Rest: The Uses of Photographs in American Studies," *American Quarterly* 29, no. 3 (1977): 280–303; and John Szarkowski, *Looking at*

*Photographs: 100 Pictures from the Collection of the Museum of Modern Art* (New York: Museum of Modern Art, 1973) and *The Photographer's Eye* (New York: Museum of Modern Art, 1966). A forthcoming publication by Katharine T. Corbett and Howard S. Miller is worth watching for; it will be based in part on their so far unpublished essays "Which Thousand Words," presented at the 1980 meeting of the Organization of American Historians in San Francisco and Miller's "Another Look at Urban Living," presented at the 1979 meeting of the same group in New Orleans.

Practical applications of reading photographs are offered in Glen E. Holt, "Chicago through a Camera Lens: An Essay on Photography as History," *Chicago History* 1, no. 3 (1971): 158–69 and Harold M. Mayer and Richard C. Wade, *Chicago: Growth of a Metropolis* (Chicago: University of Chicago Press, 1969). Carefully assembled photographs on various themes that justify a second look include: William Crawford, *The Keepers of the Light* (Dobbs Ferry, N.Y.: Morgan and Morgan, 1979); Chester Higgins, Jr., and Orde Coombs, *Some Time Ago: A Historical Portrait of Black Americans, 1860–1950* (Garden City, N.Y.: Doubleday, 1980); Paul Kagan, *New World Utopia: A Photographic History of the Search for Community* (New York: Penguin, 1975); Julia Hirsch, *Family Photographs: Content, Meaning, and Effect* (New York: Oxford University Press, 1981); Jeffrey Simpson, *The American Family: A History in Photographs* (New York: Viking, 1976); and George Talbot, *At Home: Domestic Life in the Post-Centennial Era, 1876–1920* (Madison: State Historical Society of Wisconsin, 1976).

Works on the history of photography abound. Among the better ones are Ben Maddow, *Faces: A Narrative History of the Portrait in Photography* (Boston: New York Graphic Society and Little, Brown, 1977); and three by Beaumont Newhall: *The Daguerreotype in America* (New York: Duell, Sloan, and Pierce, 1961); *The History of Photography* (New York: Museum of Modern Art, 1964); and *Photography: A Short Critical History* (New York: Museum of Modern Art, 1958). A very interesting essay on a slice of the history of photography is James C. Curtis and Sheila Grannon, "Let Us Now Appraise Famous Photographs: Walker Evans and Documentary Photography," *Winterthur Portfolio* 15 (Spring 1980): 1–23.

Photography as a research tool is discussed in Howard Becker, "Photography and Sociology," *Studies in the Anthropology of Visual Communication*, Fall 1974, pp. 3–26; John Collier, *Visual Anthropology: Photography as a Research Method* (New York: Rinehart and Winston, 1967); Jon Wagner, ed., *Images of Information: Still Photography in the Social Sciences* (Beverly Hills: Sage, 1979); Mary-Ellen Jones, *Photographing Tombstones*, Technical Leaflet no. 92 (Nashville: American Association for State and Local History, 1977); and Walter Rundell, Jr., "Photographs as Historical Evidence: Early Texas Oil," *American Archivist* 41, no. 4 (1978): 373–98. Technical aspects of lens choices are laid out simply by Gary Gore in "Zooming in on History: Basic Camera Lenses," *History News* 35, no. 9 (September 1980): 9.

Two quite different works on photographic criticism are: Nathaniel Lyons, ed., *Photographers on Photography: A Critical Anthology* (Englewood Cliffs, N.J.: Prentice-Hall, 1966), and Susan Sontag, *On Photography* (New York: Farrar, Straus and Giroux, 1977). An interesting analysis of photography is offered by Otto Bettmann, *The Good Old Days: They Were Terrible* (New York: Random House, 1974); another by Janet Malcolm is *Diana and Nikon: Essays on the Aesthetic of Photography* (Boston: David R. Godine, 1980).

Clearly the most important work on the technical aspects of the collection, care, and use of historical photographs is the one by Weinstein and Booth, cited above. Also to be noted are Georgia Eubanks, "Building a Photo Archives," *Public Libraries* 18, no. 2 (Summer 1979), 27–28; and Paul Vanderbilt, *Evaluating Historical Photographs: A Personal Perspective*, Technical Leaflet no. 120 (Nashville: American Association for State and Local History, 1979). A publication begun in 1979, *PhotographiConservation* (information may be obtained from Rochester Institute of Technology, Rochester, New York, 14623) is important for anyone wishing to work as a specialist in this area, and such people may also want to consult Henry Wilhelm, *The History and Preservation of Contemporary Photographic Materials* (forthcoming). Also useful is James H. Conrad, *Copying Historical Photographs: Equipment and Methods*, Technical Leaflet no. 139 (Nashville: American Association for State and Local History, 1981).

On movies as a resource, see Dorothy Weyer Creigh, *Old Movies: A Source of Local History Programs*, Technical Leaflet no. 100 (Nashville: American Association for State and Local History, 1977); the author recounts the history of home movie-making and gives information on how to acquire films from the National Archives and Record Service. See also Richard Noble's *Archival Preservation of Motion Pictures: A Summary of Current Findings*, Technical Leaflet no. 126 (Nashville: American Association for State and Local History, 1980).

# ·8·

# Artifacts

TRACES OF HISTORICAL EVENTS ARE FOUND IN THINGS AS well as words. Taken together, things are labeled "material culture" but are in fact only the creations of culture. The inspiration for making them comes from the bundle of knowledge, beliefs, norms, and values that compose a culture, and they therefore represent events and ideas in the lives of people. To put it another way, material culture is the part of the nearby physical environment that has been transformed from the natural state by human action for human purposes. To understand human action and human purposes in a community, it makes sense to look carefully and in many different ways at things—artifacts—from its past.

Studying the material culture of a community gives one the chance to learn from anonymous men and women who left no written record but played important parts in events. Because so little written history has been recorded by women, the study of material culture is particularly useful in learning about many aspects of women's history. Examining traces in the material culture helps historians halt the flow of history at a given point, to take out a thin slice of time, and to probe it carefully. Artifacts place the past in three-dimensional terms. Perhaps there is even a fourth dimension to the study of things, for seeing and touching things from the past gives a sense of what it was like to have lived in an earlier time, what it was like to have been there.

Changing the subject of study from words and pictures to artifacts involves shifting from the conceptual world to the perceptual world, a move begun in the previous chapter. Words are abstractions; so are pictures. They represent images and ideas conceived in our minds. In contrast, artifacts are concrete. They can be seen, heard, touched, smelled, and tasted. They are

Scenes showing the interiors of homes, factories, and businesses with people going about their daily lives, are, unfortunately, rare. What questions can such photographs suggest and answer about individuals or the community?

real things that can be weighed and measured and counted. If artifacts are to be more than merely perceived and appreciated, they must be understood in words—that is, handled conceptually.

Before turning to a model for the study of artifacts, a more specific definition is necessary. Robert Chenhall, who has developed "a logical system for naming things" to be used in museum cataloging—that is, for identifying things with words—divides artifacts into ten categories; an eleventh category is the catchall for unclassifiables. His categories show the range of artifacts subject to study by historians and suggest starting points for individuals who wish to extend the range for their own purposes. Anyone doing extensive work with artifacts or attempting to locate a particular one in a museum using this system would do well to study Chenhall's detailed elaboration. His system is built on these categories:

1. Structures. Originally created to serve as shelter from the elements or to meet some other human need for a relatively permanent location.
2. Building furnishings. Intended to be used in or around buildings for the purpose of providing comfort, care, and pleasure to the occupants.
3. Personal artifacts. Designed to serve the personal needs of individuals—clothing, adornment, body protection, grooming aids, or symbols of beliefs or achievements.
4. Tools and equipment. Made to be used in carrying on an activity such as an art, craft, trade, profession, or hobby; the tools, implements, and equipment used in the process of modifying available resources for some human purpose.
5. Communication artifacts. Originally created for the purpose of facilitating human communication.
6. Transportation artifacts. Devised as vehicles for the transporting of passengers or freight.
7. Art objects. Intended for aesthetic purposes or as a demonstration of creative skill and dexterity; the essential requirement is that the artifact was created for no apparent utilitarian purpose.
8. Recreational artifacts. Invented for use as toys or in carrying on the activities of sports, games, gambling, or public entertainment.
9. Societal artifacts. Made to be used in carrying on governmental, fraternal, religious, or other organized and sanctioned societal activities.
10. Packages and containers. Originally produced for the packing and shipping of goods and commodities; for some containers a precise function cannot be determined.

## Analyzing Artifacts

These categories suggest that artifacts are the silent carriers of vast amounts of information about the past, which the historian must find ways of extracting.

When we examine an artifact, a number of questions spring immediately to mind: Who made it? Of what is it made? For what was it used? How old is it? But rather than querying at random, it is preferable to approach artifacts with knowledgeable, systematically devised sets of questions.

# Public Sale

As we are leaving the farm, we will sell at public sale the following described property six and one-fourth miles south and two miles west of Leigh, eleven and three-fourths miles north and four miles east of Columbus, or three miles east and one mile north of the Henke garage site on

## MONDAY, NOVEMBER 9th

Sale starts at 10:30 o'clock

Lunch stand on grounds.

### 3 — — HEAD OF HORSES — — 3

1 team of bays, mare and gelding, 7 years old, weight 2700.

1 bay mare, smooth mouth, weight 1150.

### 11 — — HEAD OF CATTLE — — 11

3 Holstein milk cows
5 spring calves
1 2-year old heifer

1 Ayrshire milk cow
1 bucket calf

### 15 HEAD OF HOGS

15 head of spring shoats, weight 180 pounds, vaccinated

### POULTRY

5 dozen Austra White pullets
4 dozen White Rock pullets

### FARM MACHINERY, ETC.

1 10-20 McCormick-Deering tractor
1 2-bottom 14-in. Little Wonder tractor plow
1 16-in. Moline sulky plow
1 16-in. John Deere walking plow
1 7-ft. Deering binder
1 Deering corn binder
1 Dain hay stacker
1 Dain hay sweep
1 10-ft. John Deere hay rake
1 5-ft. McCormick mower
1 5-ft. McCormick-Deering mower
1 grapple fork
1 Nisco manure spreader
1 hay rack and truck
1 John Deere lumber wagon, like new
2 old lumber wagons
1 spring buggy
1 McCormick-Deering corn planter, 80 rods wire
1 John Deere 3-section harrow
1 10-ft. John Deere disc pulverizer
1 8-ft. alfalfa disc
1 disc cultivator
1 4-shovel riding cultivator
1 walking cultivator
1 2-hole Sandwich corn sheller
1 John Deere hand sheller
1 grain elevator, complete
1 snap corn cutter
1 fanning mill
1 buzz saw
1 2-wheel trailer
1 Hoosier endgate seeder
1 John Deere box seeder
1 6-in. burr grinder
1 McCormick-Deering cream separator
1 1½-horse gas engine

1 harrow cart
1 Slip scraper
1 30-ft. 5-in. rubber belt
1 steel wheel-barrow
60 oak fence posts
Some steel posts
Some hog fencing
2 sets of harness
1 set fly nets
1 saddle
1 blacksmith forge
1 grindstone
3 steel water tanks
1 50-gallon hog waterer
1 12-ft. steel culvert
3 oil barrels
2 10-gallon cream cans
2 vises and anvils
1 work bench and tools
2 loading chutes
Some household goods and many other articles too numerous to mention.

### GRAIN AND HAY

800 bu. ear corn in crib
250 bu. oats
300 bu. barley oats
140 bu. halo
5 tons alfalfa in barn
2 stacks millet hay
2 acres Atlas sorgo in shock
2 stacks alfalfa, 3rd and 4th cutting
2 tons prairie hay in barn
1 stack straw

TERMS: Cash, or make arrangements with your banker before the sale. All property bid in at bidder's risk. No property to be removed until settled for.

## Gottfried Marty Sr. & Son, Owners

Col. Adolph Vasek & Son, Auctioneers.

Bank of Leigh, Clerk.

This advertisement reveals something about the sellers' material possessions and the business practices connected with their sale. Why would one need to know the year of the sale (1942) to draw accurate inferences about their relative economic circumstances?

A classic, comprehensive model for devising questions to ask of artifacts was developed some years ago by E. McClung Fleming of the Winterthur Museum in Delaware. The general framework of that model is as useful for beginning students of nearby history as it is for the most advanced of scholars, and it provides the basis for the questions that we propose for use in coming to terms with artifacts. The Fleming model is built around an analysis of five basic properties, and it suggests four operations as essential to artifactual analysis.

The five basic properties provide a formula for including and interrelating all the significant facts about an artifact. The properties of an artifact are its *history*, *material*, *construction*, *design*, and *function*. *History* includes where and when it was made, by whom and for whom and why and successive changes in ownership condition, and function. *Material* involves what the object is made of—woods, fibers, ceramic bodies, metals, glass, and so on. *Construction* has to do with the techniques of manufacture employed, workmanship, and the way parts are organized to bring about the object's function. *Design* includes the structure, form, style, ornament, and iconography of the object. *Function* embraces both the uses (intended functions) and the roles (unintended functions) of the object in its culture, including utility, delight, and communication.

The four operations to be performed on the five properties yield answers to most of the important questions we want to ask about an artifact. The operations are identification (including classification, authentication, and description), which results in a body of distinctive facts about the artifact; evaluation, which results in a set of judgments about the artifact, usually based on comparisons with other examples of its kind; cultural *analysis*, which examines the various interrelationships of an artifact and its contemporary culture; and *interpretation*, which suggests the meaning and significance of the artifact in relation to aspects of our own culture. Each of these questions may involve each of the five properties of the artifact, and each successive operation is dependent upon those preceding it. Identification is the foundation for everything that follows; interpretation is the crown. [Emphasis added]

Taking the first of the four operations as the starting point suggests the initial question to ask about an artifact: What is it? To answer that question and the rest, one relies on information that the artifact itself yields upon direct examination (intrinsic data) and information brought to bear on it from outside sources (extrinsic data). The quest for intrinsic data can lead one to submit an artifact to laboratory analysis, perhaps to determine the kind of wood or metal or other material of which it is made. Searching for extrinsic data may send one to guidebooks or catalogs or may call for comparisons with artifacts already identified. In other words, answering the questions about an artifact may require considerable research.

To say what an artifact is, as Fleming suggests, requires first that it be classified, perhaps by function (what is it used for?), by the material of which it is made, by construction, or by subject matter (the classification system developed by Chenhall, referred to above, is a subject-matter system—with the subject matter defined in part by the artifact's function). It also requires authentication (as to the genuineness of its materials, its construction, and other claims made for it), and description (exact specification of its dimensions, weight, color, shape, texture, and so on). To be systematic in the use of the model, one would ask "what is it?" about the artifact's history, material, construction, design, and function—not an effort one accomplishes with a glance at the object and a stroke of the pen!

The historical aspect of artifactual analysis of this nicely crafted cradle would take one back from the basement in which it is now stored to better days almost a century ago. The history of the cradle is known by only a few people. Only if these people write about the cradle or if others interview them will the history be recorded.

Evaluation may be even more demanding. The first kind is rendered as a subjective judgment concerning the artifact's aesthetic quality and workmanship, the skill and taste of the craftsmanship that went into it, the effectiveness of its overall design, and the expressiveness of the form, style, and ornament it displays. In the other kind of evaluation, the artifact is compared in objective terms with similar artifacts as to size, cost, rarity, and date of origin. Again, both sorts are applied to all five properties of the artifact.

So, too, is the third operation, cultural analysis, which seeks to examine the relation of the artifact to aspects of the culture that created it. It is in the application of this operation that the historian clearly goes beyond the antique collector, to whom this matter is of incidental concern. The principal focus is on the function of the artifact, examination of which touches directly on questions of human action and human purpose referred to at the beginning of this chapter. Whether the function is utilitarian (as with a tool), social (as with an instrument of communication), or artistic (as with a decorative object), it provides the key to the knowledge, beliefs, ideas, norms, and values of the culture from which the artifact comes.

Obviously, great knowledge and skill are required in using this key in the most sophisticated way, but amateurs can use it if they are mindful of their own limitations and sensitive to the rules regarding the use of historical traces spelled out in chapter 3. It is helpful, too, to keep in mind that the practices governing the use of artifacts are similar to those for the use of written documents (and remember, too, the origin of the term "document" in *docere*, "to teach"). Material documents "teach" in much the same way as written documents.

The fourth of the operations, interpretation, is concerned with the relationship between what is learned about the artifact and some key feature of contemporary life. This relationship, Fleming says, must be sufficiently intense or rich to have self-evident meaning, significance, or relevance. It may have to do with a person or event important to the audience to whom the interpretation is directed, to some distinctive feature of the artifact that might be especially appreciated in a given context, to a special accomplishment—perhaps a first or a biggest or a fastest—in which it played a part, or to some notable characteristic of the times.

Cracking the subtle code of the artifact, to use the apt expression of one writer, is a task that is fraught with temptations, five of which are sufficiently common and serious to merit mention here. The first is the temptation to examine an artifact in isolation, as a thing separate from the culture of which it is a part and thus to draw erroneous conclusions about it. The second is almost the opposite: it is the tendency to see the artifact as representing a larger piece of a culture than it does. A single object should not be asked to explain too much about those who made and used it. Third, people often view an artifact only in terms of the present, that is, they identify, evaluate, analyze, and interpret it too exclusively in terms of the culture and the time period of the person studying it. Fourth, concern for the function of artifacts sometimes prompts disregard for their aesthetic value. Finally, there is the temptation, to which Americans are particularly vulnerable, to see all artifacts on a progress continuum, with each one accounting for a step in the long march from the primitive to the modern. This continuum requires each artifact to be genealogically relevant, and many are not.

## Why Use Artifacts?

The study of an artifact, it is easy to see, is a rigorous exercise. What benefits does it hold for historians of the nearby? It helps them understand how earlier generations solved daily problems; it reveals the interplay between the aesthetic and the practical, the decorative and the functional; it gives us a feel for the quality of life in another time and place; and it provides insights into tastes, customs, manners, and styles of living. In sum, it helps historians to know and understand an earlier culture and the events that went into the making of it.

## Locating Artifacts

A natural question arises at this point: Who finds the artifacts worthy of study, and where do they find them? In the most fundamental sense, artifacts are the principal concern of archaeologists, but archaeologists do more than discover material for study. They verify it, provide for its preservation, measure and describe it, photograph it—especially if relocation to another site is impossible or infeasible—classify and arrange it in logical order, and prepare it for analysis by others. Their purpose is to prepare artifacts for historical study, but that is not to say that archaeologists must abandon them to historians. Nor is it to be inferred that the archaeological processes enumerated here are off limits to historians. The fields of archaeology and history may be distinct, but those who operate in them cannot avoid crossing field lines.

Archaeologists dig. When the digging requires unearthing, literally, historians are well advised to know their limits. Locating lost sites, identifying known sites, determining their nature and extent, locating known features within them, securing data for restoration or reconstruction, actual excavation of a site, salvaging threatened sites—these are all tasks best left to trained archaeologists.

But when archaeology is defined as a "technique for discovering and conserving evidence of all times and places, both above and below ground," the limits for historians are expanded, and most particularly so for historians of the nearby. The cardinal rule in doing above-ground archaeology is: do not damage, disturb, or destroy any material that is potentially the subject of archaeological and historical study. Furthermore, archaeological material should be removed from its location only if it cannot be studied there or if removal is essential to its protection. For advice and assistance on archaeological questions, historians should turn to the state historic preservation officer (who is required by law to employ professional archaeologists) or to the National Park Service, the Corps of Engineers, state geological and archaeological agencies, or to archaeologists in academic institutions.

A relatively new area of study within the broader field of archaeology is filled with challenges for the local historian. It is called "industrial archaeology," defined by Kenneth Hudson, one of its pre-eminent practitioners, as "the discovery, recording, and study of the physical remains of yesterday's industries and communications." The technique of his specialty, Hudson says, is to examine such matters as the conditions of work in a particular period and the attitude of employers, workers, and the general public to those conditions; what the different parties—workers, owners, managers, financiers, investors—derived from the process, plant, or method of working in the way of income, satisfaction, accidents, ill health, and standards of living; the techniques and equipment used in getting the job done; the scale of an industrial operation; and the condition of the physical environment in which workers and their families lived. This is a broad undertaking; in fact, it is a virtual invitation to historians to help, for the artifacts of industry cannot reveal all these things by themselves. The insights and knowledge of historians must be brought to bear on them.

If industrial archaeology holds a natural appeal for local historians, and it should, especially if industries have played a part in the history of the locale, another area of study probably holds greater appeal. The only reason for calling the study of artifacts found around the house "household archaeology" is to point out that the methods of identification, evaluation, analysis,

Advertising devices are one variety of artifact. During the early years of the automobile era, businesses trying to attract the attention of passing motorists erected buildings representing their product or service (an oil derrick or a coffee pot, perhaps) or put up other unusual structures to catch the eye (Dutch windmills were quite popular). These artifacts suggest a different approach to advertising as well as a different type of business organization from the standardized emblems of modern-day road signs. The Fish Inn restaurant pictured here lasted longer than many structures of this type.

and interpretation are applicable to them in the same way that they are to things found underground or at industrial sites.

That such household artifacts as old furniture, tools, dishes, pottery, clothing, and decorative art are called antiques should pose no problem for historians. They can and should be studied in the same way as other cultural artifacts, and the information they yield is similar. In some respects the precise effort and intense care that antique collectors and dealers put into identifying and authenticating antiques set an example for historians. The difference is that antique collectors stop short; cultural analysis and interpretation are not their principal concerns, as they are for historians. Another difference is that for historians an artifact does not have to be old to be of interest or value; for antique collectors and dealers it is often age that confers value, and it is value expressed in monetary terms that inspires interest.

Purists would exclude persons interested in antiques from the fraternity of historians. Instead, let historians say: broaden your interests and join us; meanwhile, we will learn what we can from you.

## Museums

Of what use are museums to students of material culture? That depends, of course, on the museum. In their broadest purpose, they are conservatories of material culture. The good ones are also interpreters of it. They subject their holdings, one by one, to the scrutiny called for in the model used in this chapter, and they arrange their exhibits so that the artifacts in them tell the story of another time and place in terms that make sense today.

But museum directors are caught in a welter of dilemmas. Without charging admission, many of them cannot survive, but if fees are too high, public use declines. Tax and private voluntary support are unpredictable. Museums see themselves as teaching institutions; many of their users regard them as entertaining diversions. To teach well they must offer carefully planned exhibits; preparation of exhibits is often too costly for museum budgets. Funds for research, an activity of great importance for museums, are severely limited. But their greatest dilemma is that while they are called upon to preserve with the greatest of care the objects in their collections, especially since many of the objects are appropriately called "one of a kind," they also want to see those objects studied and used—which means exposing them to the wear and tear that come with handling.

One problem for the user of museums, including the historian, is that too often the use that is allowed is merely passive. The object, locked under glass or secured behind ropes and railings, may merely be looked at. Another problem associated with the use of museum-held artifacts in historical research derives from the fact that the artifacts are not only lifted out of contexts that help to give them meaning but are placed, quite often at least, next to completely incongruous artifacts, thus detracting from meaning all around. This problem occurs on the most grandiose scale at Henry Ford's Greenfield Village at Dearborn, Michigan, as noted in chapter 1.

Another problem is that museum curators and users are tempted to give museums a "good old days" approach, tending to simplify and glorify the past. (At one museum they call this the "goodness and granola" approach: "Life was simpler and better then, and if America would only return to the old values, the old ways of doing things . . .") In so doing, they also emphasize white, male, middle- and upper-class success stories. With but a few exceptions, museums are not good sources for finding out about the lives of blacks, and, encouraging as they do a consensus view of history, one finds little in them about such things as labor conflict, populist discontent, or feminist or minority protest. Knowing the history of a museum helps one understand the biases occurring there: Henry Ford's at Greenfield Village, for example, and the Rockefellers' at Williamsburg and Eli Lilly's at Conner Prairie. Because most such museums were founded by successful white men, their bias is to some extent consistent. Government-sponsored museums, such as the Smithsonian, tend to be more multifaceted in their ways of doing things because of their sources of support and the constituencies they serve.

Still another problem is that the artifacts held by museums are select samples; the museum user must trust that the curator's selection is representative of a given time, place, and culture—a genuine trace of an event—or that its uniqueness justifies its inclusion in a museum collection. Furthermore, a museum's artifacts are rarely cataloged and indexed in the same way that written documents are recorded in archives, although accredited museums will know where their artifacts are. In any case, finding the precise object one is looking for often requires considerable effort. It is no wonder, then, that museums are better at evoking wonder and excitement and stimulating interest in the past then they are at focusing on specific problems.

Museologists and curators are fully aware of these problems, and they are struggling to overcome them. Some museums are working diligently to catalog and index their holdings. Some are distinguishing between serious students and casual visitors and are making objects available under controlled conditions for scholarly study. Some are abandoning the practice of taking contributions of objects, willy-nilly, from the good citizens of the community in return for promises of prominent display, which means that the eclectic jumbles that have characterized many exhibits can be discontinued. Conscious efforts are being made to create exhibits that tell a story with learning rather than entertainment in mind. The story is told through imaginative arrangement of the exhibits rather than by placing long explanations next to each object.

Some museums are attempting to teach by creating living, functioning museums. Conner Prairie Pioneer Settlement, north of Indianapolis, for example, is a frontier village fixed in 1836. Instead of listening to the prepared speeches by interpreters, visitors chat with the storekeeper, attend school, watch the blacksmith and the potter at work, smell the bread being baked in the fireplaces (and perspire with the cook if they visit in summer months), stroll through the barns, and generally make themselves at home. The interpreters, speaking in the first person, present tense, engage in conversations with visitors. (Visitor: "Was this house an underground railroad stop?" Interpreter, with a suspicious look: "You with the law?" Who else would ask about the underground railroad in 1836?) This is entertainment, of course, but it is also education. For special groups, there are extraordinary learning opportunities as the staff conducts "live-ins," with the participants doing chores alongside the "residents."

Ideally, community historians should come to see themselves as partners with museums in their communities. In so doing, they can become part of a movement to open up museums and to make them more responsive to community interests. They can assist in acquiring museum-worthy objects; perhaps they can even help in researching and caring for them. Certainly, by observation and personal study, historians can learn something from museums about the conservation of artifacts in their own possession.

This chapter began by asserting that traces of historical events are found in things as well as words. Not only will persons who work with artifacts as traces in ways this chapter recommends come to see the past in different ways, but their sensitivity to the importance of things as carriers of meaning will help them see their own environment as a living museum.

## Notes

This chapter has referred to and quoted from : Robert G. Chenhall, *Nomenclature for Museum Cataloging: A System for Classifying Man-Made Objects* (Nashville: American Association for State and Local History, 1978), pp. 42–53; E. McClung Fleming, "Artifact Study: A Proposed Model," *Winterthur Portfolio* 9 (1974): 153–73; and Kenneth Hudson, *World Industrial Archaeology* (Cambridge: Cambridge University Press, 1979), pp. 2, 13–14.

## For Further Information

The most comprehensive collection of essays on topics treated in this chapter is Ian M. Quimby, ed., *Material Culture and the Study of American Life* (New York: Norton, 1978); essays in it that merit special mention are "How Much Is a Piece of the True Cross Worth?"

by Brooke Hindle and "Doing History with Material Culture" by Cary Carson. Thomas Schlereth's *Artifacts and the American Past* (Nashville: American Association for State and Local History, 1980) contains nine essays, some of them previously published (and cited below in their original place of publication). Also by Schlereth is *Material Culture Studies in America* (Nashville: American Association for State and Local History, forthcoming); in addition to a bibliographical essay, this book includes basic articles in the field. Related works include: Patrick H. Butler III, *Material Culture as a Resource in Local History* (Chicago: Newberry Library, 1979); John Chavis, "The Artifact and the Study of History," *Curator* 7, no. 2 (1964):156-162; Siegfried Giedion, *Mechanization Takes Command: A Contribution to Anonymous History* (New York: Oxford University Press, 1955); Craig Gilborn, "Pop Pedagogy," *Museum News* 47, no. 4 (December 1968): 12–18; John A. Kouwenhoven, "American Studies: Words or Things?" in Marshall Fishwick, ed., *American Studies in Transition* (Philadelphia: University of Pennsylvania Press, 1964), pp. 1–16; George Kubler, *The Shape of Time: Remarks on the History of Things* (New Haven: Yale University Press, 1962); Jules David Prown, "Mind in Matter: An Introduction to Material Culture Theory and Method," *Winterthur Portfolio* 17 (1982): 1-19; Harold Skramstad, "American Things: A Neglected Material Culture," *American Studies: An International Newsletter* 10, no. 3 (spring 1972): 11–22; John T. Schlebecker, "The Use of Objects in Historical Research," *Agricultural History* 51 (1977): 200–208; Alexander Wall, "The Voice of the Artifact," *History News*, 27, no. 10 (October 1972); Wilcomb E. Washburn, "Manuscripts and Manufacts," *American Archivist* 27 (1964): 245–50; Kenneth Ames, "Material Culture as Non-Verbal Communication: A Historical Case Study," *Journal of American Culture* 3 (1980): 619–641. A journal on material culture that had been around for eight years took on a subtitle with volume 9 in July 1977, becoming *Pioneer America: The Journal of Historic American Material Culture*; it is published by the Pioneer America Society at Louisiana State University. Another journal, begun in 1964, added a subtitle in 1979: *Winterthur Portfolio: A Journal of American Material Culture* (University of Chicago Press). An occasional article in *Technology and Culture* may be helpful to students of artifacts; an example is Ruth Schwartz Cowan's "The Industrial Revolution in the Home: Household Technology and Social Change in the Twentieth Century," *Technology and Culture* 17, no. 1 (1976): 1–23.

Works on material culture in early American life include: James Deetz, *In Small Things Forgotten: The Archaeology of Early American Life* (New York: Doubleday, 1977); E. McClung Fleming, "Early American Decorative Arts as Social Documents," *Mississippi Valley Historical Review* 45, no. 2 (September 1958): 276–284; Brooke Hindle, *Technology in Early America: Needs and Opportunities for Study* (Chapel Hill: University of North Carolina Press, 1966); Ivor Noel Hume, *All the Best Rubbish: Being an Antiquary's Account for the Pleasures and Perils of Studying and Collecting Everyday Objects from the Past* (New York: Harper and Row, 1974), and *A Guide to Artifacts of Colonial America* (New York: Knopf, 1970).

Books that deal with artifacts in the contexts in which they are found include: John A. Kouwenhoven, *Made in America: The Arts in Modern Civilization* (New York: Doubleday, 1948), a wide-ranging and provocative book; and Russell Lynes, *The Domesticated Americans* (New York: Harper and Row, 1957), an exploration of the interplay between material culture and manners.

Two extensive bibliographies of works dealing with artifacts are: Lynn R. Bailey, *From Adze to Vermilion: A Guide to the Hardware of History, and the Literature of Historic Sites Archeology* (Pasadena, Calif.: Socio-Technical Books, 1971); and Richard Hulan and Stephen S. Laurence, *A Guide to the Reading and Study of Historic Site Archaeology*, Museum Brief No. 5 (Columbia, Mo.: 1970). Works on specific kinds of artifacts are virtually limitless in number. Examples include: Robert Abels, *Early American Firearms* (New York: World Publishing, 1950); Michael and Ariane Batterberry, *Mirror, Mirror: A Social History of Fashion* (New York: Holt, Rinehart and Winston, 1977); Louise Ade Boger, *The Dictionary of World Pottery and Porcelain* (New York: Scribner's, 1971); Claudia B. Kidwell and Margaret C. Christman, *Suiting Everyone: The Democratization of Clothing in America* (Washington, D.C.: Smithsonian Institution Press, 1974); Eric Sloane, *ABC Book of Early Americana: A Sketchbook of Antiquities and American Firsts* (Garden City, N.Y.: Doubleday, 1963), and *A Museum of Early American Tools* (New York: Ballantine, 1964); John Michael Vlach, *The Afro-American Tradition in Decorative Arts* (Cleveland: Cleveland Museum of Art, 1978), contains a particularly striking section on graveyard decoration; and Philip D. Zimmerman, "A Methodological Study in the Identification of Some Important Philadelphia Chippendale Furniture," *Winterthur Portfolio* 13 (1979): 192–208.

Some of the better books on antiques are: Louise A. Boger and H. Batterson Boger, comps. and eds., *The Dictionary of Antiques and the Decorative Arts: A Book of Reference for Glass, Furniture, Ceramics, Silver, Periods, Styles, Technical Terms, Etc.* (New York: Scribner's, 1957); Ann Kilborn Coles, *Antiques: How to Identify, Buy, Sell, Refinish, and Care for Them* (New York: David McKay, 1957); Mary Durant, *The American Heritage Guide to Antiques* (New York: American Heritage Press, 1970); Helen Haywood, ed., *The Connoisseur's Handbook of Antique Collecting: A Dictionary of Furniture, Silver, Ceramics, Glass, Fine Arts, Etc.* (London: Connoisseur, 1960); F. Lewis Hinckley, *A Directory of Antique Furniture: The Authentic Classification of European and American Designs for Professionals and Connoisseurs* (New York: Crown, 1953), copiously illustrated and highly analytical in technical terms; Dorothy H. Jenkins, *A Fortune in the Junk Pile: A Guide to Valuable Antiques* (New York: Crown, 1963); John T. Kirk, *The Impecunious Collector's Guide to American Antiques* (New York: Knopf, 1975); Dennis Mullenix, *Antiques: A Browser's Handbook* (New York: Harper and Row, 1977); Harold L. Peterson, *How Do You Know It's Old? A Practical Handbook on the Detection of Fakes for the Antique Collector and Curator* (New York: Scribner's, 1975); and "Antique Farm Equipment: Researching and Identifying," *History News*, Technical Leaflet No. 101, (Nashville: American Association for State and Local History, 1977).

On industrial archaeology, see: R. A. S. Hennessey, "Industrial Archaeology in Education," *History Teacher* 9, no. 1 (1975): 29–41; Kenneth Hudson, *Industrial Archaeology: An Introduction* (London: John Baker, 1963); Theodore Anton Sande, *Industrial Archeology: A New Look at the American Heritage* (Brattleboro, Vt.: Stephen Greene Press, 1976); and David Weitzman, *Traces of the Past: A Field Guide to Industrial Archaeology* (New York: Scribner's, 1980).

General works on museums are: Edward P. Alexander, *Museums in Motion: An Introduction to the History and Functions of Museums* (Nashville: American Association for State and Local History, 1979); G. Ellis Burcaw, *Introduction to Museum Work* (Nashville: American Association for State and Local History, 1975); Ralph H. Lewis, *A Manual for Museums*

(Washington, D.C.: National Park Service, 1976); and Alma S. Wittlin, *Museums: In Search of a Usable Future* (Cambridge, Mass.: MIT Press, 1970). More specialized are: Per E. Guldbeck, *The Care of Historical Collections* (Nashville: American Association for State and Local History, 1972); Raymond F. Pisney, *What Makes a Good Museum?* (Verona, Va.: McClure, 1975); Linna Place and others, "The Object as Subject: The Role of Museums and Material Culture Collections in American Studies," *American Quarterly* 26, no. 3 (1974): 281–294 Frederick L. Rath, Jr., *Care and Conservation of Collections: A Bibliography on Historical Organization Practices* (Nashville: American Association for State and Local History, 1977); Fred Schroeder, *Designing Your Exhibits: Seven Ways to Look at an Artifact*, Technical Leaflet No. 91 (Nashville: American Association for State and Local History, 1977); and Richard Chase, "Museums as Learning Environments," *Museum News* 54 (September/October 1975): 37–43. A good introduction to museums as they may be understood through their exhibits is Arminta Neal, *Exhibits for the Small Museum: A Handbook* (Nashville: American Association for State and Local History, 1976).

An old but interesting book on historic house museums is Laurence Vail Coleman's *Historic House Museums* (New York: American Association of Museums, 1933). Brief but very comprehensive is Thomas J. Schlereth's "Historic Houses as Learning Laboratories: Seven Teaching Strategies," Technical Leaflet No. 105 (Nashville: American Association for State and Local History, 1978). Also by Schlereth is "The Historic Museum Village as a Learning Environment," *Museologist*, June 1977, pp. 10–18.

Directories of museum villages, somewhat dated by now, include: *Restored Village Directory: An Illustrated Directory Listing of Restored, Recreated and Replica Villages of Historic Interest in the United States and Canada*, 3rd ed. (New York: Quadrant Press, 1973); Mitchell R. Allegre, *A Guide to Museum Villages: The American Heritage Brought to Life* (New York: Drake, 1978); Irvin Haas, *America's Historic Villages and Restorations* (New York: Arco Publishing, 1974); and Nicholas Zook, *Museum Villages, U.S.A.* (Barre, Mass.: Barre, 1971). Some such places are included in *The American Heritage Book of Great Historic Places* (New York: American Heritage Press, 1973).

An interesting controversy regarding the purpose and future of museums took shape in a pair of articles in *Museum News*: Wilcomb Washburn, "Are Museums Necessary?" 47, no. 2 (October 1968): 9–10 and Ian Quimby, "Reply to Washburn" 47, no. 4 (December 1968): 10–11. *Museum News* is published six times a year by the American Association of Museums. Other provocative articles relating to museums include: Loris Russell, "Problems and Potentialities of the History Museum," *Curator* 6, no. 4 (1963): 341–349; David Lowenthal, "The American Way of History," *Columbia University Forum* 9 (Summer 1966): 27–32; Daniel Boorstin, "Past and Present in America: A Historian Visits Colonial America," *Commentary* 25 (1958): 1–7; and Robert B. Ronsheim, "Is the Past Dead?" *Museum News* 53, no. 3 (November 1974): 16–18, 62.

# ·9·

# Landscapes and Buildings

CULTURE, DEFINED SIMPLY, IS WHAT YOU NEED TO KNOW TO be one of the folk. Material culture is what the folk have made with what they know.

Where can you go to see the natural landscape without the intrusions of material culture? Roads, bridges, and automobiles are everywhere. Lining the roads are motels, restaurants, and gas stations. On the horizon you see the urban skyline, churches, silos, and watertowers. The natural surroundings have been so thoroughly altered by the doings of people that they are intertwined with, even lost in, the cultural landscape. And yet, most people do not see the cultural landscape, and if they do, they don't think about what they see. Perhaps the reason is that they are unaware of the clues to culture, past and present, that their environment holds.

## Surveying the Cultural Landscape

A survey of the cultural landscape shows, for one thing, the nature and extent of change over time. In urban areas, particularly, there is a commonly appearing cycle of (1) construction; (2) abandonment; (3) conversion; (4) abandonment; (5) demolition; and (6) new construction. Sometimes the cycle skips a phase, but its essential motion persists. In rural areas—and for this reason (and others) rural areas often hold greater appeal for local historians and preservationists than urban areas—the full cycle is less frequent and slower, but it occurs there, too. The process ends with abandonment.

Studying change over time in the cultural landscape invites consideration of migration patterns, the opening and closing of transportation routes, evolving architectural fashions and changing tastes in living space, and the displacement of older commercial districts by new shopping centers. In every instance, of course, the traces found in the landscape must be supplemented by information derived from written documents.

The cultural landscape also offers evidence of neighborhood or regional differences. In a city, the differences might be apparent in the width of streets or size of lots; regionally, in house styles and in materials used in construction. At the same time, the cultural landscape shows the growing similarities of cities and towns in one part of the country with those in others. Put another way, our surroundings reveal the wide diffusion of the more common ingredients of material culture.

Shopping centers provide an object lesson for study. A century ago, the general stores, dispensers of goods that can almost be described as home grown, home made, and home packaged, fell victim to mass production and distribution of standardized products. Chain store outlets, mail order houses, large department stores, and specialty stores that handled these products had little trouble in displacing general stores. Today downtown shopping areas and their smaller counterparts in scattered parts of cities, and even the town squares in smaller communities, have been supplanted by look-alike shopping centers. Visitors to Disneyland or Walt Disney World must surely be struck by the similarities between these plastic, self-conscious entertainment centers and the bright, shiny, world-within-a-world shopping centers. The chain stores that occupy them, the brand-name merchandise they offer, and the national advertising they display (within the uniform restrictions imposed by the center's management) make them astonishingly predictable. As we contemplate the place of shopping centers in American life, we might ask what became of the central commercial districts and town squares left behind. What happened to the men and women who once shopped there, and where do those who live near the abandoned areas now shop?

Also giving the cultural landscape the appearance of a growing sameness are the ubiquitous fast-food restaurants. They offer everyone something to study. Sociologists can consider relationships between their increasing popularity and changes in family size, greater numbers of mothers who are employed, and the increase in single-parent homes. Economists can examine the effect on American life of these restaurants' dependence on a labor force of young people paid at minimum wage or the ties between efficiency and waste in fast-food marketing techniques. Anthropologists can

Changes in the built landscape of the community are clues to movement in the location of various activities, alteration of economic patterns, and quite possibly other developments. Perhaps nothing has signified the rearrangement of twentieth-century communities as much as the rise of shopping centers. Exploring the consequences of their evolution is a worthy and sizable task, as historian Neil Harris hints in this capsule description of their development.

*Early shopping centers, like so many modern innovations, developed in California during the 1920s and '30s. Living in the first set of urban communities built entirely around the automobile, Californians quickly discovered the advantages of placing groups of stores around or within parking areas. Similar arrangements soon appeared in other parts of the country. Richard Neutra designed a small shopping center for Lexington, Kentucky; New Jersey had the Big Bear Shopping Centers, built around giant groceries, with parking space for up to 1,000 cars.*

*In the '30s also, chain and department stores, both vital to the future centers, began to adapt their businesses to the increasingly affluent suburbs and the ever mobile automobile. Until then, retail location in large American cities had been generally a function of existing transportation lines. But as automobile usage spread, downtown location became more problematic. "The automobile emancipated the consumer but not the merchant," the* Architectural Forum *noted in 1949, and well before then firms like Macy's and Sears Roebuck had begun building in the suburbs or on the peripheries of metropolitan centers.*

*It was the union of department stores with the older ideal of grouping easily accessible smaller stores that produced the first regional centers. This was supplemented, of course, by the explosion of highway construction during the Eisenhower era. The years from the early '50s to the late '60s were the golden era of shopping center construction. By the end of the '60s more than 10,000 shopping centers of every size and shape had been built. The huge shift of wealth and population to the suburbs guaranteed their profits. Large department stores—like Hudson's in Detroit and Dayton's in Minneapolis—were eager to get a piece of this action. Instead of simply opening up more branches, department stores began to organize their own centers, hire architects and developers, and get mortgages from life insurance companies, whose huge supply of capital enabled them to influence the suburban landscape as powerfully as their huge downtown skyscrapers shaped the center cities.*

*Source*: Neil Harris, "Spaced-Out at the Shopping Center," *New Republic*, December 13, 1975, p. 23.

Popularization of the automobile had remarkable consequences for the landscape, not only for the streets and roads cars required, but also for the structures built to service them. This corner service station left little doubt as to its purpose.

study the symbolism of the rituals of fast-food restaurants. And nutritionists can concern themselves with the long-term effects of a steady fare of hamburgers and french fries on the health of those who eat them regularly.

Historians are interested in all of these matters, of course, but perhaps most in ways in which fast-food restaurants are indicators of change over time. What do such places, virtual extensions of the automobile, say about mobility in American life? How have they helped to encourage ideas of equality? If equality is taken to mean "indistinction"—and there is significance to the assumption that it can be so taken—indistinction is apparent in the customary self-service, the attire required of patrons, the time of the day they may be patronized, the absence of tipping, and the age of their patrons. Historians might want to know how erasing distinctions has become important through the years.

People who investigate the past of the local cultural landscape will also have more specific interests: how have fast-food restaurants resulted from changed traffic patterns? Or, in turn, how have they changed such patterns? What structures, if any, were demolished to make room for them? Were they the first commercial structures on a given strip? In a given locality, how many are in the abandoned or converted stage while new ones are being built? What has been their effect on the neighborhoods in which they are located?

## Understanding the Cultural Landscape

To see the cultural landscape more intelligently and to give order to questions about it, models for analysis and interpretation are helpful. As a general principle, see the whole, and see its parts. Seeing the landscape whole means looking for relationships—between buildings and open spaces, between building and building, between the cultural and the natural landscapes, between commercial and residential areas, between old and new. It means looking for form (the principle of coherence), balance (this element offsets that element), harmony (good visual sounds), and unity (things fit

The transformation of the landscape by the automobile is everywhere apparent: in cities, in towns, at the edge of town (as shown here), and in the country.

Streetcars still dominated city streets when this photograph was taken, but the take-over by automobiles was in the making.

together to give the impression of oneness) in its constituent parts (look also for shapelessness, imbalance, incongruity, and disorder). It involves identifying time points on the cycle of construction, abandonment, conversion, and demolition. Seeing the landscape whole may entail observing the effects of distinctive features of the natural and cultural landscapes on the geographic space. How did natural features—a river, for example—shape a city? How did a railroad reshape it? And how did an interstate highway or an airport reshape it again?

Seeing the parts means focusing on traffic patterns, sharp changes in the character of neighborhoods caused by transportation routes (highways or railroad tracks, for example), pronounced changes in the nature of communities at night and by day, places where things are made, where deals are made, and where the action is, seeing dumps, greens, woods, cemeteries, and pavement.

Grouping the parts of the landscape by categories prepares you to use them in historical research. Variations in streetlights, for example, prompt one to ask why one style stops and another begins in a given community in which the houses show little age difference. Sidewalks and curbs lead the observer to wonder why some parts of a community have them and others do not. Counting churches and church-related agencies in an area invites one to consider why those of one denomination predominate. What was the effect on development of the fact that country clubs and cemeteries sur-

---

Apparently minor changes in technology or practice can have large consequences for community life. The introduction of parking meters on the streets of a central business district produced conflict and change in a Minnesota town.

*In Old Benson, one could stop one's car in the middle of the street while one exchanged civilities with a neighbor. The street operated like a general all-purpose meeting place where the ladies stopped to chat, where children shouted greetings to one another, where boys gathered with their bicycles to plan a raid on one of the nearby apple orchards, and where young men and women made a date. The street symbolized the sociability and sharing of a self-oriented community.*

*In New Benson, the street is being converted into an efficient thoroughfare and municipal parking area calculated to speed individuals on their business or to return a small fine for overparking into the public treasury. To the new-style Bensonite the stalling, traffic-blocking proclivities of the old-timers are "dog-patchy" examples of rural nostalgia. They wish to give their town the look of streamlined efficiency of the metropolis.*

Farmers, who regarded their patronage as vital to Benson's prosperity, saw the meters as an indication that they were no longer as welcome as before. In other communities, downtown parking meters have been credited with encouraging patronage of suburban shopping centers with free parking and thus have stimulated a fundamental shift in community commercial patterns, tax revenues, and crime rates. Small and indirect influences should not be overlooked in seeking explanations for complicated changes, such as the decline of a central business district.

*Source*: Don Martindale and R. Galen Hanson, *Small Town and the Nation: The Conflict of Local and Translocal Forces* (Westport, Conn.: Greenwood, 1969), p. 173.

rounded a subdivision? How did the developers exploit these features in their plans and promotions? What explains the survival of one old, incongruous business establishment, such as a feed store and grain elevator, on the edge of a ghetto? In rural areas, why does one bend in the road prosper while another becomes a ghost town? Why do farms in some areas seem so similar, in others so different?

Focusing narrowly on one specific type of artifact invites the use of the Fleming model, outlined in the previous chapter. A study of manhole covers (as reported, for example, in *The Manhole Covers of Los Angeles*, by Robert and Mimi Melnick) or fire hydrants in a locality calls for comparative

Aerial views of a neighborhood may help historians trace and question its development. At the center of this view is the little frame church shown on pages 44-45. A look at that church in these surroundings prompts one to ask: How did proximity to a streetcar line affect the church's growth and outlook? What were the reasons for locating the church one block off the main thoroughfare? What were the consequences of that decision? How did the absence of a street to connect this subdivision with the more modest one adjacent to it affect the character of the congregation? What effect did the apparently blatant violation of zoning ordinances—placing a modest frame structure in a community of substantial brick homes—have on relations with the community?

identification and descriptions, evaluations, cultural analyses, and interpretations. Their history, materials, construction, design, and function all invite attention. Indeed, the model is applicable to artifacts of all sizes and varieties, from decorative knobs to street signs to grave markers to statues and monuments and even to buildings.

Buildings deserve special attention here because they are not only the most prominent artifacts on the cultural landscape but the centers of human activity as well. People walk around them, go into them, move up and down and about in them, look at them from the outside and out of them from the inside; work, play, eat, sleep, relax, entertain, make love, worry, and squabble in them. Buildings interact with the economic, social, aesthetic, and physical lives of those who use them. People and buildings exist in an organic relationship.

As the centers of human activity, buildings can correctly be called functional entities on the cultural landscape. They are also structural entities, made of concrete materials and ordered according to certain form and design principles. And they are symbolic, representing at least the necessities of

Buildings and streets take on a different character at night.

one or more persons at a given time and place. They may also carry messages about the hopes, circumstances, and traditions of those who built them.

To understand buildings, then, historians must pay attention to their function, their structure, and their symbolism. Although sensitivity to the relationship between these three elements is of critical importance in studying buildings, it is often useful to examine them separately. While an architectural primer is beyond the scope of this chapter, some suggestions for looking at buildings may prepare one for more detailed study of styles and types.

In considering a building's function, one should try to determine what the architect and the builders conceived to be the *main purposes* of the structure, the *organizational idea* they used to accomplish these purposes, the relationship between *spatial arrangements* and purposes, the provisions made for *movement* within the spaces, *allowances for adaptation* in the event that the building's purposes changed, and the sensitivity of the architect to the *needs of the people* for whose use the building was intended.

Regarding the structure itself, one should look for signs of originality and imagination in its design, creative use of materials, appropriateness to the site and surroundings, evidence of concern for proportion (the relations of the parts to each other and to the whole), scale (the proportions as they relate to people), balance (symmetrical or asymmetrical), rhythm (repeated elements giving order), unity (indications that the building is a whole), and character (the distinctive blend of features).

Sometimes one finds buildings that exhibit few or none of the design qualities traditionally regarded as particularly desirable, such as those just listed. More often than not this lack results from the architect's or builder's ineptitude, but you should be aware that some contemporary architects have consciously sought to reject the traditional and to display instead permissiveness, chaos, ambiguity, wit, and whimsy. For them, the character of a building can be defined just as well by these qualities as by the traditional ones.

Finding symbolism in a building is trickier than identifying either its functions or its structural design features. It is tempting to see symbolism where none exists, and it is probably incorrect more often than not to assert that a given piece of architecture represents "the spirit of the age." More accurately, it represents the spirit of the architect, who may or may not have been in touch with the spirit of the age (assuming that one exists). For example, postmodern architecture of the late 1960s and 1970s, the kind

As this industrial scene in Ensley, Alabama, shows, rural remnants survived for a time in the shadow of sprouting smokestacks. What multiple effects did the advent of industry bring farmers?

referred to in the previous paragraph, may reflect the frenzy, restlessness, and disillusionment with reason that is thought to have characterized these years. But maybe architects sensed this mood more keenly than others, and therefore their work is not really representative or symbolic. The same could be said of the work of great architects like Louis Sullivan and Frank Lloyd Wright; perhaps their creations are notable because they were out of step with their age, not because they reflected the values and spirit of the times.

In what sense, then, is there symbolism in buildings? Buildings express things unintentionally, and such expressions are worth observing. For example, until very recently architects could assume the availability of cheap energy. The energy required to run a skyscraper, with its seasonal climate controls, elevators, and other services, and to bring people to work in it could be discounted as a cost consideration. The buildings of the cheap energy era symbolize an attitude; those of the new era are certain to reflect new necessities. It is not the spirit of the age, then, but its realities that initiate changes in style. Changes dictated by necessity are worth looking for.

We can go back to the Gothic cathedral, a great architectural invention, for another example. It is tempting to regard the Gothic cathedral as symbolic of the spirit of an age, as evidence of the grandeur of devotion and single-minded godliness. The structure was in fact a solution to a very practical problem. The kings and bishops found that if they could ally themselves with the rich burghers by erecting new buildings, they could break the power of the monastic orders and feudal lords. The spirit of later ages that built Gothic cathedrals was probably the spirit of imitation.

The best thing to do, then, is to look for the economic and social realities that are reflected in architecture and to be cautious about drawing inferences about things to be seen symbolically, about something as amorphous as the spirit of the times.

Once one becomes sensitive to the interplay between function, structure, and symbolism, it is natural to turn one's attention to architectural styles and to learn to identify them. Persons who wish to gain some real competence in identification should carry with them John J.-G. Blumenson's *Identifying American Architecture: A Pictorial Guide to Styles and Terms, 1600–1945*. This book is particularly helpful to persons who deal specifically with individual buildings or groups of buildings in their research, for it contains a pictorial glossary of terms they will want to use in building descriptions. Another useful book is Carole Rifkind's *A Field Guide to American Architecture*.

But the use of appropriate terminology is only the first step in preparing a history of a building. Consider the case of a house. It will contain much more than a visual account of its style. The whole facade—foundation, exterior covering material, roof, chimney, windows, doorways—needs to be described; so, too, do attachments, outbuildings, nearby grounds, and walkways. Comparisons with nearby houses are helpful. The descriptions should be accompanied by measurements. If the plans for the structure are available, they should be verified, for actual construction often fails to follow plans. One will want to discover the date of construction, which should appear in the property abstract, ordinarily in the possession of the owner or the mortgage holder. This document should also include details regarding legal transactions involving the house, particularly its ownership. The original plat, possibly available at the city hall or county courthouse, gives dates for the development of an area, shows street, driveway, sewer, and other utility locations, gives a sense of the larger scene in which the house is located, and often contains the building code of the community and the restrictions imposed by the developer. If insurance documents can be traced, they are likely sources of information, and city directories, some of which go back many years, provide at least the names and occupations of people who lived in the house at given times. The names enable the researcher to go to federal census reports, now available to 1910, for additional details. Photographs show the house as it appeared before and after adaptations as well as how it was used. Scrapbooks, diaries, and letters, if they can be located, offer clues to the dynamic relationship between the house and those who lived in it.

Pieces of furniture once used in the house may suggest how the house was lived in. Impressions stamped in the underside of porcelain fixtures in bathrooms and kitchens, particularly in older houses, may provide useful dates, but inferences must be drawn from such traces with great care. The dates may apply to remodeling rather than to original construction. Sleuthing in the house might reveal sliding doors that have been hidden, walls that have been removed, and doors that have been relocated. Careful removal of paint and wallpaper lets one discover interior redecorations.

Another way of finding out how the people lived in an old house is to become a backyard archaeologist. The trash pit, long since covered over, may lead to the recovery of traces from another day. Since bottles are the hardiest survivors, medicinal practices and tastes in liquor might be discerned. Flatware is a favorite find because it is so datable. Almost everything found in a trash pit is an ordinary object not likely to have been preserved otherwise.

All of this activity may be very interesting for the historian of a single house, but does it have any usefulness in a universal sense? Potentially, yes, if one studies a number of houses. "For most people in most cultures," cultural geographer Peirce F. Lewis writes, "a house is the single most important and expensive thing they will ever build or buy. Most people avoid building eccentric houses for the same reason they avoid eccentricity in haircuts, clothing, styles, speech patterns, and religion—each is such a basic expression of unspoken cultural values that deviations from accepted standards are taken as evidence of an unstable and untrustworthy personality and invite unfavorable comment from one's neighbors. In short, one's house is more than mere shelter; it is a personal and social testament. Axiomatically, no major changes in domestic house-types will occur in most cultures without basic shifts in the culture itself." For this reason, he argues,

Inventions can alter the way people live and interact with each other in a community. Memories of the arrival of indoor plumbing, electricity, automobiles, or television are often vivid and revealing. They are well worth seeking out. This reminiscence of one small town's early experience with another vital innovation, the telephone, suggests more than one effect.

*Father went down the school house to a meeting, and the next morning he was telling us that they were organizing a telephone company to build a line and put in phones for the farmers. Mother said, "We don't need any!" Father thought we better join as it would cost more if we waited and had to build our own line from the school house up to our place. Now when they were buliding the line they would build it up to our gate, and we would only have to pay for the line up our long lane. We lived about a quarter of a mile back in the field.*

*When they started to build our line, they called it the 400 line. I think it was the first farmer-owned built out of town. Our number was 406, and our ring was one short and two longs. The 500 line was built about the same time, and it went out to the folks that lived in and around Section Six. The 600 line went south out of town and ended up in Gilbert. The Gilbert Co-op Grain Company's number was 617.*

*I can remember when the men started to build the line. All of the neighbors worked. Some of them dug holes and put in the poles. Others rolled out the wire. Mr. Springman fixed a hook on the end of a long slim rod to lift the wire up from the ground to the bracket on the telephone pole. Then the men could pull the wire tight. I thought that was something when he came along lifting up the wire.*

*A lot of things went on over a country phone. Sometimes there was plenty of "rubbernecks." One winter evening I got bored and asked Mother if I could call Uncle Julius and have him play a few Edison phonograph records so I could hear them over the telephone. I called up and thought I talked to Uncle Julius. He said to hang up and he would ring me back. It would take a little time to set the phonograph up so it would play right into the phone. He got it fixed and played me three or four records. I thanked him and thought I had a lot of fun. A day or so later Mother was telling Uncle Martin what a kick I got when Uncle Julius played the records for me over the phone. Then Uncle Martin laughed and said, "That was me that played the records." Uncle Martin and Mother thought they had a good joke on me. To make matters worse I learned some time later that four or five other folks heard me make the call and listened in on my music too.*

*Source*: Guy Johnson, "The Boy on Kiegley's Creek," unpublished manuscript in the possession of the authors.

studying houses is an excellent way to gain insights into a culture, into diversity between regions of a larger culture, and into the nature of slow but steady change over time.

Pursuing this idea, historians of the environs nearby will discover that the amount and use of space within houses can tell us about the activities carried out there, the degree of individual privacy, the relative standing of children and adults or of males and females, and the concern for amenities of the people who lived in them. Here are clues to the place and roles of women in earlier times.

This chapter has attempted to show that the cultural landscape is filled with material traces from the past. The task for the historian is to see them and then use them to understand and reconstruct events and ideas of earlier times. The suggestions given here are little more than starting points.

## Notes

Works quoted or cited in this chapter are: John J.-G. Blumenson, *Identifying American Architecture: A Pictorial Guide to Styles and Terms, 1600–1945*, 2nd ed., rev. (Nashville: American Association for State and Local History, 1981); Peirce F. Lewis, "The Geography of Old Houses," *Earth and Mineral Sciences* 39 (1970): 33–37; Robert and Mimi Melnick, *Manhole Covers of Los Angeles* (Los Angeles: Dawson's Book Shop, 1974); and Carole Rifkind, *A Field Guide to American Architecture* (New York: New American Library, 1980).

## For Further Information

General and interpretive works on the cultural landscape, many of which are well illustrated, include: Peter Blake, *God's Own Junkyard: The Planned Deterioration of America's Landscape* (New York: Holt, Rinehart and Winston, 1964), written, the author says, not in anger but in fury; Grady Clay, *Close-Up: How to Read the American City* (New York: Praeger, 1973); Gordon Cullen, *Townscape* (New York: Reinhold, 1961); Fran P. Hosken, *The Language of Cities* (New York: Macmillan, 1968); Lawrence Halprin, *Cities*, rev. ed. (Cambridge, Mass.: MIT Press, 1972); W. G. Hoskins, *The Making of the English Landscape* (London: Hodder and Stoughton, 1963); John Brinckerhoff Jackson, *American Space* (New York: Norton, 1972); Peirce F. Lewis, "Axioms of the Landscape: Some Guides to the American Scene," *Journal of Architectural Education* 30 (September 1976): 6–9; Penelope Lively, *The Presence of the Past: An Introduction to Landscape History* (London: William Collins, 1976); Kevin Lynch, *What Time Is This Place?* (Cambridge, Mass.: MIT Press, 1972); Peter F. Smith, *The Syntax of Cities* (London: Hutchison 1977); I-fu Tuan, *To-*

*pophilia: A Study of Environmental Perceptions, Attitudes, and Values* (Englewood Cliffs, N.J.: Prentice-Hall, 1974); Christopher Tunnard and Boris Pushkarev, *Man-Made America: Chaos or Control* (New Haven: Yale University Press, 1963); Mary T. Watts, *Reading the Landscape of America*, rev. ed. (New York: Macmillan, 1975); Richard Saul Wurman, *Making the City Observable* (Cambridge, Mass.: MIT Press, 1971); Ervin H. Zube, editor, *Landscapes: Selected Writings of J. B. Jackson* (Amherst: University of Massachusetts Press, 1970); Paul Zucker, *Town and Square from the Agora to the Village Green* (Cambridge, Mass.: MIT Press, 1970). Journals include *Landscape*, published three times a year, and *Landscape Architecture*, a bimonthly publication of the American Society of Landscape Architects.

On shopping centers, see Neil Harris, "American Space: Spaced-Out at the Shopping Center," *New Republic*, December 13, 1975, pp. 23–26; William Severini Kowinski, "The Malling of America," *New Times*, May 1, 1978, pp. 30–55; and Louis G. Redstone, *New Dimensions in Shopping Centers and Stores* (New York: McGraw-Hill, 1973), a comprehensive work intended for architects, designers, and developers. Cultural implications of fast-food restaurants are treated in Conrad P. Kottak, "Rituals at McDonald's," *Natural History* 87, no. 1 (January 1978): 75–81 and Max Boas and Steve Chain touch on landscape considerations in *Big Mac: The Unauthorized Story of McDonald's* (New York: Mentor, 1977); also see *White Towers* (Cambridge, Mass.: MIT Press, 1979), by Paul Hirshorn and Steven Izenour.

Streets and their adornments are the subject of: Robert I. Alotta, *Street Names of Philadelphia* (Philadelphia: Temple University Press, 1975); Frederick Fried and Edmund Gillon, *New York Civic Sculpture* (New York: Dover, 1976); James Goode, *The Outdoor Sculpture of Washington, D.C.* (Washington, D.C.: Smithsonian Institution Press, 1974); Carole Rifkind, *Main Street: The Face of Urban America* (New York: Harper and Row, 1977); Bernard Rudofsky, *Streets for People: A Primer for Americans* (Garden City, N.Y.: Doubleday, 1969); Robert Sommer, *Street Art* (New York: Links, 1975); and Robert L. Vickery, Jr., *Anthrophysical Form: Two Families and Their Neighborhood Environments* (Charlottesville: University of Virginia Press, 1972), contains a good section on private streets of St. Louis.

Specific features of the cultural landscape are considered in: T. Allen Comp, *Bridge Truss Types: A Guide to Dating and Identifying*, Technical Leaflet No. 95 (Nashville: American Association for State and Local History, 1977); Wayne Craven, *Sculpture in America* (New York: Crowell, 1968); H. Roger Grant and Charles W. Bohi, *The Country Railroad Station in America* (Boulder, Colo.: Pruett, 1978), and "The Country Railroad Station as Corporate Logo," *Pioneer America* 11 (August 1979): 117–129; Carroll Meeks, *The Railroad Station: An Architectural History* (New Haven: Yale University Press, 1956); Sara Pressey Noreen, *Public Street Illumination in Washington, D.C.: An Illustrated History* (Washington, D.C.: George Washington University, 1975); Rene Smeets, *Signs, Symbols and Ornaments* (New York: Van Nostrand Reinhold, 1975). Susan and Michael Southworth, *Ornamental Ironwork: An Illustrated Guide to Its Design, History and Use in American Architecture* (Boston: David R. Godine, 1978); Robert Sommer, *The Mind's Eye: Imagery in Everyday Life* (New York: Delacorte, 1978) offers useful ideas for improving one's sensitivity to the material environment.

On grave markers, see: Roberta Halporn, *Lessons from the Dead: The Graveyard as a Classroom for the Study of the Life Cycle* (Brooklyn: Highly Specialized Promotions, 1979);

Leonard Huber, *New Orleans Architecture: The Cemeteries* (Gretna, La.: Pelican, 1974), contains a useful bibliography; Mary-Ellen Jones, *Photographing Tombstones: Equipment and Techniques*, Technical Leaflet No. 92 (Nashville: American Association for State and Local History, 1977); John J. Newman, *Cemetery Transcribing: Preparations and Procedures*, Technical Leaflet No. 9 (Nashville: American Association for State and Local History, 1971); David Weitzman, "Resting Places," the best chapter in *Underfoot: An Everyday Guide to Exploring the American Past* (New York: Scribner's, 1976).

Books and articles intended to foster understanding of architecture include: R. W. Brunskill, *Illustrated Handbook of Vernacular Architecture* (New York: Universe, 1971); William Caudill, William M. Pēna, and Paul Kennon, *Architecture and You: How to Experience and Enjoy Buildings* (New York: Watson-Guptill, 1978); Carl W. Condit, "Technology and Symbol in Architecture," *Humanities in Society* 1, no. 3 (1978): 203–19; Gerald A. Danzer, "Buildings as Sources: Architecture and the Social Studies," *High School Journal* 57, no. 5 (1974): 204–13; David R. Goldfield, "Living History: The Physical City as Artifact and Teaching Tool," *History Teacher* 8, no. 4 (1975): 535–56; Alfred Browing Parker, *You and Architecture: A Practical Guide to the Best in Building* (New York: Delacorte, 1965); and George Sullivan, *Understanding Architecture*, a children's book with appeal for adults (New York: Frederick Warner, 1971).

On architectural styles, see: John Poppeliers, S. Allen Chambers, and Nancy B. Schwartz, *What Style Is It?* (Washington, D.C.: Preservation Press, 1977) reprinted from three 1976 issues of *Historic Preservation*; and Marcus Whitten, *American Architecture since 1780: A Guide to Styles* (Cambridge, Mass.: MIT Press, 1969).

The better commentaries on American architecture include: Wayne Andrews, *Architecture, Ambition and Americans* (New York: Harper, 1947) and *Architecture in America: A Photographic History from the Colonial Period to the Present* (New York: Atheneum, 1980); Carl W. Condit, *American Building: Materials and Techniques from First Colonial Settlements to the Present* (Chicago: University of Chicago Press, 1969), and *American Building Art: The Nineteenth Century* (New York: Oxford University Press, 1960); James Marston Fitch, *American Building:* vol. 1, *The Historical Forces That Shaped It* 2nd ed. (Boston: Houghton Mifflin, 1966), and *American Building:* vol. 2, *The Environmental Forces That Shaped It*, 2nd ed. (Boston: Houghton Mifflin, 1976); Siegfried Giedion, *Space, Time and Architecture: The Growth of a New Tradition*, 3rd ed. (Cambridge, Mass.: Harvard University Press, 1954); Alan Gowans, *Images of American Living: Four Centuries of Architecture and Furniture as Cultural Expression* (Philadelphia: Lippincott, 1964); Henry Russell Hitchcock, *Architecture: Nineteenth and Twentieth Centuries* (New York: Penguin, 1977); William Dudley Hunt, Jr., *Encyclopedia of American Architecture* (New York: McGraw-Hill, 1980); and Vincent Scully, *American Architecture and Urbanism* (New York: Praeger, 1969); and G. E. Kidder Smith, *The Architecture of the United States: An Illustrated Guide to Notable Buildings*, 3 vols. (Garden City, N.Y.: Doubleday, 1981): vol. 1, *New England and the Mid-Atlantic States*; vol. 2, *The South and the Midwest*; vol. 3, *The Plains States and the Far West*.

On postmodern architecture, see: C. Ray Smith, *Supermannerism: New Attitudes in Post-Modern Architecture* (New York: Dutton, 1977) and Robert Venturi, *Complexity and Contradiction in Architecture* (New York: Museum of Modern Art, 1977); also by Venturi, *Learning from Las Vegas* (Cambridge, Mass.: MIT Press, 1977). Psychological aspects of architecture are treated in: David Canter and Terrence Lee, eds., *Psychology and the Built*

*Environment* (New York: Wiley, 1974), a highly technical work, and Robert Sommer, *Tight Spaces: Hard Architecture and How to Humanize It* (Englewood Cliffs, N.J.: Prentice-Hall, 1974).

Analytical works on house forms are: Lucius F. and Linda V. Ellsworth, "House-Reading: How to Study Historic Houses as Symbols of Society," *History News* 35, no. 5 (May 1980): 9–13; Henry Glassie, *Folk Housing in Middle Virginia* (Knoxville: University of Tennessee Press, 1975), and "Eighteenth-Century Cultural Process in Delaware Valley Folk Building," *Winterthur Portfolio* 7 (1972): 29–57; John Fraser Hart, *The Look of the Land* (Englewood Cliffs, N.J.: Prentice-Hall, 1975), examines houses in rural environments; D. Geoffrey Hayward, "Home as an Environmental and Psychological Concept," *Landscape* 20 (October 1975): 2–9, offers a five-step method for analyzing American homes; Fred Kniffen, "Folk Housing: Key to Diffusion," *Annals of the Association of American Geographers* 55 (1965): 549–77; Fred Kniffen, "Louisiana House Types," in Phillip L. Wagner and Marvin W. Mikesell, eds., *Readings in Cultural Geography* (Chicago: University of Chicago Press, 1962); Amos Rapoport, *House Form and Culture* (Englewood Cliffs, N.J.: Prentice-Hall, 1969); John E. Rickert, "House Facades of the Northeastern United States: A Tool of Geographic Analysis," *Annals, Association of American Geographers*, 57 (1967): 211–38.

Linda Ellsworth, *The History of a House and How to Trace It*, Technical Leaflet No. 89 (Nashville: American Association for State and Local History, 1976), offers a good starting point for doing the history of a house.

Also on houses are: Ettore Camesasca, ed., *History of the House* (New York: Putnam's, 1971), a large and attractive book; Jan Cohn, *The Palace or the Poorhouse: The American House as a Cultural Symbol* (East Lansing: Michigan State University Press, 1979); David P. Handlin, *The American Home: Architecture and Society, 1815–1915* (Boston: Little, Brown, 1979); Wilbur D. Peat, *Indiana Houses of the Nineteenth Century* (Indianapolis: Indiana Historical Society, 1962); Stephen Gardiner, *The Evolution of the House* (New York: Macmillan, 1974); Elise Lathrop, *Historic Houses of Early America* (N.Y.: Tudor, 1936); Harold R. Shurtleff, *The Log Cabin Myth: A Study of the Early Dwellings of the English Colonists in North America* (Cambridge, Mass.: Harvard University Press, 1939); *Nineteenth-Century Houses in Lawrence, Kansas* (Lawrence: University of Kansas Museum of Art, 1968). On house interiors: William Seale, *The Tasteful Interlude: American Interiors through the Camera's Eye*, 2nd. ed., rev. (Nashville: American Association for State and Local History, 1981) and *Recreating the Historic House Interior* (Nashville: American Association for State and Local History, 1979); and Gwendolyn Wright, *Building the Dream: A Social History of Housing in America* (New York: Pantheon, 1981).

Two works on the urban landscape that suggest new directions for historical research are: Devereaux Bowly, Jr., *The Poorhouse: Subsidized Housing in Chicago, 1895–1976* (Carbondale: Southern Illinois University Press, 1978), and Louis Cain, *Sanitation Strategy for a Lakefront Metropolis* (DeKalb: Northern Illinois University Press, 1978).

Four works with interpretation as their theme are: William T. Alderson and Shirley Payne Low, *Interpretation of Historic Sites* (Nashville: American Association for State and Local History, 1976); Paul L. Benedict, *Historic Site Interpretation: The Student Field Trip*, Technical Leaflet No. 19 (Nashville: American Association for State and Local History,

1971); Shirley Payne Low, *Historic Site Interpretation: The Human Approach*, Technical Leaflet No. 32 (Nashville: American Association for State and Local History, 1965); Freeman J. Tilden, *Interpreting Our Heritage* (Chapel Hill: University of North Carolina Press, 1967), reflects a National Park Service point of view.

On archaeology and its variations: John L. Cotter, "Above-Ground Archaeology," *American Quarterly* 27, no. 3 (August 1974): 266–80; James Deetz, *Invitation to Archaeology* (Garden City, N.Y.: Natural History Press, 1967); Jean C. Harrington, *Archaeology and the Historical Society* (Nashville: American Association for State and Local History, 1965); Ivor Noel Hume, *Historic Archaeology: A Comprehensive Guide for Both Amateurs and Professionals to the Techniques and Methods of Excavating Historical Sites* (New York: Knopf, 1969) and "Archaeology: Handmaiden to History," *North Carolina Historical Review* 41 (1964): 215–25; and Thomas J. Schlereth, "Above-Ground Archaeology: Discovering a Community's History through Local Artifacts," in *Local History Today*, Thomas Krasean, ed. (Indianapolis: Indiana Historical Society, 1979), pp. 53–83; this excellent essay appears in revised form as chapter 9 in Schlereth's *Artifacts and the American Past* (Nashville: American Association for State and Local History, 1980), pp. 184–203.

# ·10·

# Preserving Material Traces

MATERIAL TRACES FROM THE PAST ARE IMPORTANT IN THE
study of history, and historians may have a role to play in preserving them. It
is a role sometimes misunderstood, and so, to counter misconceptions, we
begin a chapter devoted to a consideration of ironies, issues, and processes in
historic preservation with a statement regarding purposes and benefits.

## Historic Preservation: Purposes and Benefits

For historians, the most important aim of historic preservation, though
not by any means an exclusive one, is to give people a sense of "what it was
like to have been there." Seeing, touching, and moving about in the remains of the past permit us to feel its scale, its texture, its uses of space and
distance, and its attitude toward time and place. Meeting the past in a
material way sometimes stirs feelings of pride, patriotism, or admiration.
Sometimes it gives insights into such things as work, hardship, illness,
eating habits, and forms of education, recreation, and entertainment in
other times and places.

If the cultural value of historic preservation is so obvious and significant,
how is it possible to explain the fact that so many of the buildings that have
been listed on the National Register of Historic Places have been demolished? Or that landmarks are regularly turned into rubble and hauled
away? Why has "progress at any price" for so long characterized the American outlook? Are the arguments for preservation so weak, the benefits so
trifling, that they fail to persuade? Or are the people who must be convinced
simply dense, indifferent, and insensitive? To turn the question a bit: Are
there any practical arguments for preservation, any tangible benefits to be

gained from it, something the historian would not necessarily be looking for?

First, preservation sometimes makes good economic sense. Preserving is sometimes cheaper than building anew. Site clearance and excavation are unnecessary; construction time and expense and cost of materials are already spared. Streets and utility lines are probably in place, and landscaping costs are likely to be lower than they would be for a new structure. Nor should we overlook the conservation of energy. There are indirect benefits as well. Land values, for example, may be stabilized through preservation and whole communities saved. Tourism may increase, bringing in outside dollars.

Another tangible benefit of preservation is aesthetic. Stylish old buildings, or even unstylish ones with distinctive character, are marks of beauty, stability, and continuity on the cultural landscape, especially as they stand in contrast to the structures likely to replace them after demolition. If nothing else, they add diversity to the environment. Preserved buildings may offer specific educational benefits. The structures themselves and their contents are usually worthy subjects for study, and it seems natural to use them as centers for historical exhibits and for the broader study of history,

One midwestern community tried to "save" its downtown by making it look like a suburban shopping center, but the arcade wrecked the facades of some grand old buildings.

architecture, and material culture. Preservation may usefully contribute to forming community spirit when people work together to restore a single building as a centerpiece in their community or, better, when individuals and families restore an entire neighborhood. Community pride is an inevitable by-product. Preservation can also be used to approach social problems in intelligent ways. The high social and economic cost of high-rise, low-rent public housing increases the attractiveness of preserving, restoring, and putting to use row houses or flats for subsidized housing.

Now, if all these benefits can be identified and demonstrated in practice, we must ask why historic preservation in the United States has been what Peirce Lewis, in what may be an overstatement, has called a "thundering failure."

## Ironies in Movements for Historic Preservation

Part of the explanation for this can be found in the ironies that abound in efforts at historic preservation—ironies that we can merely note here.

First, since cultural benefits are not economic in nature, cultural issues cannot reasonably be debated in economic terms. The irony associated with doing so is compounded by the fact that promotion of the economic benefits of preservation is sometimes self-defeating. For example, if the case for preserving a structure of genuine historical significance rests on claims that economic benefits will flow from preservation, what happens when cost-benefit analyses show otherwise? Disregarding for the moment the possible manipulation of facts and figures by either side, let us suppose the figures are indisputable. Does the preservationist then join in the call for the bulldozer or lose credibility by switching claims? And what happens when the economic benefits of preserving a historic district or building prove too great? Can the character of a structure be maintained when it is overrun with more tourists than it can handle? Is the building visited by multitudes the same building that existed before the crowds found it, or has it become something else? Or consider how new tourist-handling facilities, widened streets, and increased traffic alter the texture of a single neighborhood or an entire historic district.

The preservation of neighborhoods, particularly in urban areas, is similarly problematic. Is it not ironic, for example, that the first casualties of a preserved neighborhood are often the people with the deepest roots there? When blocks of row houses become the target of middle-class preservers—

sometimes styled "urban frontiersmen"—property values rise so much and so rapidly that the indigenous population is displaced. Is it more important to restore a neighborhood or to save a people? How can the charge of elitism be refuted in situations that displace people? Is "gentrification," as the displacement process is sometimes called, ever justified?

Then, too, how are decisions made regarding what should be preserved? When we preserve the ordinary, it quickly becomes the extraordinary. Its value rises, it attracts attention, and imitators appear. This is often the point at which displacement of the indigenous population occurs. If we preserve the extraordinary, the special structures in a community, it does not take long for them to be idealized, to become regarded as typical and representational when in fact they are not. Still, choices must be made. Just as we cannot remember everything we have ever learned, so a society cannot retain everything it has ever built or made. The whole landscape cannot be locked in time.

Also ironic, to some, at least, is the realization that much so-called historic preservation is merely preservation. Individuals who are romantic, sentimental, or nostalgic pay little heed to the historic—that is, to the significant—when they preserve buildings. If nostalgia is a growth industry, some creations of the preservation movement are its lead products. There is nothing wrong, of course, with preservation, but *historic* preservation should be what the designation implies.

Government programs, despite commitments to preservation going back at least to 1906, have sometimes been the most destructive forces in urban areas. Consider the record of urban renewal. What, do you suppose, occupied the land where government-financed projects now stand? The next time you drive on an interstate highway through the heart of the city, notice the rows of stately buildings watching vigilantly over the highway. What view did they have before the highway came through? Preservationists consider many government actions not as ironic betrayals of the popular interest but as flagrant violations of existing laws.

Perhaps the ultimate irony is that preservationists' worst and most ardent foes are sometimes other preservationists. The movement (or movements) quite naturally attracts men and women who find in it both a faith and an ideology. Compromise comes hard to such persons, and preservation questions must necessarily be met at least sometimes with compromise, as the following list of issues shows.

## Issues in Historic Preservation

*Progress*. Perhaps it is true that, until very recently at least, America's past has always seemed to lie somewhere out in the future. Plans for tomorrow were always more important to us than our remembrances of yesterday. The future called for bigger, faster, and more—more in quantity, more comfortable, more convenient. Such plans were not created by builders and designers and wreckers of the landscape. They simply planned the instruments to place the country where it thought it had a right to be. Destruction of the landscape can rightly be regarded as reflecting the collective will of the people. How, the preservationist must ask, can this will be changed so that it shows different understandings of progress? And what gives some people—preservationists specifically—the right to define progress for others? To complicate matters still further, how do we approach this question when progress has already brought some people rewards to which they feel entitled while denying such benefits to others? Can the former decide for the latter that their idea of progress is wrong?

*Money*. Acquisition of properties to be preserved can be expensive, as are repairing or restoring them and maintaining them. If private investors provide the money, how are public interests to be protected? How can nonprofit organizations raise enough money through donations to be effective? What government funds are available, how can they be obtained, and how should they be used?

*Technical demands*. Preservation is an exciting but demanding business. Anyone who has worked with old buildings knows how difficult it is to cope with deterioration of inside and outside walls, foundations, floors, ceilings, and roofs; to know how to combat crumbling masonry, peeling paint, falling plaster, and broken windows; to find ways of conserving energy or of remedying plumbing and electrical deficiencies—to say nothing of solving landscaping and parking problems.

*Property rights*. What is to keep property owners from doing as they please with their property—including tearing it down or altering it beyond recognition? Who has the right to impose the "public good" on owners of private property? This issue, of course, involves zoning, understood as the tool by which people collectively establish standards to preserve the beauty and integrity of their communities.

*Zoning and building codes*. Suppose a property is acquired. Will zoning laws permit its use in ways that may be at odds with the character or design of the community in which it is located? Can it be brought into conformity with building codes without destroying it? How does a sprinkler system, for example, affect the historic atmosphere of a building a century old?

*Tax laws.* Since the Tax Reform Act of 1976, tax laws have been more favorable to preservation than they were previously. Amendments in 1980 and 1981 have made them even more favorable. How can they be used most effectively? Does tax abatement lower the tax base and lead to reduction of government services? Do tax incentives benefit the upper classes' interests at the expense of the welfare of the lower classes?

*What to do with a preserved building.* Simply preserve it? Reconstruct it entirely? Relocate it? Adapt it for new uses? To which point in its existence should it be restored, if restoration is the purpose? What should be done about changes or additions? Is restoration worthwhile if only the facade can be returned to its original appearance?

*Save a building? Or save a neighborhood?* These are critical questions. Preservationism was once conceived almost entirely as the saving of isolated, representative, or unique structures. House museums in urban areas show the consequences, in many instances unavoidable. Yet does it not make sense to avoid such consequences where possible by saving entire districts rather than isolated buildings?

Such questions provide background for turning to matters on which local historians involved in preservation efforts need to be informed, specifically: (1) the history of preservation and preservation laws; (2) how to place historic buildings, sites, and districts on appropriate registers; and (3) how to deal with technical aspects of acquisition, restoration, rehabilitation, and adaptive use of historic places.

## Preservation Laws

The history of the most significant laws affecting the preservation of historic places shows an evolving commitment to making preservation possible and successful. The first act of Congress having to do with historic preservation, the Antiquities Act of 1906, gave the president power to designate nationally significant historic resources and authorized cabinet members to grant permits for archaeological work; the actions of the president and cabinet members could apply only to lands belonging to the United

Research in the National Archives helped Michael Musick find a historical house to buy. "I always wanted to live in an old home," he explained, "particularly one associated with the Civil War." He visited Bolivar, West Virginia, a small community adjacent to Harpers Ferry which had served as the background for an 1862 Mathew Brady Civil War photograph he had found in the Archives. The buildings shown in the picture that were still standing included the circled house. Neighbors gave him the name of the owner.

Armed with this evidence, Musick returned to the archives to consult maps and Civil War claim files. He found that the house's original owner had petitioned for government compensation, attaching a receipt from a colonel acknowledging that Union soldiers had occupied the house during the war and used the picket fence around the house for firewood. Census records for 1850 through 1900 provided further information about owners and tenants of the house. After he had verified his discovery and learned more, Musick was able to buy and restore the house of which he had dreamed.

The Twenty-second New York State Militia, Bolivar, West Virginia, 1862, by Mathew Brady.

The historic house that Michael Musick bought for restoration in Bolivar, West Virginia, after tracing it through National Archives records and a Mathew Brady Civil War photograph.

A before-restoration detail of the well-preserved decorative woodwork on the Musick house.

*Source*: Michael Musick and the National Archives and Records Service, Washington, D.C.

States. Ten years later, the National Park Service Act created the Park Service and gave it authority to administer historic sites as well as scenic parks.

In 1935, with the enactment of the Historic Sites Act, a national policy was established for preserving sites, buildings, and objects of national significance, regardless of ownership. The law authorized the secretary of the interior to identify historic buildings and sites by conducting surveys, to acquire some of them, and to administer the ones acquired while aiding in the preservation of others through cooperative agreements. The act also created the National Historic Landmarks Program.

In 1966, a Conference of Mayors report, *With Heritage So Rich*, indicated the growing interest in preservation and pointed to the need for a more comprehensive, coordinated national preservation program focusing on the cultural environment as a whole rather than on its outstanding parts. Four new laws broadened and strengthened the federal role in historic preservation. The Department of Transportation Act and the Federal Highway Act declared it a national policy of making special efforts to preserve the natural beauty of the countryside. The Demonstration Cities and Metropolitan Development Act relaxed restrictions that had previously prevented the use of urban renewal funds for historic preservation, and it authorized new historic preservation programs in urban areas.

The most important of the four 1966 laws was the National Historic Preservation Act. This act considerably strengthened the 1935 legislation by calling for the creation of the National Register of districts, sites, buildings, structures, and objects significant in American history, and it afforded limited protection for properties listed in the National Register by requiring that federal agencies take them into consideration in the evaluation of federally funded, licensed, or permitted projects. It also inaugurated a matching grants-in-aid program to states and the National Trust for Historic Preservation (a federally chartered private organization) and established an Advisory Council on Historic Preservation to review federal actions related to preservation and to advise the president and Congress on these matters. The National Environmental Policy Act of 1969 enlarged the interpretation of impact to include the man-made environment. Under this act, federal agencies are required to evaluate and explain publicly the impact of their projects on both natural and cultural resources and to make every effort to eliminate or mitigate damaging effects.

Executive Order No. 11593 ("Protection and Enhancement of the Cultural Environment") issued by the president on May 13, 1971, and codified by Congress in 1980, explicitly requires every federal agency to make an inventory of historic properties in their custody, to nominate them to the National Register, and to adopt measures to ensure their preservation. Because some federal agencies have been slow to comply, citizens should be alert for violations.

The Tax Reform Act of 1976, extended for three years in 1980, seeks to discourage destruction of historic buildings and to make their rehabilitation economically feasible, principally by allowing large tax incentives in the form of deductible costs and depreciation provisions for their rehabilitation, providing the rehabilitation meets certain standards established by the secretary of the interior. To qualify, the buildings must be on the National Register or in a district certified by the secretary of the interior. It also encourages charitable donations of historic properties. The Economic Recovery Tax Act of 1981 established new incentives to encourage the preservation and reuse of buildings by replacing the earlier provisions with a 25 percent investment tax credit and changing property depreciation terms to allow recovery of investment costs in fifteen years, rather than over the useful life of the property.

For many years, all preservation activities were centered in the National Park Service in the Department of the Interior. To cope with the demands on the Park Service brought by the growing size and scope of preservation efforts, the Advisory Council on Historic Preservation was recently made an independent agency of the executive branch, and in 1978 the National Register of Historic Places and three other agencies sharing responsibility for preservation were pulled together in the Heritage Conservation and Recreation Service, still in the Department of the Interior. In 1981 the HCRS was abolished, and its programs were returned to the National Park Service.

## The National Register

The key element in the preservation laws is the National Register, since listing on the Register provides some protection against destruction and may make it possible to secure funding for restoration. The protection was lessened in 1980 with the enactment of a provision allowing the owner's objection to block the placement of a property on the Register. In the event of such objection, the property may still be listed as eligible, so that it is at least protected from the negative effects of federal projects. Persons seeking to preserve historic places in their communities must know how to register them. Each state designates an agency headed by a state historic preservation officer to work with the Register, most commonly the state historical society, department of natural resources, department of conservation, or department of cultural affairs. The criteria for evaluation of places nominated are uniform nationally. They read as follows:

The quality of significance in American history, architecture, archaeology, and culture is present in districts, sites, buildings, structures, and objects that possess integrity of location, design, setting, materials, workmanship, feeling, and association, and:

A.    that are associated with events that have made a significant contribution to the broad patterns of our history; or

B.    that are associated with the lives of persons significant in our past; or

C.    that embody the distinctive characteristics of a type, period, or method of construction, or that represent a significant and distinguishable entity whose components may lack individual distinction; or

D.    that have yielded, or may be likely to yield, information important in prehistory or history.

Ordinarily cemeteries, birthplaces, or graves of historical figures, properties owned by religious institutions or used for religious purposes, structures that have been moved from their original locations, reconstructed historic buildings, properties primarily commemorative in nature, and properties that have achieved significance within the past 50 years shall not be considered eligible for the National Register. However, such properties will qualify if they are integral parts of districts that do meet the criteria or if they fall within the following categories:

A.    a religious property deriving primary significance from architectural or artistic distinction or historical importance; or

B.    a building or structure removed from its original location but which is significant primarily for architectural value, or which is the surviving structure most importantly associated with a historic person or event; or

C.    a birthplace or grave of a historical figure of outstanding importance if there is no other appropriate site or building directly associated with his productive life; or

D.    a cemetery that derives its primary significance from graves of persons of transcendent importance, from age, from distinctive design features, or from association with historic events; or

E.    a reconstructed building when accurately executed in a suitable environment and presented in a dignified manner as part of a restoration master plan, and when no other building or structure with the same association has survived; or

F.  a property primarily commemorative in intent if design, age, tradition, or symbolic value has invested it with its own historical significance; or

G.  a property achieving significance within the past 50 years if it is of exceptional importance.

Working with the designated state historic preservation officer is essential in the registration process. This officer provides the nomination forms that are required if the property is to be considered by a state review board, and approval of this board is a necessary step in the quest for a place on the National Register.

The essential part of the nomination to the National Register is an inventory or survey of the property in question (see the sample in appendix C). One way to begin this survey—of a building, let us assume—is with the historic inventory form in hand. Each piece of information might be sought as the form calls for it. Another way would be to undertake a systematic survey of the building and to draw from it the information requested on the form:

1. the name of the property
2. the location
3. the classification
4. the owner
5. the legal description
6. the property's representation in existing surveys
7. findings of architectural research: style, materials used in construction, date and extent of alterations, descriptions of unique features, an account of its current condition, and so on
8. findings of historical and archaeological research: identification of people associated with it, such as the architect, builder, and users; uses through the years, important events associated with it; other details turned up that were not previously a part of the record of the property
9. major bibliographical references to the property
10. findings of geographical research: mainly the relationship of the building with the cultural and natural environment in which it is located.

The form also calls for the name of the preparer and the signature of the state historic preservation officer. Photographs from various angles should accompany the form, and you may also wish to prepare a set of measured drawings.

While placement on the National Register carries prestige and is very important if federal grants are to be used for acquisition or restoration of a property, local inventories and landmark legislation can be equally important (see appendices D and E). The National Register protects a property if federal money is to be used; the local landmark legislation can protect a property, to some extent, from its owner or from prospective buyers.

A survey gives the information needed for nomination forms, but local historians interested in preserving the building will want to analyze the information and draw conclusions about the architectural, historical, and archaeological significance of the building to determine the feasibility of preserving it, and to consider possible uses for it should preservation seem feasible. Various questions will need to be considered: Does the building require repairs? Can it be restored through rehabilitation? To be useful, would it have to be reconstructed or possibly even relocated?

## Doing Preservation

Other questions that must be asked at this point are numerous. What kind of support for preserving the building can be gained from local governments and community groups? (Certain government programs are vital sources of funding.) What are the owner's interests in the building? What legal matters must be dealt with in a preservation effort? What is the best way to acquire the property? What use can be made of tax incentives in a preservation effort? Where will the funds for acquisition be found?

And suppose the property is acquired. Then comes a host of problems too numerous to be explored here; they will relate to scraping and painting; patching, reinforcing, and rebuilding; finding missing pieces and repairing broken ones; matching replacement parts with originals; coping with rotting, leaking, and sagging; recording work that is done, particularly the changes being made and the reasons for them; incorporating modern conveniences like electricity, plumbing, and air conditioning; satisfying building codes; providing access for the handicapped; and maintaining the building inside and out.

Historic preservation is not an endeavor which one should attempt alone. Help should be constantly sought. Preservationists should be prepared to maintain ties not only with the appropriate state agency but also with local landmark commissions and historic properties advisory councils. They should be prepared, too, to call on persons specially trained and well experienced in historic preservation. Of what does special training consist? A recent survey of degree programs in colleges and universities shows a variety of emphases, including urban planning, architecture, art history, architectural history, urban affairs, landscape architecture, geography, law, management, history, and American studies.

If the processes of preservation are so complicated and the work so hard, some people might wonder whether the effort is worthwhile. Those who believe it important, however, will make it possible for more and more people to find links with the past, to develop a sense of what it was like to have been there.

And how does one start? By starting! As one who has been active in state historic preservation remarked, it may be best for people simply to take a foolhardy plunge into preservation projects, since reliance on absolute logic is not always helpful in such work; a touch of insanity helps, and "if most folks knew the frustrations they were in for, probably nothing would ever be taken on." Perhaps such people consider the frustrations a small price for great rewards.

## Notes

The Peirce Lewis quotation is from "The Future of the Past: Our Clouded Vision of Historic Preservation," *Pioneer America* 7, no. 2 (July 1975): 1–20.

For information on the National Register of Historic Places, write to: Keeper of the National Register, National Park Service, United States Department of the Interior, 440 G Street, N.W., Washington, D.C. 20240.

The criteria of evaluation listed in this chapter appear in brochures available from the National Park Service and in the *Federal Register* 46, no. 220 (November 16, 1981): 56189, where they are incorporated in the interim rules covering the transfer of the Register from the now abolished Heritage Conservation and Recreation Service to the National Park Service. Current information is also available from the National Trust for Historic Preservation, 1785 Massachusetts Avenue, N.W., Washington, D.C. 20036.

## For Further Information

Historic preservation is the subject of much controversy involving political, social, economic, aesthetic, and other questions. For years, it seems, historic preservation has been in crisis. Betty Doak Elder, "Crossroads: Congress to Decide Preservation's Future," *History News* 35, no. 4 (April 1980): 7–13, describes the alternatives as they looked at the beginning of a new decade.

Other works touching on controversial or problematical aspects of preservation include Walter L. Bailey, "Historic Districts: A Neglected Resource," *North Dakota History* 43 (1976): 22–24; David A. Clary, "Historic Preservation and Environmental Protection: The Role of the Historian," *Public Historian* 1 (fall 1978): 61–75; Grady Clay, "Townscape and Landscape: The Coming Battleground," *Historic Preservation* 24 (1972): 34–43; E. Blaine Cliver, "Reconstruction: Valid or Invalid?" *Historic Preservation* 24 (1972): 22–24; Larry Tice, "Let's Put History Back into Historic Preservation," *Preservation News*, October 1979, p. 5; Larry Ford, "Historic Preservation and the Stream of Time," *Historical Geography Newsletter* 5 (winter 1975): 1–15; Tom Huth, "Should Charleston Go New South?" *Historic Preservation* 31 (July-August 1979); 32–38; Kevin Lynch, *What Time Is This Place?* (Cambridge, Mass.: MIT Press, 1972); Robert M. Utley, "Historic Preservation and the Environment," *Colorado Magazine* 51 (winter 1974): 1–12; Carrie Johnson, "A Dynamic Movement Looks at Itself: Preservation in the 1980s," *Historic Preservation* 32 (November–December 1980): 33–39; and *Economic Benefits of Preserving Old Buildings*, papers from the Seattle Conference of the National Trust for Historic Preservation, July 31–August 2, 1975 (Washington, D.C.: National Trust for Historic Preservation, 1975).

A good introduction to the roots of the legislation that has been a part of the recent historic preservation movement is found in *With Heritage So Rich* (New York: Random House, 1966), a report of the United States Conference of Mayors. A good case for preservation is made in Randolph Langenbach, *A Future from the Past: The Case for Conservation and Reuse of Old Buildings in Industrial Communities* (Washington, D.C.: Department of Housing and Urban Development, 1977). Advocacy in the context of success stories at the local level is found in Raymond F. Pisney, ed., *Old Buildings: New Resources for Work and Play* (Verona, Va.: McClure, 1976).

Charles B. Hosmer, Jr., lays out the history of historic preservation in *Presence of the Past: A History of the Preservation Movement in the United States before Williamsburg* (New York: Putnam's, 1965) and *Preservation Comes of Age: From Williamsburg to the National Trust* (Charlottesville: University of Virginia Press, 1981); also by Hosmer is "The Broadening View of the Historic Preservation Movement," in Ian M. G. Quimby, ed., *Material Culture and the Study of American Life* (New York: Norton, 1978), pp. 121–139.

Among the many surveys of doings in the preservation movement are: Alice Cromie, *Restored Towns and Historic Districts of America: A Tour Guide* (New York: Dutton, 1979); Elizabeth Kendall Thompson, ed., *Recycling Buildings: Renovations, Remodelings, Restorations, and Reuses* (New York: McGraw-Hill, 1977); Louis Redstone, *The New Downtowns: Rebuilding Business Districts* (New York: McGraw-Hill, 1976); Nathan Weinberg, *Preservation in American Cities and Towns* (Boulder, Colo.: Westview Press, 1979); and Tony P. Wrenn and Elizabeth D. Mulloy, *America's Forgotten Architecture* (New York: Pantheon, 1976). That preservation efforts are often too little, too late is apparent in James M. Goode, *Capital Losses: A Cultural History of Washington's Destroyed Buildings* (Washington, D.C.: Smithsonian Institution Press, 1979). Also in Mary Cable, *Lost New Orleans* (Boston: Houghton Mifflin, 1980); Jane H. Kay, *Lost Boston* (Boston: Houghton Mifflin, 1980);

David Lowe, *Lost Chicago* (Boston: Houghton Mifflin, 1975); and Nathan Silver, *Lost New York* (New York: Schocken, 1971).

Among the better guides for doing preservation or for coping with preservation problems are: Orin M. Bullock, Jr., *The Restoration Manual: An Illustrated Guide to the Preservation and Restoration of Old Buildings* (Norwalk, Conn.: Silvermine, 1966); Marsha Glenn, *Historic Preservation: A Handbook for Architectural Students* (Washington, D.C.: American Institute of Architects, 1974); Harrison Goodall and Renee Friedman, *Log Structures: Preservation and Problem-Solving* (Nashville: American Association for State and Local History, 1980); Robert H. McNulty and Stephen A. Kliment, *Neighborhood Conservation: A Handbook of Methods and Techniques* (New York: Watson-Guptill, 1976); Morgan W. Phillips, *The Eight Most Common Mistakes in Restoring Houses*, Technical Leaflet No. 118 (Nashville: American Association for State and Local History, 1979); Richard Ernie Reed, *Return to the City: How to Restore Old Buildings and Ourselves in America's Historic Urban Neighborhoods* (Garden City, N.Y.: Doubleday, 1979); Arthur P. Ziegler, Jr., *Historic Preservation in Inner City Areas: A Manual of Practice*, rev. ed. (Pittsburgh: Ober Park Associates, 1974); Robert E. Stipe, ed., *New Directions in Rural Preservation* (Washington, D.C.: U.S. Department of the Interior, 1980); Arthur P. Ziegler, Jr., and Walter C. Kidney, *Historic Preservation in Small Towns: A Manual of Practice* (Nashville: American Association for State and Local History, 1979); and Thomas J. Martin, et al., *Adaptive Use: Development Economics, Process, and Profiles* (Washington, D.C.: Urban Land Institute, 1978). Also useful is *Information: A Preservation Sourcebook* (Washington, D.C.: Preservation Press, 1979), which offers more than 400 pages of information in "fact sheet" form on basic and frequently used preservation techniques. Technical information is also available from the Technical Preservation Services Division, Office of Archaeology and Historic Preservation, National Park Service, U.S. Department of the Interior, Washington, D.C. 20240. In addition to publishing and distributing a wide variety of booklets and brochures, this agency offers a series of topical papers called *Preservation Briefs*. These briefs deal with such topics as "Aluminum and Vinyl Sidings on Historical Buildings" (No. 8, by John H. Myers) and "Conserving Energy in Historic Buildings" (No. 3, by Baird M. Smith). The same division also has available a set of reading lists on specialized topics. The general information brochures of this agency offer useful introductions to the range of federal involvement in preservation efforts.

Federal involvement is extensive and of long standing. An interesting introduction is found in F. Ross Holland, Jr., "The Park Service as Curator," *National Parks and Conservation Magazine*, August 1979, pp. 10–15. The most significant federal publication is the *National Register of Historic Places* (Washington, D.C.: U.S. Government Printing Office). Volume 1, published in 1978, lists 9,500 properties placed in the Register from its creation in 1966 through 1974; its 960 pages include more than 600 illustrations. Volume 2, 1979, lists 5,000 properties registered in 1975–1976; its 700 pages have 560 illustrations. A cumulative list of all National Register properties is printed each February in the *Federal Register*, and additions to it are printed there on the first Tuesday of each month. The *National Register* program is the responsibility of the National Park Service, U.S. Department of Interior. *How to Complete National Register Forms* (1977) is available from the National Park Service.

Also of interest here is Harley J. McKee, *Recording Historic Buildings: The Historic American Buildings Survey* (Washington, D.C.: National Park Service, 1970). The roots of this publication lie in the Historic American Buildings Survey begun as a New Deal program in 1933 and published with additional material bringing it up to date from time to time since then.

Historic preservation frequently entails legal questions. Although such questions require the special knowledge and skills of lawyers, a helpful reference book for lay persons is Nicholas Robinson, *Historic Preservation Law* (New York: Practicing Law Institute, 1979). Legal questions are considered from a local perspective in Richard Collins, Ross Netherton, and Raymond F. Pisney, eds., *Public Policy and Historic Preservation in Virginia* (Staunton, Va.: Mouseion Press, 1978). For help in local situations, see Stephen N. Dennis, *Recommended Model Provisions for a Preservation Ordinance, with Annotations* (Washington, D.C.: National Trust for Historic Preservation, 1980). Related is the National Trust's *Preservation: Toward an Ethic in the 1980s* (Washington, D.C.: Preservation Press, 1980).

The most comprehensive bibliography of materials on historic preservation is Frederick L. Rath, Jr., and Merrilyn O'Connell, *Historic Preservation: A Bibliography on Historical Organization Practices*, vol. 1 (Nashville: American Association for State and Local History, 1975). John A. Jakle, *Past Landscapes* (Monticello, Ill.: Council of Planning Librarians, 1973), is a bibliography of work done by cultural geographers in historic preservation. An earlier work, largely superseded but possibly still useful, is Gary L. Menges, *Historic Preservation: A Bibliography* (Monticello, Ill.: Council of Planning Librarians, 1969). Also useful for the range of its entries is the *National Trust for Historic Preservation Bookshop Catalogue* (1980), available at the bookshop, 740 Jackson Place, N.W., Washington, D.C. 20006.

Persons wishing to know what others are doing in preservation may consult the *Directory of Private, Nonprofit Preservation Organizations: State and Local* (Washington, D.C.: Preservation Press, 1979).

The regular publications of the National Trust for Historic Preservation are *Preservation News*, a monthly newspaper, and *Historic Preservation*, a bimonthly magazine. Both may be ordered from the National Trust, 1785 Massachusetts Ave., N.W., Washington, D.C. 20005. Still another is *The Old House Journal*, 199 Berkeley Pl., Brooklyn, New York 11217. Related to this journal is Lawrence Grow, comp., *The Old House Catalogue* (New York: Main Street Press, 1976).

# ·11·

# Research, Writing, and
# Leaving a Record

THE PRECEDING CHAPTERS HAVE DISCUSSED A WIDE variety of research methods, some of them quite specialized. Those chapters have emphasized discovering historical traces—written, oral, visual, material, and immaterial—and interpreting them. Using them purposefully to communicate information about the nearby past, however, requires moving beyond the excitement of discovery and insight to bring the evidence under control. It is therefore important to record the discoveries of the moment. If they are registered in a sloppy or indifferent manner, even the best research is wasted. But careful, organized recording with a view toward future use, is an aspect of historical research that pays off in understanding, time saved, quality, and satisfaction. Observing just a few sound principles of research, writing, and record keeping will help you avoid common mistakes, make your work more effective, and enable you to accomplish more in the time available.

## Taking Notes

Few people can remember great quantities of detailed information for long. Taking notes becomes essential for an accurate record. While it is possible to scribble notes on any scrap of paper that is handy at the moment, such jottings often prove awkward to use later. It is far better in the long run to work out a method of note taking at the outset of a project and to follow it consistently thereafter.

The material on which you choose to record information is a matter of personal preference, of course, and that choice should be dictated by the way in which you plan to present your findings. Some researchers find notebooks most satisfactory, while others prefer loose sheets or cards which can later be sorted and rearranged. Choose materials that suit your research and writing styles and stick with them. (One of the authors prefers five-by-eight-inch index cards, which he color codes according to topic by drawing narrow lines with felt-tip markers across the tops. This method facilitates sorting and assimilating when the time to write arrives. The other author dislikes the bulk of cards and uses five-by-eight-inch slips of paper instead.) A change in size or format is likely to mean that smaller items will be overlooked and creates storage problems.

The cardinal rule of note taking is to identify on every sheet the source of the information you are recording. This practice allows you to go back and check if necessary. It is also a good idea to leave some space on each note for adding information later or for coding as you prepare for writing. If you choose to use a notebook from which pages can only be removed by tearing them out, be sure to devise some system of cross-referencing and organizing so that your notes are not lost to you.

There is no substitute for neatness and accuracy in recording information. Using a pen rather than a pencil (except where the rules of the archival research room prohibit it) reduces the likelihood of smudging. Scribbling in haste may mean effort wasted. An unclear note may require going back to the source at a later time to verify information that might have been carefully recorded the first time. Writing on only one side of a card prevents you from overlooking notes later and makes card flipping unnecessary.

As you proceed to gather information, ideas for organizing and analyzing may come to you. Jot down these thoughts also. If you do not write them down until later, they may disappear altogether. Be alert, too, for illustrative material that could make your story more vivid. Here is where a photocopying machine may be used most effectively. Make a copy of the visual document you consider to be potentially useful, write on it where you found it, and file it with others that you are accumulating so that you have a set to choose from when you prepare your presentation.

Photocopiers come in handy for other purposes as well, but they must be used judiciously. Some researchers make extra work for themselves by photocopying indiscriminately everything they find. Selections must be made sooner or later; by making them sooner you are likely to save yourself time and money without damaging your finished product.

## Writing

Eventually the time will come for you to write. Even if you choose to present your findings in an audiovisual form, such presentations require a script, and the better the writing, the better the final product. Effective writing, after all, is nothing other than a process of putting ideas and evidence in a logical order and comprehensible language so that a reader or listener can understand them. If writers present a worthwhile topic in this way, they stand a good chance of interesting and persuading the audience.

The nature and extent of preparation for writing depends on the envisioned finished product. The range of options for historians of people and things nearby is broad, both in medium and in scope. End results might be presented in an audiovisual medium. A sound recording might be made to accompany a set of printed pictures or merely for use by itself. A slide-tape show can effectively convey a wide variety of information. Videotape is becoming a more accessible and economical format. More elaborate film presentations are possible, though they can be expensive and technologically complex and can demand professional involvement. Some groups have had great success communicating their research in dramatic form, either as stage presentations or through role playing in historical surroundings. Written pieces can range from short essays on single topics to full-length books. Possibilities between these extremes include scrapbooks, photo-essays, collections of vignettes, and extended articles. Sometimes short pieces can be used to present findings at early stages and as parts of longer works later. Whatever form your finished product takes, it will be more effective if you prepare it with its intended audience in mind.

Starting to write is often very difficult, even painful. The first step involves thinking through the topic and deciding what to say about it. If you are like many people, you will be tempted, when the time for writing arrives, to find an excuse to do something else. You will think of another source to check, another book to read, another library or archives to visit, another person to interview. But at some point you will have to stop gathering information and put words on paper to meet a deadline, to seek funds for a preservation project, or simply to assess for yourself the work you have done.

Some people find it helpful to begin their writing with an outline. Some are committed to very formal and detailed outlines, while others are satisfied with a general idea as to how they hope to develop their story. An outline, formal or informal, grows from a conceptual scheme. Typically there is an

Some writers find that catastrophes offer a good focus for stories. They are dramatic, they unfold in a natural sequence, and they can cause important changes. The response of individuals and institutions to crisis can provide clues to their character and role within the community. Of course, the importance of one event in the overall history of a family or community ought not to be exaggerated. This description of a northern Indiana disaster, written by a student, provides an example of how both narrative and analysis can be incorporated into an interesting account.

*The worst explosion and fire in the Calumet Region's history were caused by the world's largest hydroformer on Saturday, August 27, 1955. The hydroformer made high octane fuel which was blended with other gasoline stocks to create fuel for high compression auto engines. The explosion occurred because an experiment backfired. When the hydroformer blew up at the Standard Oil Refinery, some of Whiting's residents did not know what to think; some thought an atomic bomb had hit their town. The first explosion and fire occurred at 6:15 a.m. and burned uncontrollably throughout the day. As the flames spread, a 60 million-barrel storage tank blew up as late as 4:00 p.m.*

*The series of explosions that rocked the Standard Oil Refinery on that day blew out most of the windows in a three mile radius, including most of Whiting and parts of East Chicago and Indiana Harbor. The Stiglitz Park District of Whiting was the worst hit. The initial blast hurled hunks of two-inch steel up to 30 feet long out of the refinery. One chunk nearly 50 feet long flew two city blocks, smashed through a food store and flattened an automobile. At least 50 homes close to the explosion were demolished.*

*Firemen from ten cities responded to the explosion and fire, including firemen from Gary, Hammond, East Chicago, Whiting, Oak Forest, Midlothian, Oak Park, Blue Island, and Dolton.*

*A grocery store at 1829 129th Street in Whiting was demolished by the steel roof of the huge hydromate unit. When Douglas Stepullin, the owner of the grocery store, arrived on the scene, all that remained of his store was a huge scar on the earth. Some of the store's merchandise was thrown across the street.*

*The Plewniak household at 2638 Schrage Avenue in Whiting was slumbering at 6:14 a.m. on August 27, 1955. Frank Plewniak and his wife, Joan, were sleeping in a front bedroom, while their two small sons were asleep in another bed in the rear of the house. Suddenly!—an ear-splitting explo-*

sion rocked the house. Seconds later, a 10-foot steel pipe torpedoed through the roof of the house. A child's scream pierced the air. The terrified parents rushed into the children's bedroom. Upon arrival in the room, they found Ronald Plewniak, 8, crying in his bed. His right leg had been severed by the 10-foot pipe. Ronald's three year old brother, Richard, was unconscious in his crib. He was pinned beneath the pipe. Richard Plewniak died one half hour later at Saint Catherine Hospital in East Chicago, Indiana.

Ronald Plewniak is now thirty years old. After his graduation from college, he was given a life-time job with the Standard Oil Company.

Twenty-five other people were injured. There was one death which was indirectly related to the explosion. Walter Rhea, 61, a foreman at the refinery, died of a heart attack as he arrived on the disaster scene.

Standard Oil bought up most of the residential property in the area worst hit by the explosion and fire. The area was bounded on the east by Indianapolis Boulevard, on the south by 129th Street and on the west by Louisa Avenue. Neither the newspapers nor the people that I interviewed mentioned where the owners of this property moved. . . .

Standard Oil's loss was estimated at 19 million dollars. They received 18 million dollars in insurance payments, but I could not find any records where the insurance company paid individuals for their damaged property. Due to the huge amount by the insurance company, Standard Oil was able to replace most of the equipment burned by the fire with new and improved facilities. By 1956, they were back to normal operating procedures.

This explosion has been described as the worst fire in the Calumet Region's history. However, most of the people who were interviewed cannot remember what happened on Saturday, August 27, 1955. I believe that this is the case because the newspaper played the explosion down. They reported as little as possible. The release by Standard Oil was only a rehash of what was said in the newspapers. While researching this paper, Standard Oil refused to discuss the matter and offered no information technical or otherwise.

Source: Ruthie Williams, "The Explosion of Standard Oil, August 27, 1955," in *Steel Shavings*, edited by Ronald D. Cohen (Gary: Indiana University Northwest, 1978), pp. 25–27.

interplay between a rudimentary notion of the purpose you have in mind and the material with which you are working. The lack of any idea, at least as a starting point, is likely to be a handicap, since that means that you are working aimlessly, without a goal.

Conceptual schemes need not to be elaborate. Consider the possibilities, for instance, of the following simple plan for the history of a family, an organization, or a community:

> Origins
> Dynamics
> Milestones
> Character

It is natural to focus on *origins*, as many of the questions posed in chapter 2 imply. Origins lead you to the people who knew about them, to the time and place, and to much more. In examining *dynamics*, you will look at what moved people, how power was held and used, and how decisions were made. Again, people will be at the center of your examination. Contemplating *milestones* means considering times of marked change, great occasions, measuring points on the continuum of routine, and turning points. In discerning *character* you seek to identify distinctive features that set your subject apart from others of the same general type. You are seeking to answer the simple question: "Who were these people—*really*?"

Outlines, whether formal and detailed or loose and general, are most helpful when the parts in them are expressed as questions to be answered. A mere listing of topics to be treated gives little coherence or direction to the finished product, and these are two essential ingredients of good writing. Also important are simplicity and clarity. These four qualities—coherence, direction, simplicity, and clarity—are perhaps best defined in terms of their opposites. Thus prose manifesting them will not be rambling and disjointed, aimless, tangled and confused, and vague or murky.

Keep in mind that someone fifty or a hundred years from now may be interested in the same nearby past which has absorbed your attention. Your possibility of communicating with that person improves if you avoid slang or jargon that is popular at the moment but may be incomprehensible within a few years as "in" phrases change. Cryptic comments, sarcasm, and attempts at humor also run a high risk of being misinterpreted. If you write in simple, direct English with well-defined terminology, uncomplicated, straightforward sentences, and paragraphs which follow logically, you stand the best chance of being understood in the future as well as now.

Writing about a person's personality or the nature of family and community life is seldom easy. Detailed descriptions usually provide greater accuracy and generate more interest than general labels. For example, Oliver Cook's grandfather might have been called stern, honest, quick-tempered, and forgiving, but a reader has a much better sense of him from these brief stories.

*Oliver Cook was born on March 6, 1897, in Green County, Boligee, Alabama, the fourth of Mack and Fannie Cook's seven children. His mother died when he was very young, and his father, who worked for the Alabama-Georgia Railroad, was killed by a train. The children were then reared by their maternal grandparents. Having to go to work on the farm at nine years of age, they had little time for schooling. Oliver attended school for three sessions. When the children returned from school, they had to change clothes and go to the fields. There was always something to do.*

*Oliver's grandfather was an earlier riser than the other family members. He would drink his morning coffee. When he finished, he would tap his walking stick on the floor about three times. You had better get out of bed or you would feel the stick. To this day, Oliver enjoys sleeping late into the morning.*

*When Oliver was nine years old his grandfather sent him to the store with 45¢. The store owner had Oliver do some work such as bringing in wood and lard barrels for kindling. The storekeeper paid him 45¢ also. When he got home, he showed his grandmother the money, and she told his grandfather. The next morning, his grandfather hooked up the team and drove to the store to ask the storekeeper about the money.*

*Oliver remembered his encounter with a white man named Horton when he was seven or eight years old. He was walking down the road when they met and he said, "What you say, Horton?" The man got mad and went to tell Oliver's grandfather because no black addressed a white man that way.*

*His grandfather said he would take care of the situation. He was getting ready to punish Oliver when one of his uncles asked what was going on. His grandfather said, "He called Mr. Horton 'Horton.' "*

*His uncle said, "You aren't going to whip him for calling him 'Horton?' That's his name," Horton! His grandmother added that Oliver was too young to know what he was saying. After that Horton wouldn't even look his way; if he saw him coming, he'd turn his horse around and go the other way.*

*Source*: Family History Collection, American History Research Center, University of Akron, Akron, Ohio.

Two further thoughts on writing. The best way to overcome the initial obstacle, how to start, is simply to write something relating to the beginning of your account. Never mind if the result later seems quite unusable. You can always revise or rewrite entirely. And at some point in your writing you are likely to throw up your hands and say, "Everybody already knows what I am writing! Why should I write it down? It all seems so useless!" This is a common reaction. The fact is, though, that you think everybody knows only because you are so immersed in your material that it has become commonplace to you. How to solve the problem? Just keep writing.

Finally, writers and sponsors of publications or other creative presentations should be aware of copyright regulations, which protect for a time exclusive rights to print, record, translate, perform, or sell one's work. For works published before 1978, copyright protection extended for twenty-eight years and could be renewed once, extending protection to fifty-six years. A new law took effect January 1, 1978, and protection now extends for the life of the author plus fifty years or, in the case of older works still under copyright, for seventy-five years after publication. It is neither difficult nor expensive to register a copyright, but specific procedures must be followed. Using a copyrighted work requires the copyright holder's permission. Information on copyright can easily be obtained from the Register of Copyrights, Library of Congress, Washington, D.C. 20559.

## Preserving a Record

You can leave a record of your work, of course, regardless of whether you write, tape, or film anything. A good way to make your efforts useful to others is to contribute material prepared or collected to an archives, library, or museum, or, if none exists with a particular interest in the history of your area, to establish one. The preservation of documents, oral interview tapes or transcripts, and material objects which have enduring value and are not duplicated elsewhere ensures that other nearby historians later on will be able to achieve their own understanding of the past. Some future historian may have questions or ideas different from yours and may not be satisfied with your version of the past alone, any more than you would be content with only one source of information. If you ensure that worthwhile historical traces available to you are preserved along with the accounts you produce, then people who become interested in the same family, building, neighborhood, church, business, community, or whatever will be able to understand the basis for your view and will have as good or better an opportunity to draw their own conclusions. Such an endeavor can make a great contribution to nearby history.

In the course of your own investigation of the nearby past, you may well have encountered one or more repositories with holdings relating to your locality or topic and with an interest in acquiring additional material, most likely part of a public or university library in the area, a local historical society or museum, or a similar institution. If no such facility exists, the creation of one in a local library, high school or college, church, community center or other appropriate institution can be a worthwhile undertaking. Whether you place materials with an existing archives or museum or create a new repository, certain matters need to be considered in order to ensure that the materials will be well preserved and used.

The first standard for judging any repository must be the strength of its commitment to preserving and making accessible its holdings. If resources or interest in historical collections run low after a few years, materials may be lost to succeeding generations. Those institutions which already have a long history of caring for historical materials are most likely to survive and retain their interests in years to come. A library, which has the narrow purpose of acquiring and preserving documents and enjoys reasonably steady financial support, may be a better choice for a repository than a community center with a wide range of programs, changing leadership with varied interests, and uncertain funding. Of course, the library may be the victim of a tax-payers' revolt, while the community center may remain a stable and vital institution for generations, so there are no absolute guarantees. But whether you contribute to an existing repository or create a new one, it is wise to consider its possible circumstances fifty or a hundred years in the future. At the very least, it is worth knowing that should the institution at some time not wish or not be able to maintain historical collections, it will act responsibly to transfer them to other appropriate and capable hands rather than abandoning them.

A second important consideration is location with respect to your topic. In doing your own research, you have no doubt realized the value of having all related materials in a single place. Not only does such an arrangement save a researcher's time and expense, but it contributes to a better understanding by archivists, librarians, and curators of the range of sources available on a subject. It is therefore generally better, if possible, to add to an existing collection rather than to divide materials concerning an individual,

family, organization, or community. While having a separate repository for
your particular materials may seem attractive, in the long run they may as a
result be overlooked. Of course, if no institution exists with an interest in or
an ability to handle your material, or if the appropriate one is at too great a
distance to allow reasonable access to those most interested, the establishment of a new repository may be the only solution.

Beyond having a firm commitment to maintaining materials, a repository
needs to be prepared to provide adequate care and protection, publicity, and
reasonable access for purposes of research. While the techniques of preserving historical documents and artifacts are logical and are not excessively
complicated, they are rather specialized. In order to ensure that an existing
institution or a newly created one can properly handle the materials en-
trusted to it, its personnel ought to have knowledge and training in appropriate archival or curatorial methods. The staff also need sensitivity to the
past and concern for its preservation. A number of universities conduct
courses in archival administration, museum curatorship, or historical preservation, while the Society of American Archivists (300 South Wells
Street, Suite 810, Chicago, Illinois 60606) and the American Association
for State and Local History (708 Berry Road, Nashville, Tennessee 37204)
offer a wide variety of publications and programs to inform individuals and
institutions about proper procedures and methods. This is not the place for
an extended discussion of archival-curatorial theory and technique, but a
few comments on basic policies may be useful in assessing the capabilities of
existing institutions to handle historical materials successfully and the
standards that newly created repositories should be expected to meet.

Repositories must be able to make intelligent judgments regarding the
value of material offered to them. Not everything from the past is equally
worth keeping, especially when resources of time, money, and space are
limited, as they always seem to be. Documents and objects must be appraised
and their historical importance assessed, so that valuable traces are preserved but not buried under a mountain of trivial or duplicate material.
Appraisals are some of the most difficult judgments that archivists and
curators must make. Items preserved must be those which seem likely to
shed light on matters that either now or at some future time will be regarded
as historically significant or interesting. Is the information contained in a
document or an artifact unique, or can it be found elsewhere? Does its
preservation present problems which outweigh its value? Is the material
likely to be used? The more the archivist or curator knows about the past,

A local history society which was encouraging the preservation of historically valuable records distributed this checklist so that the churches would have a clear idea of what to save or collect.

I. Church records to be preserved in perpetuity

A. *Constitutions and articles of incorporation*, at least one copy of each edition, including also auxiliaries, affliated agencies, or subsidiaries;

B. *Calls* issued and accepted by pastors and others who serve the parish; *assignments* of church workers by hierarchical officials;

C. *Deeds*, leases, titles, policies, surveys, and descriptions of church properties;

D. *Contracts*, blueprints, plans, specifications, and related documents;

E. *Mortgages* (even if retired—don't burn them);

F. *Membership lists*, possibly in serial, with designation of charter members;

G. *Minutes* of voting bodies, boards, councils; related documents which have produced resolutions or actions;

H. *Sunday bulletins*, newsletters, announcements to the members of the congregation, news releases;

I. *Ledgers* of official acts: baptism, confirmation, marriage, and burial records;

J. *Official correspondence* relating to membership status, pastors, and others employed by the congregation; relating to denominational or organizational affliations;

K. *Treasurers' reports* and financial files required by law;

L. *Histories* of the congregation: narrative, statistical, and chronological;

M. *Records of educational agencies* regarding such things as enrollments, teachers, policies, terms, materials, and tuition;

N. *Reports* of all official committees and commissions;

O. *Reports* filed with judicatories;

P. *Membership changes*, transfers, disciplinary cases, excommunications, expulsions, etc.;

Q. *Officers*, lists of the congregation and all boards, committees, commissions, auxiliary agencies and organizations, etc.;

R. *Biographical* and vital data of members to the extent that it can be recorded.

II. Church records that we recommend be kept only temporarily

A. General correspondence (2 years);

B. Copies of calls and contracts offered but not accepted (2 years);

C. Communications with members that do not have legal or historical value (2 years);
D. Programs and other printed materials not covered in any of the above categories: keep two copies in permanent files for programs of special occasions, one copy of others; discard duplicates periodically, perhaps annually;
E. Communion announcement cards and related types (1 year);
F. Financial records: remittance envelopes, deposit slips, canceled checks, weekly financial reports (5 years);
G. Miscellaneous: when in doubt, retain.

III. Materials to be actively sought for inclusion in church archives
A. Photographs related to the life of the church: formal ones may include confirmation pictures, for which a complete file (with identifications) is desirable; weddings, church staff, church officers; informal ones of picnics, socials, and gatherings; exterior and interior shots of buildings and properties; aerial views of church and community;
B. Community documents that relate to the place of the church in the community; examples of cooperation or conflict between church and community;
C. Written records and recollections of members willing to provide them;
D. Tapes of interviews with selected members; transcriptions of the tapes;
E. Tape recordings (audio or video) of sermons—randomly selected ones as well as those made on special occasions;
F. Tape recordings of choirs and renditions by organists;
G. Artifacts of the church "keepsake" variety.

*Source*: Normandy (Missouri) Area Historical Association. Parts I and II are adapted from bulletins of the Concordia Historical Institute, August R. Sueflow, Director, 801 DeMun Avenue, St. Louis, Missouri 63105.

other historical resources, and the process of research, the wiser the decisions he or she can make as to what to save. No wonder that the growing career fields of archives, museums, and historical preservation require individuals with training and interest in history.

Once a repository accepts material, it assumes an obligation to care for it and to make it accessible. Thus, an archivist or curator might conclude that something is worth preserving and might still feel that his or her particular institution should not accept it because it lacks relevance to that institution's other holdings or because there are no resources to care for it. Such a decision does not indicate indifference or hostility. No archives or museum can collect everything, and a different or new repository may be needed to provide an adequate home for worthwhile material.

A repository must be able to arrange newly acquired materials in good order, to provide safe, secure storage so that material will not be damaged or lost, and to take steps to preserve fragile, aged items. The staff must also keep track of each acquisition, record its provenance or history, and prepare catalogs, inventories, and other finding aids, so that potential users will be able to determine the contents of the repository and to locate those items which they wish to examine. Furthermore, the institution must publicize its own existence and holdings through the *National Union Catalog of Manuscript Collections*, scholarly and popular publications, and other means so that interested parties will become aware of its resources. Protecting, arranging, describing, and publicizing materials in their care are important responsibilities for archivists and curators.

Aiding people who wish to use materials is an obvious duty but one which must be balanced with a responsibility to protect donors and guard the items for future use. Individuals and heirs, businesses, and institutions have rights and interests which deserve respect. Archives, manuscripts, audiovisual documents, and material objects are placed in repositories in the belief that they ought to be preserved but not necessarily that they should be made public immediately. Furthermore, many individuals identified in family, business, or government documents have not participated in the decision to deposit the information in an archives and may not wish to have their privacy invaded. Donors should consider such matters and discuss possible areas of concern with archivists or curators.

Any responsible institution will recognize and defend legitimate rights of privacy and will do its best to assure that researchers do likewise. It is reasonable and appropriate for use of some types of sensitive material to be restricted for a period of time. In addition, donors may properly ask, and institutions may insist, that researchers not publish or otherwise publicly repeat names of living persons or other designated confidential information without permission of the repository, donor, and possibly other persons involved. Archivists and curators should explain the conditions under which materials may be used, and researchers should pay careful heed. If donor, protector, and user cooperate, traces of the past can be physically preserved and made available without damage.

If you decide to place material which you own or for which you bear responsibility in a library, archives, or museum, you should reach an understanding with the institution about the nature of donation and the rights and obligations of the recipient. A written agreement to this effect is a normal and very important procedure by which both donor and repository acknowledge their acceptance of the specified terms. Satisfactory forms for gifts of family histories, documents, oral histories, and objects may be found in appendix B.

Depositing historical materials in an archives or museum is an act of generosity and concern for future generations, but nevertheless it requires thoughtful consideration to ensure proper care for the items. Creating a new repository is an even more weighty matter, for it involves assuming responsibility to see that traces of the past continue to be preserved, protected, and

Photographs of the nearby world are as important to preserve as any other historical document. Sometimes a photograph taken for a particular purpose can provide information on other matters as well. This picture of a city sewer project, for instance, records the appearance of a neighborhood's buildings, streets, and other public utilities. Proper identification, storage, and care of photographs will extend their life and usefulness.

made available. Fortunately, in either case there are trained specialists, educational institutions, and professional organizations willing and able to provide advice and assistance. The creation and support of archives, libraries, museums, and similar institutions is a fine means of leaving a record. But whether you write about your own research, produce a tape, film, exhibit, or drama, or contribute to an historical repository, you are furthering in a valuable way the understanding of nearby history.

## For Further Information

Other works on this subject, different in emphasis or less comprehensive, include: John Cummings, *A Guide for Writing Local History* (Lansing: Michigan Bicentennial Commission, 1974)—a very elementary book; Thomas E. Felt, *Researching, Writing, and Publishing Local History* (Nashville: American Association for State and Local History, 1976); Mark Friedberger and Janice Reiff Webster, "Social Structure and State and Local History," *Western Historical Quarterly* 9 (1978): 297–314; Richard W. Hale, Jr., *Methods of Research for the Amateur Historian* Technical Leaflet No. 21 (Nashville: American Association for State and Local History, 1969); W. G. Hoskins, *Fieldwork in Local History* (London: Faber and Faber, 1976) and *Local History in England* (1959; London: Longman, 1972); Kirk Jeffrey, *Writing a Community History: Some Suggestions for Grassroots Historians* (Chicago: Newberry Library, n.d.); Donald D. Parker, *Local History: How to Gather It, Write It, and Publish It* (New York: Social Science Research Council, 1944); R. B. Pugh, *How to Write a Parish History* (London: Allen and Unwin, 1954); Sam Bass Warner, *Writing Local History: The Uses of Social Statistics* Technical Leaflet No. 7 (Nashville: American Association for State and Local History, 1970); David Weitzman, *Underfoot: An Everyday Guide to Exploring the American Past* (New York: Scribner's, 1976).

Books dealing with nearby history in schools include Robert Douch, *Local History and the Teacher* (London: Routledge and Kegan Paul, 1967); and Schools Council History 13–16 Project, *History around Us: Some Guidelines for Teachers* (Edinburgh: Holmes McDougall, 1977). A book that shows how to examine town newspapers, firehouses, post offices; how to make maps; how to create family museums and archives; and other things is James Robertson, ed., *Old Glory: A Pictorial Report on the Grass Roots History Movement and the First Hometown History Primer* (New York: Warner Paperback, 1973). A book that seeks to place nearby history in a larger context and suggests different forms for future family and community histories is David Russo, *Families and Communities: A New View of American History* (Nashville: American Association for State and Local History, 1974).

The best handbook for researchers and writers of history, amateur as well as professional, is Jacques Barzun and Henry F. Graff, *The Modern Researcher*, 3rd ed. (New York: Harcourt Brace Jovanovich, 1977). On writing, of the many books available, see particularly Jacques Barzun, *Simple and Direct: A Rhetoric for Writers* (New York: Harper and Row, 1976); William Zinsser, *On Writing Well: An Informal Guide to Writing Nonfiction*, 2nd ed. (New

York: Harper and Row, 1980); and William Strunk and E. B. White, *The Elements of Style*, 3rd ed. (New York: Macmillan, 1978).

To find local institutions concerned with preserving, collecting, investigating, or celebrating the past, consult the *Directory of Historical Societies and Agencies in the United States and Canada* (Nashville: American Association for State and Local History).

There are several excellent references for those establishing their own nearby history archives or attempting to assess the quality of an existing repository: Theodore R. Schellenberg, *Modern Archives: Principles and Techniques* (Chicago: University of Chicago Press, 1956) and *The Management of Archives* (New York: Columbia University Press, 1965); Ruth B. Borden and Robert M. Warner, *The Modern Manuscripts Library* (New York: Scarecrow, 1966); Lucile M. Kane, *A Guide to the Care and Administration of Manuscripts*, 2nd ed. (Nashville: American Association for State and Local History, 1966); O. Lawrence Burnette, Jr., *Beneath the Footnote: A Guide to the Use and Preservation of American Historical Sources* (Madison: State Historical Society of Wisconsin, 1969); Kenneth W. Duckett, *Modern Manuscripts: A Practical Guide for Their Management, Care, and Use* (Nashville: American Association for State and Local History, 1975); H. G. Jones, *Local Government Records: An Introduction to Their Management, Preservation, and Use* (Nashville: American Association for State and Local History, 1980). A very good brief overview is David H. Hoober, *Manuscript Collections: Initial Procedures and Policies*, Technical Leaflet 131 (Nashville: American Association for State and Local History, 1980).

The Society of American Archivists (330 S. Wells St., Suite 810, Chicago, Illinois 60606) has published a series of basic how-to-do-it manuals: *Archives and Manuscripts: Appraisal and Accessioning* by Maynard Brichford, *Arrangement and Description* by David B. Gracy II, *Reference and Access* by Sue E. Holbert, *Security* by Timothy Walch, *Surveys* by John Fleckner, and *Exhibits* by Gail Farr Casterline. The society has also produced more specialized manuals: *Business Archives: An Introduction* by Edie Hedlin and *Religious Archives: An Introduction* by August R. Suelflow. Other manuals on administration of archives, cartographic and architectural records, funding, and public programs are in preparation. The monthly *History News* and quarterly *American Archivist* frequently contain articles, book reviews, technical reports, and other information of value to historians working on topics relating to their immediate environment.

Other matters of concern to the historian of the nearby world are addressed in David E. Kyvig, "Family History: New Opportunities for Archivists," *American Archivist* 38 (1975): 509–19; Robert A. Weinstein and Larry Booth, *The Collection, Use and Care of Historical Photographs* (Nashville: American Association for State and Local History, 1976); and James Bartlett and Douglas Marshall, *Maps in the Small Historical Society: Care and Cataloging*, Technical Leaflet 111 (Nashville: American Association for State and Local History, 1979).

# ·12·

# Linking the Particular and the Universal

EACH COMMUNITY, LOCAL INSTITUTION, STRUCTURE, AND family is unique, and at the same time each shares characteristics with others of its kind. Every one occupies a different location in time, space, and circumstance which gives it an individual identity. But similar organization, design, motivation, or behavior joins it with others in important respects. Uniqueness assures that any exploration of nearby history will present its own challenges and revelations. The existence of shared characteristics, on the other hand, means that any historian of the nearby world can benefit from an awareness of what other students of the past have done, particularly those who have examined similar phenomena elsewhere.

The historian who wishes to understand a topic never regards it as existing in a vacuum. A much better appreciation of any particular subject can be attained by considering related matters, both the history of comparable phenomena and simultaneous developments in other areas which may affect the object of interest. The behavior of similar individuals or institutions and the nature of contemporary developments can often shed light on the subject of concern. If, as British historian H. P. R. Finberg suggests, family, community, national, and international history form a series of concentric circles, one must always be considered in relation to the others. Furthermore, all families in a community or communities in a society are circumscribed by the same conditions and thus have much in common. Therefore, any historian of the nearby past is wise to consider the questions, methods, and insights of other historians concerned with related times or topics. As a result some of the links between the personal and the commonplace, the particular and the universal, may become evident.

There is also something to be gained from observing how other historians

217

have examined the past. Whether or not their questions, methods, assumptions, and conclusions correspond to one's own, the process of comparing one's approach to others, past and present, can help clarify what one is doing and why. Historians approach their work differently from sociologists, economists, political scientists, and other students of human society. Historians regard a broad variety of past conditions and phenomena—social, economic, political, cultural, and intellectual—as interrelated, and they have used many different techniques and analytic schemes to study the complex process of change over time. Not every historian accepts the same approach to understanding the past, of course, and debate over various points of view has long been and will undoubtedly continue to be a vital part of the study of history. Discussions of questions and methods help all historians clarify their own assumptions, priorities, and beliefs.

Since the 1960s a growing number of academic historians have become interested in family and community history, joining the many independent historians and genealogists who were already concerned about the past of a particular family or place. The academics brought new questions and research methods to the field, both broadening and altering the direction of study. It is useful to consider the causes and effects of the rise of this "new social history" as well as the gulf which previously separated academic from other historians. Doing so helps make apparent the relationship between the two.

## The Evolution of American Local History

American historical writing began as the consideration of the nearby past. William Bradford's *Of Plymouth Plantation*, accounts of early Massachusetts Bay by John Winthrop and Cotton Mather, and numerous similar works on New England villages reflected the initial Puritan concern with showing a corrupt world how their religiously committed community could, with God's favor, overcome hardship and establish a more moral society. The secular historiography of the seventeenth, eighteenth, and early nineteenth century focused as well on the settlement and development of individual colonies or towns, usually with an upper-class perspective and a large measure of local pride and self-promotion. Long after the Revolution ended, that tumult was still being described colony by colony, for Americans continued to identify themselves in state and local rather than national terms. In the new nation, state and local historical societies began to gather records and present accounts of the past that were understandably self-centered. The Massachusetts Historical Society was founded in 1794, and similar institutions followed, in New York in 1804, thereafter in other Atlantic coast states and, seemingly as soon as they settled, in western states as well.

Not until George Bancroft's ten-volume *History of the United States of America from the Discovery of the Continent* began to appear in 1834 (the last volume was not published until forty years later) was a successful effort made to describe the American past from a national rather than a state or local perspective. Not for another fifty years would a national historical association be created, and an additional half century would pass before a national archives came into being. Preoccupation with local affairs and conditions, tinged perhaps with sectional self-justification, kept historical attention firmly focused on the nearby past until after the Civil War.

Much nineteenth-century historical writing came from wealthy gentlemen for whom history was an absorbing pastime. Bancroft and the other patrician historians were romantics who also wrote poetry and prose, regarded history as literature, and preferred descriptive narrative to abstract analysis. They focused on heroic individuals and colorful episodes which served to extol the virtues and progress of Anglo-American democracy. Toward the end of the nineteenth century, these locally oriented patricians were joined by the commercial historians described in chapter 4, who for their own reasons produced volume after volume of uncritical, relentlessly cheerful local history. Both types focused on long-established leading citizens and community successes, ignoring lower-class groups (especially those racially, culturally, religiously different) and community conflict, intolerance, or failure. However much a part of the local past, such matters were not part of the story they wished to remember or sell.

In the 1870s and 1880s a new type of historian began to appear: the professional scholar, trained in German-style graduate school seminars and committed to the belief that systematic, critical analysis of historical records could lead to an accurate, indeed scientific, understanding of the past. History courses in college curricula increased rapidly, leading universities began awarding the Ph.D. in history, and in 1884 a group of these new professionals formed the American Historical Association. At first, nonacademic historians were encouraged to participate in the AHA. The academic historians, however, were committed to a belief in the importance of specialized research leading to a cooperatively produced overview. They also held to the notion that they were serving society and culture by concentrating on national history. Many came to scorn nonprofessionals, whose approaches and interests differed from their own, and they tended to dismiss local history as uncritical, unscientific, and inaccurate, which indeed was often true, and of little importance, which was very shortsighted.

For their part, many local historians had little interest in matters outside the immediate realm of family and community, and they soon abandoned the AHA to the academics. The gulf between academic, nationally oriented history and nonacademic, locally oriented history grew deeper and deeper during the first half of the twentieth century. Few historians outside the universities embraced the methods or analytical approaches of the professionals, while academics generally ignored the subject matter of local history.

Before the 1960s only a handful of academic historians devoted serious attention to local history, and they often examined the local scene only for examples of national developments. The history of cities provided something of an exception. In 1940 Arthur M. Schlesinger, Sr., argued that cities had transformed America and demanded the attention of scholars. Schlesinger himself had offered an impressionistic national overview of American urban history in *The Rise of the City* (New York: Macmillan, 1933), and his lead was followed by Carl Bridenbaugh, *Cities in the Wilderness: The First Century of Urban Life in America, 1625–1742* (New York: Ronald Press, 1938), and *Cities in Revolt: Urban Life in America, 1743–1776* (New York: Knopf, 1955); studies of particular cities such as Harold C. Syrett, *The City of Brooklyn, 1865–1898* (New York: Columbia University Press, 1944), and Bayrd Still, *Milwaukee* (Madison: State Historical Society of Wisconsin, 1948); and multivolume compendia by Bessie Pierce, *A History of Chicago*, 3 vols. (New York: Knopf, 1937–57), Blake McKelvey, *Rochester*, 4 vols. (vols. 1–3, Cambridge, Mass.: Harvard University Press, 1945–56; vol. 4, Rochester: Christopher, 1961), and Constance M. Green, *Washington*, 2 vols. (Princeton: Princeton University Press, 1962–63). A rare and noteworthy specialized study of an aspect of a community's past was Oscar Handlin, *Boston's Immigrants, 1790–1880: A Study in Acculturation* (Cambridge, Mass.: Harvard University Press, 1941).

Smaller communities received attention mostly from a few historians interested in testing Frederick Jackson Turner's view that the frontier stimulated democracy. Lewis Atherton, *Main Street on the Middle Border* (Bloomington: Indiana University Press, 1954), an examination of town life

The growth of cities produced distinctive activities, organizations, and a physical world that attracted the interest of academic historians.

through an analysis of the institutions found along the typical main street, was an innovative effort to summarize the nature of midwestern towns. Interesting generalizations also emerged from the brief examination of five Ohio Valley cities in Richard C. Wade, *The Urban Frontier: The Rise of Western Cities, 1790–1830* (Cambridge, Mass.: Harvard University Press, 1959). Merle Curti, *The Making of an American Community: A Case Study of Democracy in a Frontier Community* (Palo Alto: Stanford University Press, 1959), was both an impressive use of local records, census and property lists, newspapers, and letters to write a sophisticated community history of Trempeleau County, Wisconsin, and a pioneering attempt by an academic historian to base analytical generalizations upon a careful study of one locality's history. Atherton, Wade, and Curti all found support for Turner's ideas in their studies of frontier towns.

The history of the family received even less notice than communities. A sociologist's impressionistic survey, Arthur W. Calhoun, *A Social History of the American Family from Colonial Times to the Present*, 3 vols. (Cleveland: A. H. Clark, 1917–19), and Edmund S. Morgan's outstanding colonial studies, *The Puritan Family* (1944; rev. ed., New York: Harper and Row, 1966), and *Virginians at Home* (Williamsburg: Colonial Williamsburg, 1952), stood practically alone. Utopian communities, business enterprises, schools, and churches attracted some attention, but generally for their distinctiveness rather than for their connection with the nearby area.

## The New Social History

The 1960s represented a turning point in the attitude of academic historians toward family and community history. Increasing numbers began to realize that concentration on national history and emphasis on progress, shared experience, and democratic values had taken no account of major elements in the American past. Social protest movements of the time made many historians conscious that their picture of the American past had not even included, much less accurately portrayed, blacks and other ethnic minorities, poor people, opponents of wars, or women. Recognition that the experience of ordinary people was as vital to historical understanding as knowledge of federal policy regarding such persons produced calls for "history from the bottom up."

Aware that the techniques employed to study leadership groups could not be used to study those who did not engage in the same types of activities or leave the same sorts of records, academic historians began to consider different approaches. The value of family and community history became apparent. The individual experiences of ordinary people were most accessible through the study of their immediate social institutions, families, and communities; these in turn could serve as case studies for understanding national patterns. The advent of computers brought the possibility of handling vast amounts of information about large numbers of obscure people contained in census and other compiled records. By the 1970s research activity in graduate schools and other academic centers had shifted perceptibly toward the new social history, studies of ordinary people, workers, slaves, immigrants, families, and nonelite communities, often with statistical patterns replacing the named individuals of more traditional history.

Academic historians pursuing the new social history remain interested in general patterns of development, not just the isolated experience of one community, one institution, or one family. They find the descriptive narrative on which the pure local historian has usually focused to be useful but not sufficient. Instead they concentrate on questions which facilitate the analysis and comparison of local situations in a search for universals. Their questions nevertheless deserve the attention of those concerned only with a particular place, for they suggest lines of inquiry which can enrich any effort to understand the nearby past.

Among the many questions which professional historians have been asking about communities and their components, those dealing with patterns of structure and growth have been especially prominent. Questions of community or family size, organization, and change over time are basic. It often proves surprisingly difficult to determine conclusively the size and makeup of a population, much less comprehend the factors influencing change. Related issues which have provoked considerable inquiry involve migration, assimilation of outsiders, and physical, social, and economic mobility. The movement of individuals and groups from place to place and within a social pyramid can be a principal factor in family or community change. Questions of tension and conflict have attracted attention because of what they can reveal about values and interests, divisions, authority, and the decision-making process within a household or larger institution.

A host of questions centers around the effects of modernization, the rise of urban, industrial mass society sensitive to the efficient use of time and oriented to the concept of progress: the alteration of the physical environment, the creation of bureaucratic structures to perform various functions, and the increase of individual autonomy and anonymity, what one historian labeled "privatism," within the community. Associated questions include the division of labor and authority within families, between sexes, and between family and community as well as the treatment of childhood, adolescence, and aging. The nature, extent, and quality of changes produced by modernization are among the most important being addressed by academic social historians.

## Early American Communities

Historians of colonial America were among the first to concentrate on questions of community and family structure and evolution. This focus developed naturally from the great interest in American Puritanism and the much observed shift from religious solidarity and intensity to secularism and individuality. Intellectual historians had scrutinized Puritan sermons and analyzed Puritan thought, but the connections to behavior often had not been made despite the obvious relevance of community study to that of a congregational religious system.

Sumner Chilton Powell, *Puritan Village: The Formation of a New England Town* (Middletown, Conn.: Wesleyan University Press, 1963), used church and town records for an innovative examination of how Puritan settlers adapted English town patterns in establishing Sudbury, Massachusetts, in the 1640s as well as how power and property were initially distributed within the community. A more complex analysis focusing on the first two decades of Massachusetts Bay's principal settlement appeared in Darrett B. Rutman, *Winthrop's Boston: A Portrait of a Puritan Town, 1630–1649* (Chapel Hill: University of North Carolina Press, 1965). Through church records, private papers, and government records, Rutman traced the link between the religious ideas of Boston's founders and the nature of community governance, the evolution of commerce and land distribution, the general outlines of social activity, and the gradual decline of church dominance.

A trio of books, published in 1970 though foreshadowed for a half decade in their authors' articles, provided a more detailed and quantitative look at seventeenth-century New England family and community structure and growth. John Demos, *A Little Commonwealth: Family Life in Plymouth Colony* (New York: Oxford University Press), looked specifically at the cramped physical environment, close family relationships, and social responsibilities that tied the seventeenth-century community and family so closely together. A more extended analysis of another community, Philip J. Greven, Jr., *Four Generations: Population, Land, and Family in Colonial Andover, Massachusetts* (Ithaca: Cornell University Press), used vital, town, probate, and deed records to determine family characteristics and land ownership patterns. Greven found that as the community grew and land became more scarce, many fathers could no longer provide each son with a farm, ties between generations loosened, the tendency to delay marriage while awaiting inheritance declined, and instead more people married earlier and moved away. A similar pattern of development was seen by Kenneth A. Lockridge, *A New England Town: The First Hundred Years: Dedham, Massachusetts, 1636–1736* (New York: Norton), though his focus was less on family than on community evolution. With the close connection of purposeful church and civil leadership as well as the high degree of economic equality, Lockridge saw early Dedham as a utopian commune. Community growth, leading to land scarcity, social and economic division, and conflicts, transformed Dedham from a cooperative Puritan commonwealth into an individualistic, secular town.

Another 1970 book, *Peaceable Kingdoms: New England Towns in the Eighteenth Century* (New York: Knopf), was based on an examination of records from fifteen towns. Its author, Michael Zuckerman, contended that even as the influence of Puritanism ebbed, community solidarity and consensus remained strong. This was contrary to Lockridge's view and to those of Charles S. Grant, *Democracy in the Connecticut Frontier Town of Kent* (New York: Columbia University Press, 1961), and Richard L. Bushman, *From Puritan to Yankee: Character and the Social Order in Connecticut, 1690–1765* (Cambridge, Mass.: Harvard University Press, 1967). The issue of whether communities from the seventeenth century to the twentieth remained cohesive or were disintegrating would continue to intrigue and divide historians.

Subsequent colonial community studies broadened the base of inquiry. Paul Boyer and Stephen Nissenbaum, *Salem Possessed: The Social Origins of Witchcraft* (Cambridge, Mass.: Harvard University Press, 1974), used a study of landholding, social structure, and authority within the community as the basis for a new and impressive analysis of the deep-seated causes of the conflict which produced the famous Salem witchcraft trials of 1692. Using town records from seventy-four New England towns, by far the largest sample to date, Edward M. Cook, Jr., analyzed the economic, family, and church background of the men who became community political leaders in the era of the American Revolution. In *The Fathers of the Towns: Leadership and Community Structure in Eighteenth-Century New England* (Baltimore: Johns Hopkins University Press, 1976), Cook concluded that in political matters, citizens deferred to those of high social-economic status who were already proven community leaders.

The nature of community life and solidarity during the revolutionary crisis were described in Robert A. Gross, *The Minutemen and Their World* (New York: Hill and Wang, 1976), an outstanding study of Concord, Massachusetts; Christopher M. Jedrey, *The World of John Cleaveland: Family and Community in Eighteenth-Century New England* (New York: Norton, 1979); and Donald W. White, *A Village at War: Chatham, New Jersey, and the American Revolution* (Rutherford, N.J.: Fairleigh Dickinson University Press, 1979). Two excellent studies, James T. Lemon, *The Best Poor Man's Country: A Geographical Study of Early Southeastern Pennsylvania* (Baltimore: Johns Hopkins University Press, 1972), and Stephanie Grauman Wolf, *Urban Village: Population, Community, and Family Structure in Germantown, Pennsylvania, 1683–1800* (Princeton: Princeton University Press, 1976), found a greater degree of individualism and concern with economic progress and a lesser concern with social control in the middle colonies than in New England. Each of these works contributed to a general understanding of colonial cohesion and development as well as to appreciation of the unique circumstances of individual communities.

Not surprisingly, community historians focusing on the national period carried forward the examination of some of the same issues raised by scholars of the colonial period. The process of community formation and development remained a central interest. James S. Young, *The Washington Community, 1800–1828* (New York: Columbia University Press, 1966), examined the physical setting and growth as well as the social structure of the new national capital, shedding light on how the local environment both mirrored and influenced early federal political conflict.

Midwestern frontier community development, which had earlier drawn the attention of Merle Curti and Richard Wade, received sophisticated treatment from Don Harrison Doyle, *The Social Order of a Frontier Community, Jacksonville, Illinois, 1825–70* (Urbana: University of Illinois Press, 1978). Doyle looked closely at voluntary association within an evolving town. These varied membership organizations, he concluded, both defined and limited strife, contributing to stability and cohesion within a dynamic, growing community.

An impressive social-economic-political comparison of the post–Civil War rise of five Kansas communities, Robert R. Dykstra, *The Cattle Towns* (New York: Knopf, 1968), found that conflict between farmers and businessmen and among various groups of townspeople was as normal as cooperation and that both helped shape the course of community growth. Dykstra uncovered little evidence of the placid consensus which Michael Zuckerman thought characterized the eighteenth-century New England town. Instead, he perceived that internal conflict was a central factor in community evolution and blamed town boosters, local historians, and academics alike for suppressing views of divisiveness on the questionable assumption that progress only resulted from harmony.

The peculiar circumstances of western communities formed in the midst of some economic boom were examined in James B. Allen, *The Company Town in the American West* (Norman: University of Oklahoma Press, 1966), and Gunther Barth, *Instant Cities: The Urbanization and Rise of San Francisco and Denver* (New York: Oxford University Press, 1975).

## Modern Communities

Much of the academic study of nineteenth- and twentieth-century American community history has centered on the issue of modernization. As it is generally used by historians, the term "modernization" connotes a radical change in the basic character of life, a shift from a preindustrial society which anticipated a repetitive cycle of seasons and a continuation of traditional practices and organizations to an industrial society predicated on a faith in the possibility of progress, attuned to a search for efficiency through education, science, and technological advancement, and inclined to urbanization and the growth of bureaucracy. Some observers even suggest that America has already entered a "postmodern" era of diminishing faith in technological and bureaucratic solutions, skepticism about the values of life in huge bureaucratic organizations and urban settings, and doubts as to whether further social progress is possible. Whether or not they believe that the "modern" age is over, its analysts regard it as fundamentally different from the era preceding it.

Modernization is a complex concept and a social process with no easily datable beginnings or limits. Some historians regard the modernizaton process as having begun in the eighteenth or early nineteenth century. Others argue that America was "born modern," exhibiting an interest in innovation and efficiency and a faith in progress from the time of settlement onward.

The early stages of modernization received sensitive treatment in Michael H. Frisch, *Town into City: Springfield, Massachusetts, and the Meaning of Community, 1840–1880* (Cambridge, Mass.: Harvard University Press, 1972), and Stuart M. Blumin, *The Urban Threshold: Growth and Change in a Nineteenth-Century American Community* [Kingston, N.Y.] (Chicago: University of Chicago Press, 1976). Frisch and Blumin identified a change in the citizen's very idea of community as a village became a thriving city, in Kingston's case because of the opening of the Delaware and Hudson canal and in Springfield's case because of the Civil War and the federal armory in the town's midst. Looking especially at political structures and processes, Frisch found the small town severely limited in both community institutions and functions but with a strong sense of social cohesion. As Springfield grew into an industrial city, its institutions became larger in scale as well as more formal, and citizens identified with particular interest groups. Growth and the development of divisions carried the community beyond the reach of personal association, but produced among residents a sense of interdependence. Blumin, looking more closely at economic and social developments, saw a similar pattern. "Community, in other words, was changing from an informal, direct sensation to a formal, perceived abstraction," concluded Frisch (p. 247).

Other useful examinations of pre–Civil War modernization can be found in John Borden Armstrong, *Factory under the Elms: A History of Harrisville, New Hampshire, 1774–1969* (Cambridge, Mass.: MIT Press, 1969); Anthony F. C. Wallace, *Rockdale: The Growth of an American Village in the Early Industrial Revolution* (New York: Knopf, 1978); Susan E. Hirsch, *Roots of the American Working Class: Industrialization of Crafts in Newark, 1800–1860* (Philadelphia: University of Pennsylvania Press, 1978); and Thomas Dublin, *Women at Work: The Transformation of Work and Community in Lowell, Massachusetts, 1826–1869* (New York: Columbia University Press, 1979).

The post–Civil War modernization process has received the greatest attention. Robert H. Wiebe, *The Search for Order, 1877–1920* (New York: Hill and Wang, 1967), a very influential broad view of modernization (though he never uses the term), suggested that at the end of the Civil War, American communities generally remained islands unto themselves but thereafter the impact of railroads, telegraphs, and other new technologies helped bind the nation together, end local isolation, and standardize taste and behavior.

The rush to industrialize, urbanize, and absorb large numbers of immigrants created momentary confusion but eventually produced a new social order. Large bureaucracies evolved to manage both government and business, and new types of communities of middle-class professionals arose, organizations based on shared expertise and interest rather than geographical proximity. In a modern urban setting, according to Wiebe, individuals found greater independence and anonymity but lost the sense of shared values and practices which characterized older, smaller communities.

One of the earliest and still most useful community modernization studies was Sam Bass Warner, Jr., *Streetcar Suburbs: The Process of Growth in Boston, 1870–1900* (Cambridge, Mass.: Harvard University Press, 1962). Warner analyzed the influence of electric street railways and the extension of public utilities on the expansion and shaping of an industrial city. These developments permitted the middle classes to withdraw to new suburban settlements and leave the central city to immigrants and the poor, fragmenting the community.

The modernization process in other communities has been examined in different ways. Among the most helpful of such studies are Stanley Buder, *Pullman: An Experiment in Industrial Order and Community Planning, 1880–1930* (New York: Oxford University Press, 1967); Robert M. Fogelson, *The Fragmented Metropolis: Los Angeles, 1850–1930* (Cambridge, Mass.: Harvard University Press, 1967); Zane L. Miller, *Boss Cox's Cincinnati: Urban Politics in the Progressive Era* (New York: Oxford University Press, 1968); Harold M. Mayer and Richard C. Wade, *Chicago: Growth of a Metropolis* (Chicago: University of Chicago Press, 1969); Don Martindale and R. Galen Hanson, *Small Town* [Benson, Minnesota] *and the Nation: The Conflict of Local and Translocal Forces* (Westport, Conn.: Greenwood, 1969); and Roy Lubove, *Twentieth Century Pittsburgh: Government, Business and Environmental Change* (New York: Wiley, 1969); and Gunther Barth, *City People: The Rise of Modern City Culture in Nineteenth-Century America* (New York: Oxford University Press, 1980).

The quantity of community modernization studies has grown recently. Some of the most interesting have been Michael P. Weber, *Social Change in an Industrial Town: Patterns of Progress in Warren, Pennsylvania, from Civil War to World War I* (University Park: Pennsylvania State University Press, 1976); Alan Dawley, *Class and Community: The Industrial Revolution in Lynn* (Cambridge, Mass.: Harvard University Press, 1976); Carl V. Harris, *Political Power in Birmingham, 1871–1921* (Knoxville: University of Tennessee

Press, 1977); Alan D. Anderson, *The Origin and Resolution of an Urban Crisis: Baltimore, 1890–1930* (Baltimore: Johns Hopkins University Press, 1977); Tamara Hareven and Randolph Langenbach, *Amoskeag: Life and Work in an American Factory City* (New York: Pantheon, 1978); Daniel J. Walkowitz, *Worker City, Company Town: Iron and Cotton-Worker Protest in Troy and Cohoes, New York, 1855–84* (Urbana: University of Illinois Press, 1978); John T. Cumbler, *Working-Class Community in Industrial America: Work, Leisure, and Struggle in Two Industrial Cities* [Lynn and Fall River, Massachusetts], *1880–1930* (Westport, Conn.: Greenwood, 1979); Howard L. Preston, *Automobile Age Atlanta: The Making of a Southern Metropolis, 1900–1935* (Athens: University of Georgia Press, 1979); and Zane L. Miller, *Suburb: Neighborhood and Community in Forest Park, Ohio, 1935–1976* (Knoxville: University of Tennessee Press, 1981).

The case of a town that did not cope well with modernization is treated in Herman R. Lantz, *A Community in Search of Itself: A Case History of Cairo, Illinois* (Carbondale: Southern Illinois University Press, 1972). A special type of modern town is examined in Charles E. Funnell, *By the Beautiful Sea: The Rise and High Times of that Great American Resort, Atlantic City* (New York: Knopf, 1975).

## Social Mobility and Assimilation

An early and continuing concern of academic historians investigating modernizing communities has been the matter of population mobility: changes in social-economic status, geographical movement, and assimilation of new arrivals into a society. Stephan Thernstrom's pioneering work, *Poverty and Progress: Social Mobility in a Nineteenth Century City* (Cambridge, Mass.: Harvard University Press, 1964), used census data on Newburyport, Massachusetts, from 1850 to 1880 to test the long-popular notion of rapid social-economic advancement by the working class, the American "land of opportunity," or "rags to riches," image. Thernstrom concluded instead that of those who remained in the community, most individuals within their lifetime and families from one generation to the next climbed the social-economic ladder slowly and by small steps. Most strikingly, fewer than half the workers in the community at the time of one census remained ten years later; movement into and out of Newburyport was rapid.

Thernstrom's work inspired a host of similar mobility studies, among them Peter R. Knights, *The Plain People of Boston, 1830–1860: A Study of*

*City Growth* (New York: Oxford University Press, 1971); Howard P. Chudacoff, *Mobile Americans: Residential and Social Mobility in Omaha, 1880–1920* (New York: Oxford University Press, 1972); Thernstrom's own *The Other Bostonians: Poverty and Progress in the American Metropolis, 1880–1970* (Cambridge, Mass.: Harvard University Press, 1973); Robert Doherty, *Society and Power: Five New England Towns, 1800–1860* (Amherst: University of Massachusetts Press, 1977); Gordon W. Kirk, Jr., *The Promise of American Life: Social Mobility in a Nineteenth-Century Immigrant Community, Holland, Michigan, 1847–1894* (Philadelphia: American Philosophical Society, 1978); Peter R. Decker, *Fortunes and Failures: White-Collar Mobility in Nineteenth Century San Francisco* (Cambridge, Mass.: Harvard University Press, 1978); and Clyde Griffen and Sally Griffen, *Natives and Newcomers: The Ordering of Opportunity in Mid-Nineteenth Century Poughkeepsie* (Cambridge, Mass.: Harvard University Press, 1978). The similar Canadian experience was treated in Michael B. Katz, *The People of Hamilton, Canada West: Family and Class in a Mid-Nineteenth Century City* (Cambridge, Mass.: Harvard University Press, 1975). The basic impression of high geographical and modest social working-class mobility was confirmed, although significant differences between ethnic groups were perceived, especially by Thernstrom and the Griffens. Calculations of mobility rates are difficult and disputed, but the evidence of rapid in-and-out movement has many implications for nearby history, not the least of which is the importance to communities of institutions and forces which promote stability and cohesion in the face of substantial population turnover.

Assimilation of new groups into the modernizing community is closely tied to the process of social and geographic mobility but also raises issues of ethnic differences and their impact. Not only did communities have a great influence on newcomers, but the immigrants often had a shaping effect on the place where they settled. This influence was first recognized in sophisticated political histories of communities: J. Joseph Huthmacher, *Massachusetts People and Politics, 1919–1933* (Cambridge, Mass.: Harvard University Press, 1959); Frederick C. Luebke, *Immigrants and Politics: The Germans of Nebraska, 1880–1900* (Lincoln: University of Nebraska Press, 1969); and John M. Allswang, *A House for All Peoples: Ethnic Politics in Chicago, 1890–1936* (Lexington: University of Kentucky Press, 1971).

More complex social and economic aspects of community interaction were identified in Thernstrom, *The Other Bostonians*, Griffen and Griffen,

Although more of the new social history community studies seem to have focused on Massachusetts than on any other place, nearby historians elsewhere will usually find that some academic historians have studied their locality as well. If the community itself has not been examined, statewide or regional studies will often prove helpful. Indeed the less urbanized South, West, and Midwest have been dealt with more often at the state than at the local level. For instance, Iowa, a middle-sized state in the middle of the country, has not yet generated much community-level academic study, but it has been the subject of a number of excellent state or regional studies which include: Leland L. Sage, *A History of Iowa* (Ames: Iowa State University Press, 1974); Joseph F. Wall, *Iowa: A Bicentennial History* (New York: Norton, 1978); Allan G. Bogue, *From Prairie to Corn Belt: Farming on the Illinois and Iowa Prairies in the Nineteenth Century* (Chicago: University of Chicago Press, 1963); Robert Swierenga, *Pioneers and Profits: Land Speculation on the Iowa Frontier* (Ames: Iowa State University Press, 1968) and *Acres for Cents: Delinquent Tax Auctions in Frontier Iowa* (Westport, Conn.: Greenwood, 1976); Donald L. Winters, *Farmers without Farms: Agricultural Tenancy in Nineteenth-Century Iowa* (Westport, Conn.: Greenwood, 1970); Don S. Kirschner, *City and Country: Rural Responses to Urbanization in the 1920s* (Westport, Conn.: Greenwood, 1970); Richard J. Jensen, *The Winning of the Midwest: Social and Political Conflict, 1888–1896* (Chicago: University of Chicago Press, 1971); Clarence A. Andrews, *A Literary History of Iowa* (Iowa City: University of Iowa Press, 1972); Morton M. Rosenberg, *Iowa on the Eve of the Civil War: A Decade of Frontier Politics* (Norman: University of Oklahoma Press, 1972); and Glenda Riley, *Frontierswomen: The Iowa Experience* (Ames: Iowa State University Press, 1981). The local history and the state historical society can be very helpful in determining what has been published on your state.

*Natives and Newcomers*, Gerd Korman, *Industrialization, Immigration, and Americanizers: The View from Milwaukee, 1866–1921* (Madison: State Historical Society of Wisconsin, 1967); Humbert S. Nelli, *Italians in Chicago, 1880–1930: A Study in Ethnic Mobility* (New York: Oxford University Press, 1970); Dean R. Esslinger, *Immigrants and the City: Ethnicity and Mobility in a Nineteenth-Century Midwestern Community* [South Bend, Indiana] (Port Washington, N.Y.: Kennikat, 1975); Kathleen Neils Conzen, *Immigrant Milwaukee, 1836–1860: Accommodation and Community in a Frontier City* (Cambridge, Mass.: Harvard University Press, 1976); John Modell, *The*

*Economics and Politics of Racial Accommodation: The Japanese of Los Angeles, 1900–1942* (Urbana: University of Illinois Press, 1977); John Bodnar, *Immigration and Industrialization: Ethnicity in an American Mill Town* [Steelton, Pennsylvania], *1870–1940* (Pittsburgh: University of Pittsburgh Press, 1977); Caroline Golab, *Immigrant Destinations* [Philadelphia] (Philadelphia: Temple University Press, 1977); Virginia Yans-McLaughlin, *Family and Community: Italian Immigrants in Buffalo, 1880–1930* (Ithaca: Cornell University Press, 1977); and John W. Briggs, *An Italian Passage: Immigrants to Three American Cities* [Rochester, Utica, and Kansas City], *1890–1930* (New Haven: Yale University Press, 1978).

A considerable variation became evident when the family patterns and social experiences of different ethnic groups were compared, as was done by Josef J. Barton, *Peasants and Strangers: Italians, Rumanians, and Slovaks in an American City* [Cleveland], *1890–1950* (Cambridge, Mass.: Harvard University Press, 1975), and Thomas Kessner, *The Golden Door: Italian and Jewish Immigrant Mobility in New York City, 1880–1915* (New York: Oxford University Press, 1977). The distinctive experience of Jews received special attention in Lloyd P. Gartner, *History of the Jews of Cleveland* (Cleveland: Western Reserve Historical Society, 1978); Steven Hertzberg, *Strangers within the Gate City: The Jews of Atlanta, 1845–1915* (Philadelphia: Jewish Publication Society of America, 1978); Jeffrey S. Gurock, *When Harlem Was Jewish, 1870–1930* (New York: Columbia University Press, 1979); and Mark Lee Raphael, *Jews and Judaism in a Midwestern Community: Columbus, Ohio, 1840–1975* (Columbus: Ohio Historical Society, 1979). Ronald H. Bayor, *Neighbors in Conflict: The Irish, Germans, Jews, and Italians of New York City, 1929–41* (Baltimore: Johns Hopkins University Press, 1978), and John F. Stack, *International Conflict in an American City: Boston's Irish, Italians, and Jews, 1935–1944* (Westport, Conn.: Greenwood, 1979), took an important step beyond the study of individual ethnic groups to analyze the relations among ethnic groups that affected their assimilation and the course of a community's history.

The special circumstances of black people and the evolution of black ghettos within modern cities has been investigated in Gilbert Osofsky, *Harlem: The Making of a Ghetto, Negro New York, 1890–1930* (New York: Harper and Row, 1966); Allan H. Spear, *Black Chicago: The Making of a Negro Ghetto, 1890–1920* (Chicago: University of Chicago Press, 1967); William M. Tuttle, Jr., *Race Riot: Chicago in the Red Summer of 1919* (New York: Atheneum, 1972); David M. Katzman, *Before the Ghetto: Black Detroit in the Nineteenth Century* (Urbana: University of Illinois Press, 1973); Kenneth L. Kusmer, *A Ghetto Takes Shape: Black Cleveland, 1870–1930* (Urbana: University of Illinois Press, 1976); Harold X. Connolly, *A Ghetto Grows in Brooklyn* (New York: New York University Press, 1977); Thomas Lee Philpott, *The Slum and the Ghetto: Neighborhood Deterioration and Middle-Class Reform, Chicago, 1880–1930* (New York: Oxford University Press, 1978); and James Borchert, *Alley Life in Washington: Family, Community, Religion, and Folklife in the City, 1850–1970* (Urbana: University of Illinois Press, 1980).

Chicanos, another distinctive ethnic group, have only begun to receive the attention they deserve. The peculiar circumstances of a community on an international border is considered in Oscar J. Martínez, *Border Boom Town: Ciudad Juárez since 1848* (Austin: University of Texas Press, 1978). A larger Chicano community is examined in Richard Griswold del Costillo, *The Los Angeles Barrio, 1850–1890: A Social History* (Berkeley: University of California Press, 1980).

## Aspects of Modernity

The study of modernization has involved the examination of a great variety of topics besides mobility, assimilation, and the evolution of individual communities; they include the history of education, business and industry, middle-class professionalization, private and governmental social services, and politics. Topical studies of modernization which have notable value for nearby historians include Michael B. Katz, *The Irony of Early School Reform: Educational Innovation in Mid-Nineteenth-Century Massachusetts* (Cambridge, Mass.: Harvard University Press, 1968); Selwyn Troen, *The Public and the Schools: Shaping the St. Louis School System, 1838–1920* (Columbia: University of Missouri Press, 1975); Lawrence A. Cremin, *The Transformation of the School: Progressivism in American Education, 1876–1957* (New York: Knopf, 1961); Daniel Nelson, *Managers and Workers: Origins of the New Factory System in the United States, 1880–1920* (Madison: University of Wisconsin Press, 1975); Alfred D. Chandler, Jr., *The Visible Hand: The Managerial Revolution in American Business* (Cambridge, Mass.: Harvard University Press, 1977); Peter Friedlander, *The Emergence of a UAW Local, 1936–1939: A Study in Class and Culture* (Pittsburgh: University of Pittsburgh Press, 1975); Burton J. Bledstein, *The Culture of Professionalism: The Middle Class and the Development of Higher Education in America* (New

This 1941 photograph of a Washington, D.C., alley, with the U.S. Senate Office Building in the background, shows how close to one another poverty and substance could be found in modern cities.

York: Norton, 1976), James F. Richardson, *The New York Police: Colonial Times to 1901* (New York: Oxford University Press, 1970); Martin J. Schiesl, *The Politics of Efficiency: Municipal Administration and Reform in America, 1880–1920* (Berkeley: University of California Press, 1977); and Kenneth Fox, *Better City Government: Innovation in American Urban Politics, 1850–1937* (Philadelphia: Temple University Press, 1977). The darker side of modernization as it relates to communities is explored in Eric Monkkonen, *The Dangerous Class: Crime and Poverty in Columbus, Ohio, 1860–1885* (Cambridge, Mass.: Harvard University Press, 1975), and Roger Lane, *Violent Death in the City: Suicide, Accident, and Murder in Nineteenth-Century Philadelphia* (Cambridge, Mass.: Harvard University Press, 1979).

The impact of modernization on a community was perhaps most thoughtfully explored in Sam Bass Warner, Jr., *The Private City: Philadelphia in Three Periods of Its Growth* (Philadelphia: University of Pennsylvania Press, 1968). Warner looked at Philadelphia as the town of 1770–1780, the big city of

1830–1860, and the industrial metropolis of 1920–1930 in terms of urban growth, the economic system, use of space, social structure, government, and planning for the future. He perceived a persistent pattern of "privatism," a preoccupation with personal happiness and the pursuit of wealth. Community growth and change, prosperity, and physical form resulted from individual ambition and choice, accounting for income-segregated residential patterns, narrow-purpose government, unresolved social problems, and poor city planning. Warner considered the Philadelphia example typical of modern American cities. His assessment of the results of modernization was notably more pessimistic than the generalizations which Michael Frisch and Stuart Blumin based on equally careful studies of individual nineteenth-century communities or which Thomas Bender, *Community and Social Thought in America* (New Brunswick, N.J.: Rutgers University Press, 1978), and Robert Wiebe drew from their overviews of American community development.

Mixed views of modernization's impact are evident in several studies of communities during the Great Depression of the 1930s: Bernard Sternsher, ed., *Hitting Home: The Great Depression in Town and County* (Chicago: Quadrangle, 1970); Glen H. Elder, Jr., *Children of the Great Depression: Social Change in Life Experience* (Chicago: University of Chicago Press, 1974); and Charles H. Trout, *Boston: The Great Depression and the New Deal* (New York: Oxford University Press, 1977).

## Families

Warner's stress on privatism draws attention to the importance of the elements within the community to an understanding of its overall character. The history of businesses, churches, social agencies, and voluntary associations has generated a rich literature of general works and specific studies. In recent years the history of the family and related matters has drawn increasing attention. Many of the studies of specific communities mentioned earlier have paid considerable attention to family structure and behavior, notably Morgan, Demos, Greven, Lockridge, Wolf, Hirsch, Walkowitz, Thernstrom, Knights, Chudacoff, the Griffens, Yans-McLaughlin, Barton, and Kessner. A vast number of biographies have explored the nature and influence of individual family situations.

Several scholars have provided insight into particular aspects of family life. Child rearing has been examined in Bernard Wishy, *The Child and the*

*Republic: The Dawn of Modern American Child-Nurture* (Philadelphia: University of Pennsylvania Press, 1968); Peter Gregg Slater, *Children in the New England Mind* (Hamden, Conn.: Archon, 1977); Joseph F. Kett, *Rites of Passage: Adolescence in America, 1790 to the Present* (New York: Basic, 1977), and Paula S. Fass, *The Damned and the Beautiful: American Youth in the 1920s* (New York: Oxford University Press, 1977). The other end of the family life cycle is the focus of David Hackett Fischer, *Growing Old in America* (New York: Oxford University Press, 1977); and W. Andrew Achenbaum, *Old Age in the New Land: The American Experience since 1790* (Baltimore: Johns Hopkins University Press, 1978). Aspirations for the family as well as marital breakdown received attention in William O'Neill, *Divorce in the Progressive Era* (New Haven: Yale University Press, 1967); and Elaine Tyler May, *Great Expectations: Marriage and Divorce in Post-Victorian America* (Chicago: University of Chicago Press, 1980). The distinctive circumstances of black families were treated in John Blassingame, *The Slave Community* (New York: Oxford University Press, 1972); and Herbert Gutman, *The Black Family in Slavery and Freedom, 1750–1925* (New York: Pantheon, 1976).

Women have finally begun to receive attention from historians, both as important persons in their own right and as central figures in the family. Gerda Lerner provides an overview in *The Female Experience: An American Documentary* (Indianapolis: Bobbs-Merrill, 1977) and *The Majority Finds Its Past: Placing Women in History* (New York: Oxford University Press, 1979). Detailed examinations of women's situation in pre-1900 American society include: Lyle Koehler, *A Search for Power: The "Weaker Sex" in Seventeenth-Century New England* (Urbana: University of Illinois Press, 1980); Mary Beth Norton, *Liberty's Daughters: The Revolutionary Experience of American Women, 1750–1835* (Boston: Little, Brown, 1980); Nancy F. Cott, *The Bonds of Womanhood: 'Woman's Sphere' in New England, 1780–1835* (New Haven, Yale University Press, 1977); Anne Firor Scott, *The Southern Lady: From Pedestal to Politics, 1830–1930* (Chicago: University of Chicago Press, 1970); Kathryn Kish Sklar, *Catherine Beecher: A Study in American Domesticity* (New Haven: Yale University Press, 1977); and Julie Roy Jeffrey, *Frontier Women: The Trans-Mississippi West, 1840–1880* (New York: Hill and Wang, 1979).

Twentieth-century developments in women's social and family roles receive considerable attention in Sheila M. Rothman, *Woman's Proper Place: A History of Changing Ideals and Practices, 1870 to the Present* (New York: Basic, 1978); Barbara J. Harris, *Beyond Her Sphere: Women and the Professions* in *American History* (Westport, Conn.: Greenwood, 1978); David M. Katzman, *Seven Days a Week: Women and Domestic Service in Industrializing America* (New York: Oxford University Press, 1978); Susan Estabrook Kennedy, *If All We Did Was to Weep at Home: A History of White Working-Class Women in America* (Bloomington: Indiana University Press, 1979); Leslie W. Tentler, *Wage-Earning Women: Industrial Work and Family Life, 1900–1930* (New York: Oxford University Press, 1979); Linda Gordon, *Woman's Body, Woman's Right: A Social History of Birth Control in America* (New York: Grossman, 1976); William H. Chafe, *The American Woman: Her Changing Social, Economic, and Political Role, 1920–1970* (New York: Oxford University Press, 1972), and *Women and Equality: Changing Patterns in American Culture* (New York: Oxford University Press, 1977); and Peter Filene, *Him/Her/Self: Sex Roles in Modern America* (New York: Harcourt Brace Jovanovich, 1975).

The many specialized studies have provided support for an impressive effort to summarize the history of the American family and the role of women within it. Carl N. Degler, *At Odds: Women and the Family in America from the Revolution to the Present* (New York: Oxford University Press, 1980), draws heavily on the recent scholarship. Degler's synthesis focuses upon the tension between the centrality of women to the family and the confining aspects of family life which have inhibited and frustrated many women.

Efforts to examine men in terms of their relationship to the family have not proceeded nearly so far as studies of women. A beginning has been made, however, by Joe L. Dubbert, *A Man's Place: Masculinity in Transition* (Englewood Cliffs, N.J.: Prentice-Hall, 1979).

The great outpouring of studies by scholars, which shows no signs of slowing, suggests that academic interest in community and family history is likely to remain strong. This trend will be valuable for all historians of the nearby world. Observing the methods which other historians use to probe the past can often point the way to the answer to one's own questions. Even more important, the histories of other people, institutions, and communities enrich the understanding of one's own nearby history, the ways in which it parallels the experience of others and the respects in which it is unique.

Much obviously remains to be learned about the past, and the past of communities in particular. "Community" was once defined as an interactive population in a specific location, but in modern society physical proximity may lead to relationships or experiences shared to only a very limited extent, while strong attachment to a group may not depend on geographic closeness. Modern cities may contain a great many semiautonomous communities with ethnic, class, geographical, occupational, cultural, or other attachments, each of which has internal ties much stronger than most links to the greater community. Likewise, an individual may feel a strong bond with a group which is geographically dispersed but defines acceptable group behavior, provides support, and offers a sense of belonging, functions which are associated with membership in a community. Disgust with existing communities may lead to efforts to form new types of communities or to movement from one location to another but seldom to abandonment of all social contact or rejection of the quest for community. The attempt of most people to form a new family of some sort after death, divorce, or departure has disrupted the old family reflects the same human desire for social attachment. As long as communities continue to be a vital part of human experience, each new generation will need to reestablish their meaning. The value of nearby history for understanding one's self and circumstances will remain as constant and fresh as the need for satisfying human relationships.

## For Further Information

Since academic historians discovered the value of community and family studies, many books have appeared in addition to those discussed in this chapter. A great many master's theses and doctoral dissertations have also been written, and many extremely worthwhile articles, too numerous to mention here, have been published. New research and insights often appear first as articles and only much later, if ever, in books. The journals which regularly publish community and family history articles as well as review new books in the field include *American Quarterly*, *Feminist Studies*, *Historical Methods Newsletter*, *Journal of Family History*, *Journal of Interdisciplinary History*, *Journal of Marriage and the Family*, *Journal of Social History*, *Journal of Urban History*, *Signs*, *William and Mary Quarterly*, and the many local state, and regional historical journals.

Several edited collections of shorter essays have brought together valuable insights and examples of research methods. See Stephan Thernstrom and Richard Sennett, eds., *Nineteenth-Century Cities: Essays in the New Urban History* (New Haven: Yale University Press, 1969); Kenneth Jackson and Stanley K. Schultz, eds., *Cities in American History* (New York: Knopf, 1972); and Raymond A. Mohl and James F. Richardson, eds., *The Urban Experience: Themes in American History* (Belmont, Calif.: Wadsworth, 1973). A great deal of useful information has been gathered in Stephan Thernstrom, ed., *Harvard Encyclopedia of American Ethnic Groups* (Cambridge, Mass.: Harvard University Press, 1980). On specific cities and as models, see Allen F. Davis and Mark H. Haller, eds., *The*

*People of Philadelphia: A History of Ethnic Groups and Lower-Class Life, 1790–1940* (Philadelphia: Temple University Press, 1973); and Irwin Yellowitz, ed., *Essays in the History of New York City* (Port Washington, N.Y.: Kennikat, 1978).

Families have been explored in Charles H. Mindel and Robert W. Habenstein, eds., *Ethnic Families in America: Patterns and Variations* (New York: Elsevier, 1976); Michael Gordon, ed., *The American Family in Social-Historical Perspective*, 2nd ed., (New York: St. Martin's, 1978); John Demos and Sarane Spence Boocock, eds., *Turning Points: Historical and Sociological Essays on the Family* (Chicago: University of Chicago Press, 1978); and Nancy F. Cott and Elizabeth H. Pleck, eds., *A Heritage of Her Own: Toward a New Social History of American Women* (New York: Simon and Schuster, 1979). Tamara K. Hareven has edited several noteworthy collections of essays: *Anonymous Americans: Explorations in Nineteenth-Century Social History* (Englewood Cliffs, N.J.: Prentice-Hall, 1971); *Family and Kin in Urban Communities, 1700–1930* (New York: Franklin Watts, 1977); *Transitions: The Family and the Life Course in Historical Perspective* (New York: Academic, 1978); and with Maris A. Vinovskis, *Family and Population in Nineteenth-Century America* (Princeton: Princeton University Press, 1978).

Several attempts have been made to summarize the American experience in terms of communities and/or families. See especially Page Smith, *As a City Upon a Hill: The Town in American History* (New York: Knopf, 1966); Sam Bass Warner, Jr., *The Urban Wilderness: A History of the American City* (New York: Harper and Row, 1972); Ruth E. Sutter, *The Next Place You Come To: A Historical Introduction to Communities in North America* (Englewood Cliffs, N.J.: Prentice-Hall, 1973); Zane L. Miller, *The Urbanization of Modern America* (New York: Harcourt Brace Jovanovich, 1973); David J. Russo, *Families and Communities: A New View of American History* (Nashville: American Association for State and Local History, 1974); Howard P. Chudacoff, *The Evolution of American Urban Society* (Englewood Cliffs, N.J.: Prentice-Hall, 1975); and Carl N. Degler, *At Odds: Women and the Family in America from the Revolution to the Present* (New York: Oxford University Press, 1980).

On modernization see Richard D. Brown, *Modernization: The Transformation of American Life, 1600–1865* (New York: Hill and Wang, 1976); and Richard J. Jensen, *Illinois: A Bicentennial History* (New York: Norton, 1978). Focusing on Europe but useful for America as well is Edward Shorter, *The Making of the Modern Family* (New York: Basic, 1975).

For anyone interested in the evolution of the study of history in the United States, a good starting point is David D. Van Tassel, *Recording America's Past: An Interpretation of the Development of Historical Studies in America, 1607–1884* (Chicago: University of Chicago Press, 1960); and John Higham, *History: Professional Scholarship in America* (Englewood Cliffs, N.J.: Prentice-Hall, 1965). The most up-to-date assessment is Michael Kammen, ed., *The Past before Us: Contemporary Historical Writing in the United States* (Ithaca: Cornell University Press, 1980).

Finally, if the challenge of exploring the past seems more than you can manage, look at Emmanuel LeRoy Ladurie, *Montaillou: The Promised Land of Error*, trans. Barbara Bray (New York: Random House, 1978). This French historian used church inquisition records to assemble a detailed, intimate picture of a tiny peasant town in southwestern France at the start of the fourteenth century. This book may provide some ideas about topics of importance and the use of evidence, but at the very least it should help you to realize that the task of doing nearby history is not impossible and the result can be fascinating.

# Appendix A

*Forms to Request Information from*
*Federal Agencies*

1. Census Records
2. Passenger Arrival Records
3. Social Security Earnings Information
4. Veterans' Records

FORM **BC-600**
(6-1-81)

U.S. DEPARTMENT OF COMMERCE
BUREAU OF THE CENSUS

Form Approved:
O.M.B. No. 0607-0117

DO NOT USE THIS SPACE

CASE NO.

## APPLICATION FOR SEARCH OF CENSUS RECORDS

PURPOSE FOR WHICH RECORD IS TO BE USED (MUST BE STATED HERE) (See Instruction 1)

$ _____ (Fee)

☐ Money Order
☐ Check
☐ Other

**RETURN TO:** U.S. Department of Commerce, Bureau of the Census, PITTSBURG, KANSAS 66762

FULL NAME OF PERSON WHOSE CENSUS RECORD IS REQUESTED (Print or type)

| FIRST NAME | MIDDLE NAME | MAIDEN NAME (If any) | PRESENT LAST NAME | NICKNAMES |
|---|---|---|---|---|

DATE OF BIRTH (If unknown – estimate)

| PLACE OF BIRTH (City, county, State) | RACE | SEX |
|---|---|---|

FULL NAME OF FATHER (Stepfather, guardian, etc.)

Please give FULL name of husband or wife of person whose record is requested.

| FIRST MARRIAGE (Name of husband or wife) | YEAR MARRIED (Approximate) |
|---|---|
| SECOND MARRIAGE (Name of husband or wife) | YEAR MARRIED (Approximate) |

FULL MAIDEN NAME OF MOTHER (Stepmother, etc.)

### GIVE PLACE OF RESIDENCE AT EACH DATE LISTED BELOW

| CENSUS DATE | NUMBER AND STREET (Very important) | CITY, TOWN, TOWNSHIP (Precinct, beat, etc.) | COUNTY AND STATE | NAME OF PERSON WITH WHOM LIVING (Head of household) | RELATIONSHIP |
|---|---|---|---|---|---|
| JUNE 1, 1900 (See Instruction 2) | | | | | |
| APRIL 15, 1910 (See Instruction 3) | | | | | |
| JAN. 1, 1920 (See Instruction 2) | | | | | |
| APRIL 1, 1930 (See Instruction 3) | | | | | |
| APRIL 1, 1940 (See Instruction 3) | | | | | |
| APRIL 1, 1950 (See Instruction 3) | | | | | |
| APRIL 1, 1960 (See Instructions 3 and 9) | | | | | |
| APRIL 1, 1970 (See Instructions 3 and 9) | | | | | |

• If the census information is to be sent to someone other than the person whose record is requested, give the name and address, including Zip code, of the other person or agency.

• This authorizes the Bureau of the Census to send the record to: (See Instruction 4)

**FEE REQUIRED:** See Instructions 5, 6, and 7 on the reverse side.

A check or money order (**DO NOT SEND CASH**) payable to "Commerce — Census," must be sent with the application. This fee covers the cost of a search of not more than two census years about one person only.

Fee required . . . . . . . . . . . . $ 12.00

_____ extra copies @ $2.00 each . . $ _____

_____ full schedules @ $4.00 each . $ _____

TOTAL amount enclosed ⟶ $ _____

I certify that information furnished about anyone other than the applicant will not be used to the detriment of such person or persons by me or by anyone else with my permission.

SIGNATURE – **Do not print** (Read Instruction 8 carefully before signing)

PRESENT ADDRESS

| NUMBER AND STREET |
|---|
| CITY | STATE | ZIP CODE |

IF SIGNED ABOVE BY MARK (X), TWO WITNESSES MUST SIGN HERE

SIGNATURE                     SIGNATURE

NOTICE – Intentionally falsifying this application may result in a fine of $10,000 or five years imprisonment, or both (title 18, U.S. Code, section 1001).

# GENERAL INFORMATION

The Application on the reverse side of this sheet is for use in requesting a search of the census records and **an official** copy of the personal information found which includes age, place of birth, and citizenship. This application should be filled in and mailed to **BUREAU OF THE CENSUS, PITTSBURG, KANSAS 66762,** together with a money order or check payable to "Commerce — Census."

Birth certificates, including delayed birth certificates, are not issued by the Bureau of the Census but by the Health Department or similar agency of the State in which the birth occurred. In most Federal Censuses, the census takers obtained the age and place of birth of individuals. Copies of these census records often are accepted as evidence of age, citizenship, and place of birth for employment, social security benefits, insurance, and other purposes. *Since the place*

*of birth and citizenship were obtained only on a sample basis during the 1960 and 1970 Censuses, this information will not be shown on transcripts for those years.*

Census records for **1900** and prior years have been transferred to the National Archives and Records Service, Washington, D.C. 20408, and are considered public records. Requests for information from these Censuses should be addressed to that agency.

If you authorize the Bureau of the Census to send your record to someone other than yourself, attention is called to the possibility that the information shown in the census record may not agree with that given in your application. The record must be copied exactly as it appears and will be sent as you direct regardless of what it shows.

## INSTRUCTIONS FOR COMPLETING THIS FORM

▶ **1. Purpose**

The purpose for which the information is desired must be shown so that a determination may be made under 13 U.S.C. 8(a) that the record is required for a proper use. The statement of purpose also provides a basis for determining which census records would best serve such purpose and thereby, save the expense of additional searches.

▶ **2. Censuses 1900—1920**

A system for filing names by sound is available for these census years. Information can be furnished in many instances when only the following information is given:

The name of the person about whom the information is desired.
The name of the city or county and State where the person resided.
The name of the head of the household with whom this person was living on the various dates of these censuses.

Additional information **such as the names of brothers and sisters is helpful if it can be furnished.**

▶ **3. Censuses — years 1910—1930—1940—1950—1960—1970**

If residing in a city at the time these censuses were taken, it is necessary to furnish the house number, the name of the street, city, county, and State and the name of the parent or other head of household with whom residing at the time of the census. If residing in a small town or a rural area, give all available information as to cross-streets, road names, township, district, precinct, or beat, etc. If the district or township is unknown, give the distance from the nearest town and the direction, also the rural route number.

▶ **4. Confidential information given to other than person to whom it relates**

(a) Census information for the years 1900 and on is confidential and ordinarily will not be furnished to another person unless the person to whom it relates authorizes this in the space provided or there is other proper authorization as indicated in 4(b), 4(c), and 4(d) hereof.

(b) Minor children

Information regarding a child who has not reached legal age may be obtained upon the written request of either parent or the legal guardian.

(c) Mentally incompetent persons

Information regarding persons who are mentally incompetent may be obtained upon the written request of the legal representative supported by a certified copy of the court order naming such legal representative.

(d) Deceased persons

If the record requested relates to a deceased person, the application must be signed by (1) a blood relative in the immediate

family (parent, brother, sister, or child), (2) the surviving wife or husband. (3) the administrator or executor of the estate, or (4) a beneficiary by will, or insurance. In all cases involving deceased persons, a certified copy of the death certificate must be furnished, and the relationship to the deceased must be stated on the application. Legal representatives must also furnish a certified copy of the court order naming such legal representatives; and beneficiaries must furnish legal evidence of such beneficiary interest.

▶ **5. Fee required**

The **$12.00** fee is for a search in regular turn, based on the date the request is received, of not more than two suggested censuses about one person only. The time required to complete a search depends upon the number of cases on hand at the particular time and the difficulty encountered in searching a particular case. The normal processing time would require from two to four weeks.

Not more than two censuses will be searched and the results furnished for one fee. Should it be necessary to search more than two censuses to find the record, you will be notified to send another fee before further searches are made. Tax monies are not available for the furnishing of this information. Accordingly, even though the information is not found, if a search has been made, the fee cannot be returned.

▶ **6. Additional copies of Census information**

Additional copies of this information furnished will be prepared at a cost of $2.00 for each additional copy. Fill in the amount of money enclosed and the number of extra copies desired in the spaces provided.

▶ **7. Full schedules (For Genealogy)**

Upon request, a full schedule will be furnished. There is an additional charge of $4.00 for each full schedule requested. The full schedule is the complete one-line entry of personal data recorded for the individual. The name of the head of household may also be shown, but the names of other persons will not be listed.

▶ **8. Signature**

In general, the signature should be the same as that shown on the line captioned "full name of person whose census record is requested." When the application is for the census record concerning another person, the authority of the requester must be furnished as set forth in instruction 4 above.

▶ **9. 1960—1970 Censuses**

Since the place of birth and citizenship were obtained only on a sample basis during the 1960 and 1970 Censuses, this information will not be shown on transcripts.

FORM BC-600 (6-1-81)

244

## ORDER AND BILLING FOR COPIES OF PASSENGER ARRIVAL RECORDS

**Please follow instructions below.**
Submit a separate set of order forms for each passenger arrival.
Do not remove any of the sheets of this 3-part set. You will be billed $3.00 for each list reproduced. **Do not mail payment with your order.** This form will be returned to you and serves as your bill when we fill your order.

*Date received*

**Mail the complete set of this order to** ▶ **Passenger Arrival Records (NNCC), Washington, DC 20408**

### IDENTIFICATION OF ENTRY

| DATE OF ARRIVAL | NAME OF IMMIGRANT OR NAMES OF MEMBERS OF IMMIGRANT FAMILY | AGE | SEX |
|---|---|---|---|
| PORT OF ENTRY | | | |
| WHERE NATURALIZED *(if known)* | | | |
| SHIP NAME *(or carrier line)* | | | |
| PASSENGER'S COUNTRY OF ORIGIN | | | |

### NOTE

The National Archives has customs passenger lists dating back to 1820 with a few as early as 1787. Lists prior to 1820 that are not at the National Archives may be on file at the port of entry or the State archives in the State where the port is located. The **Morton Allan Directory of European Passenger Steamship Arrivals** may be useful in determining the name and arrival date of ships arriving at New York, 1890—1930, and Philadelphia, Baltimore, and Boston, 1904—1926.
Please fill in as much of the information called for above as possible. We will advise you if the information is inadequate to enable us to locate the entry you are seeking.
We do not maintain a list of persons who do research for a fee; however, many researchers advertise their services in genealogical periodicals, usually available in libraries.

---

**YOUR NAME & ADDRESS**

Type or print legibly PRESS HARD

Name
Number & Street
City & State

(Zip code)

**DO NOT WRITE BELOW - SPACE IS FOR REPLY TO YOU**

| ARRIVAL DATE | PORT | SHIP |
|---|---|---|

☐ THIS IS YOUR BILL — RECORD ENCLOSED ▶

| MICROFILM PUBLICATION | make check or money order payable to NATF (NNCC) |
|---|---|
| ROLL | PAGE | AMOUNT DUE ▶ $ |

☐ WE WERE UNABLE TO COMPLETE YOUR ORDER — RECORD SEARCHED FOR BUT NOT FOUND ▶

RECORDS SEARCHED

| MICROFILM PUBLICATION | SEARCHER |
|---|---|
| ROLL | PAGE | DATE SEARCHED |

☐ SEE REVERSE

☐ A SEARCH WAS NOT MADE FOR THE REASON INDICATED:

☐ 1. Our index to New York passenger arrivals covers the periods 1820 – 1846 and 1897 – 1943. We regret that we cannot undertake a page-by-page search of the lists for the period between 1847 – 1896, inclusive.

☐ 2. Masters of vessels departing from U.S. ports were not required to list the names of passengers. Therefore, we would not have a list for the passenger you have cited.

☐ 3. Our holdings of passenger lists do not include any for Pacific coast ports. The San Francisco passenger lists were destroyed by fires in 1851 and 1940. (Consult the two works by Louis J. Pasmussen, **San Francisco Ship Passenger Lists**, 4 vols., 1965; and **Railway Passenger Lists of Overland Trains to San Francisco and the West**, 1 vol., 1966.)

☐ 4. Overland arrivals into the U.S. from Canada and Mexico are not documented in passenger list records.

☐ 5. Justice Department restrictions prohibit us from making searches in Immigration and Naturalization records less than 50 years old. We suggest that you direct an inquiry to: District Director, Immigration and Naturalization Service, New York, NY 10007.

**NUMBER OF BLANK ORDER FORMS YOU WOULD LIKE SENT TO YOU** ▶

NATIONAL ARCHIVES TRUST FUND BOARD

NATF FORM 40 (12-79)

## PASSENGER LISTS IN THE NATIONAL ARCHIVES

1. We found several entries for persons of the same name arriving at the same port during the same period. Additional information, such as age, occupation, etc., will help in resolving this problem.

2. We found the requested information on the passenger index, but we regret that the corresponding passenger list is missing. A copy of the index card is enclosed.

3. We are unable to locate the passenger list for the ship listed and have found no entry on the passenger index for the requested party at that port.

4. We examined the passenger list for the requested ship and were unable to find an entry for the requested passenger.

5. The register of ship arrivals did not show any entry for the ship named.

6. Our only passenger lists for the cited port do not cover the date that you have requested, and we were unable to find an entry on the index to the lists we have.

7. You may find some help in the book **Irish and Scotch-Irish Ancestral Research** by Margaret Dickson Falley (1962). It is a guide to genealogical records and repositories in Ireland and is normally available in larger libraries.

8. Passports are issued to persons leaving the U.S., not arriving but early arrivals are frequently documented in passenger lists, which are described in the enclosed leaflet.

9. The National Archives has abstracts of Naturalization proceedings for the New England States (1787 – 1906) and the District of Columbia (1802 – 1926). For information about citizenship granted elsewhere before September 27, 1906, send inquiries to the clerk of the Federal, State, or other court that issued the naturalization certificate. The Immigration and Naturalization Service, Washington, DC 20536, can furnish information on naturalizations that occurred after September 26, 1906.

10. It should be noted that the passenger lists in our custody do not represent a complete collection. Some passenger lists of the 19th century were either lost or destroyed by dampness, fire, and other causes before records of this type were deposited in the National Archives.

246

# Social Security
# Request for Detailed Earnings Information

Decide on the information you need. Complete the request form provided below and mail it to the address shown.

**FOR YOUR INFORMATION**

TYPE I - EARNINGS, PERIOD OF EMPLOYMENT OR SELF-EMPLOYMENT (Includes names and addresses of reporting employers.)

TYPE II - YEARLY TOTALS ONLY (Does not include names and addresses of reporting employers.)

Failure to give complete and correct information will delay your request. Please be sure to copy your social security number as it appears on your social security card and sign your name on the signature line. Clearly show the calendar quarter(s) and/or year(s) requested and the person who is to receive the information. (It is important that you read the other side of this form before you complete the request.)

There usually is a charge when information from a person's (social security number holder) record is to be released to someone else. However, do not send any payment at this time. We will send a bill to the party shown below. Charges of $5.00 or less will be waived.

— — — — — — — — — — — — — — — — — (cut along this line) — — — — — — — — — — — — — — — — — — — —

## REQUEST FOR DETAILED EARNINGS INFORMATION

Name _____

Social Security Administration
Office of Central Records Operations
Baltimore, Maryland 21235

SOCIAL
SECURITY
NUMBER

DATE OF
BIRTH

| MONTH | DAY | YEAR |
|-------|-----|------|
|       |     |      |

Please send the information for the block(s) checked below to the following address:

MR.
MISS  _____
MRS      *(Name and address to whom the information is to be sent)*

☐ Type I for the calendar quarter(s) and/or year(s) _____ through _____ .
☐ Type II for the calendar year(s) _____ through _____ .

It information from your record is being sent to someone else, there usually is a charge. Please show the name and address of the party to whom the bill should be sent, if different from that shown above: _____

_____

_____

Sign your name here *(do not print)* _____ Date _____

**WARNING:** This signature *must* be that of the person whose social security number is shown above. Any false representation to obtain information from social security records is punishable by a fine of not more than $5,000 or one year in prison.

Department of Health, Education, and Welfare
Social Security Administration

Form SSA-L137 (9-79)

## INFORMATION ABOUT SIGNATURES

Information in the social security records is confidential. We can give you information from your record only if you sign your request, or from another person's record only if that person authorizes us in writing to do so.

**NOTE:** The signature should be the written signature of the social security number holder. We cannot accept printed, typed or stamped signatures.

If a mark (usually an "X") is used instead of a signature, it must be witnessed by two disinterested persons who must include their addresses.

The social security number holder must initial ANY changes made on the authorization.

Earnings information from the record of a deceased individual may be disclosed upon receipt of an authorization from the administrator, executor, or trustee of the decedent's estate, if that representative provides proof of appointment. Proof of death also must be furnished with the authorization.

## INFORMATION ABOUT SOCIAL SECURITY RECORDS

Our records do not contain earnings information for years before 1937. Exact dates of employment (month and day) cannot be given because employers are not required to show that information on their social security reports.

Quarterly information is available only for earnings reported for periods from 1938 through 1977. Our records do not show the amount of earnings in each quarter of 1937 because employers were required to report earnings semi-annually in that year. Employers are required to report earnings annually after December 31, 1977.

Because of the time required to receive and process reports, earnings information reported after 1977 may not be available from our records before February following the year the earnings were reported. For example, 1978 earnings may not be available before February 1980, and 1979 earnings not before February 1981.

Our records show the amount of earnings reported, not the amount of contributions paid. They do not necessarily show a person's total earnings for a given year. The maximum amount of earnings each employer is required to report for an employee in a year for social security purposes is $3,000 for 1937-50; $3,600 for 1951-54; $4,200 for 1955-58; $4,800 for 1959-65; $6,600 for 1966-67; $7,800 for 1968-71; $9,000 for 1972; $10,800 for 1973; $13,200 for 1974; $14,100 for 1975; $15,300 for 1976; $16,500 for 1977; $17,700 for 1978; $22,900 for 1979; and $25,900 for 1980. The same maximum amounts apply to earnings reported by self-employed persons beginning with 1951. (Self-employment was not covered before that time.)

☆ U. S. Government Printing Office: 1979—311-269/7

<table>
<tr>
<td>ORDER AND BILLING<br>FOR COPIES OF<br>VETERAN'S RECORDS</td>
<td>Please read the information and instructions on the back before completing this form.<br><br>Mail the complete set of this order to ▶     Military Service Records (NNCC)<br>National Archives, GSA<br>Washington, DC 20408</td>
<td>Date received by<br>National Archives</td>
</tr>
</table>

**1. CHECK RECORD DESIRED**

☐ PENSION

☐ BOUNTY-LAND WARRANT APPLICATION (*Service before 1856 only*)

☐ MILITARY

**REQUIRED MINIMUM IDENTIFICATION OF VETERAN**

2. VETERAN (*Give last, first, and middle names*)

3. STATE FROM WHICH SERVED

4. WAR IN WHICH, OR DATES BETWEEN WHICH HE SERVED

5. IF SERVICE WAS CIVIL WAR     ☐ UNION     ☐ CONFEDERATE

**PLEASE PROVIDE THE FOLLOWING INFORMATION, IF KNOWN**

6. UNIT IN WHICH HE SERVED (*Name of regiment or number, company, etc., or name of ship*)

7. BRANCH IN WHICH HE SERVED    ☐ INFANTRY    ☐ CALVARY    ☐ ARTILLERY    ☐ NAVY     If other, specify:

8. KIND OF SERVICE    ☐ VOLUNTEERS    ☐ REGULARS

9. PENSION OR BOUNTY LAND FILE NUMBER

10. DATE OF BIRTH

11. PLACE OF BIRTH (*City, county, State, etc.*)

12. NAME OF WIDOW OR OTHER CLAIMANT

13. DATE OF DEATH

14. PLACE OF DEATH (*City, county, State, etc.*)

16. PLACE(S) VETERAN LIVED AFTER SERVICE

15. IF VETERAN LIVED IN A HOME FOR SOLDIERS, GIVE LOCATION (*City and State*)

17. NUMBER OF THESE BLANK FORMS YOU WOULD LIKE SENT TO YOU

18. YOUR NAME AND ADDRESS

*Print or type your name and address within the block below.*

(Zip Code)

**Do NOT write below - Space is for National Archives reply to you.**

☐ THIS IS YOUR BILL

RECORDS ENCLOSED ▶    ☐ PENSION    ☐ BOUNTY LAND    ☐ MILITARY

NUMBER OF FILES FROM WHICH COPIES WERE REPRODUCED    **AMOUNT DUE** ▶ $

Please remit the above amount in the enclosed addressed envelope with the white copy of this form.

☐ WE WERE UNABLE TO COMPLETE YOUR ORDER

RECORDS SEARCHED FOR BUT NOT FOUND ▶    ☐ PENSION    ☐ BOUNTY LAND    ☐ MILITARY

☐ We found _____ pension or bounty land files and _____ military service files of the same name (or similar variations). You may order copies by returning the enclosed, marked forms.

☐ When we are unable to find a record for a veteran, this does not necessarily mean that he did not serve. You may be able to obtain information about him from the State archives.

☐ See attached forms/leaflets/information sheet.

☐ Please *complete* items 2 (give full name), 3 and 4, and resubmit.

☐ Other: _____

_____ ☐ See reverse

SEARCHER

FILE DESIGNATION

DATE

CASHIER

GENERAL SERVICES ADMINISTRATION

**GSA** FORM **6751** REV. 1-78J

249

## TYPES OF RECORDS THAT CAN BE ORDERED WITH THIS FORM

**PENSION APPLICATION FILES** based on United States (not State) service before World War I. Pension or bounty-land warrant application files usually include an official statement of the veteran's military or naval service, as well as information of a personal nature. Pensions based on military service for the Confederate States of America were authorized by some Southern States but not by the Federal Government until 1959. Inquiries about State pensions should be addressed to the State archives or equivalent agency at the capital of the veteran's State of residence after the war.

**BOUNTY-LAND WARRANT APPLICATION FILES** based on United States (not State) service before 1856. In addition to service, data, these files usually give the veteran's age and place of residence at the time the application was made.

**MILITARY SERVICE RECORDS** based on service in the United States Army (officers who served before June 30, 1917; enlisted men who served before October 31, 1912); Navy (officers and enlisted men who served before 1896); and Confederate armed forces (1861-65). We cannot provide photocopies of files for veterans whose service terminated less than 75 years ago; however, we are usually able to provide certain information from the files. Military service records rarely contain family information. The record of an individual's service in any one organization is entirely separate from the record of the service in another organization. We are ordinarily unable to accurately establish the identity of individuals of the same name who served in different organizations. If you know that an individual served in more than one organization and you desire copies of the military service record, submit a separate form for the service record in each organization.

## INSTRUCTIONS FOR COMPLETING THIS FORM

Submit a separate set of forms for each veteran. Do NOT remove any of the sheets of this 3-part set. **Do NOT mail payment with your order.** You will be billed $3.00 for each file reproduced.

Mail completed form to:
Military Service Records (NNCC)
National Archives, GSA
Washington, DC 20408

## IMPORTANT INFORMATION

When you send more than one form at a time, each form may be handled separately and you may not receive all of your replies at the same time.

When, because of the size of a file, we are unable to provide copies of all documents, we send copies of the documents we feel will be most useful to you. You may order copies of all documents in a file by making a specific request and giving us authorization to bill you 20¢ per page ($3.00 minimum).

When we indicate that we have numerous files for veterans of the same name given, we suggest that you visit the National Archives and examine the various files, or hire a professional researcher to examine the file for you. As a matter of policy, the National Archives does not perform research for individuals; therefore, we are unable to make a file-by-file check to see if the information in the numerous files matches the information you have provided.

The Board for Certification of Genealogists, 1307 New Hampshire Avenue, NW., Washington, DC 20036, can provide you with names of persons in the Washington area willing to do research for a fee. Also, genealogical researchers advertise their services in "The Genealogical Helper," the most widely circulated genealogical magazine available in most libraries having a genealogical section, or by subscription from Everton Publishers, P.O. Box 368, Logan, UT 84321.

More information about the availability of armed service records may be found in our free genealogical information leaflets and forms. These may be requested by writing to the address mentioned under "Instructions for Completing this Form."

# Appendix B
*Sample Gift Agreements*

1. Family History Deposit Agreement
2. Historical Materials Gift Agreement
3. Historical Records Gift Agreement
4. Oral History Gift Agreement

# Family History Deposit Agreement

I hereby donate this family history, entitled _____

and dated _____ , along with all literary and administrative

rights thereto, to _____ In accepting this family history,
the above named institution obtains the right to make the document available for
use by all researchers whom it deems qualified, provided the researcher agrees that
no names or other personal characteristics obtained from the document which
would identify living persons discussed therein are published or otherwise publicly
uttered without my permission and, if I so stipulate at the time of the request, the
permission of any person so identified.

Signed _____

Dated _____

# Historical Materials Gift Agreement

I hereby donate to _____ ,

hereinafter referred to as the Repository, the following materials; _____

_____

_____

_____

_____

    Title to the materials shall pass to the Repository upon their delivery to its authorized representative.

    The Repository shall administer, care for, and exhibit the materials according to accepted professional standards and practices. The Repository may loan the materials for exhibit elsewhere if in the Repository's judgment reasonable care of the materials can be provided.

    When not on public exhibit or loan, the materials shall be made available for examination by the Donor or for research by qualified persons, as determined by the Repository.

    Should any or all of the materials be deemed by the Repository to be inappropriate for retention, these may be disposed of, provided that they are first offered to

_____ .

Signed: _____ Date: _____

    This gift is accepted on behalf of the Repository, subject to the terms set forth.

Signed: _____ Date: _____

# Historical Records Gift Agreement

I hereby donate to _____ ,
hereinafter referred to as the Repository, the following materials; _____

_____

_____

_____

_____

Title to the materials shall pass to the Repository upon their delivery to its authorized representative. Such literary property rights as the Donor possesses in these materials and any others in the custody of the Repository are hereby dedicated to the public.

The Repository shall administer and care for the materials according to accepted professional standards. An inventory of the materials shall be prepared and a copy provided to the Donor. The Donor and persons designated by the Donor shall have access to the materials during the Repository's regular hours of service.

The materials shall be made available for research by qualified persons, as determined by the Repository, commencing _____ .
Thereafter, the materials may, with the Repository's permission, be copied, reproduced, and/or published.

Should part or all of the materials be deemed by the Repository to be inappropriate for retention, these may be disposed of, provided that they are first offered

to _____ .

Signed: _____ Date: _____

This gift is accepted on behalf of the Repository, subject to the terms set forth.

Signed: _____ Date: _____

# Oral History Gift Agreement

I hereby donate recordings and transcripts of interviews conducted with me by

_____ on _____ , along with all literary property

rights thereto, to _____ , hereinafter referred to as
the Curator.

The Curator shall administer and care for these materials according to accepted
professional practices.

These materials shall be made available for research by qualified persons, as

determined by the Curator, commencing _____ .
Thereafter, the materials may, with the Curator's permission, be copied, transcribed, reproduced, and/or published.

Should all or part of the materials be deemed by the Curator to be inappropriate
for retention, these may be disposed of, provided that they are first offered to

_____ .

Signed: _____ Date: _____

This gift is accepted on behalf of the Repository, subject to the terms set forth.

Signed: _____ Date: _____ _____

# Appendix C

*Sample Nomination Form:*
*National Register of Historic Places*

SOURCE: *How To Complete National Register Forms* (Washington, D.C.: National Register Division, Office of Archaeology and Historical Preservation, U.S. Department of the Interior, 1977)

# Thomas Miller House

Form No. 10-300
(Rev. 10-74)

UNITED STATES DEPARTMENT OF THE INTERIOR
NATIONAL PARK SERVICE

## NATIONAL REGISTER OF HISTORIC PLACES
## INVENTORY -- NOMINATION FORM

FOR NPS USE ONLY

RECEIVED

DATE ENTERED

SEE INSTRUCTIONS IN *HOW TO COMPLETE NATIONAL REGISTER FORMS*
TYPE ALL ENTRIES -- COMPLETE APPLICABLE SECTIONS

## 1 NAME

HISTORIC    Thomas Miller House

AND/OR COMMON    Ashton Lumber Company

## 2 LOCATION

STREET & NUMBER   Green Acres Road

_NOT FOR PUBLICATION

CITY. TOWN    Watkinsville    X VICINITY OF

CONGRESSIONAL DISTRICT
10

STATE    Ohio    CODE 39    COUNTY    Green    CODE 141

## 3 CLASSIFICATION

| CATEGORY | OWNERSHIP | STATUS | PRESENT USE | |
|---|---|---|---|---|
| _DISTRICT | _PUBLIC | X OCCUPIED | _AGRICULTURE | _MUSEUM |
| X BUILDING(S) | X PRIVATE | _UNOCCUPIED | X COMMERCIAL | _PARK |
| _STRUCTURE | _BOTH | _WORK IN PROGRESS | _EDUCATIONAL | _PRIVATE RESIDENCE |
| _SITE | PUBLIC ACQUISITION | ACCESSIBLE | _ENTERTAINMENT | _RELIGIOUS |
| _OBJECT | _IN PROCESS | X YES RESTRICTED | _GOVERNMENT | _SCIENTIFIC |
| | _BEING CONSIDERED | _YES UNRESTRICTED | _INDUSTRIAL | _TRANSPORTATION |
| | | _NO | _MILITARY | _OTHER |

## 4 OWNER OF PROPERTY

NAME    Charles Ashton, III

STREET & NUMBER   Grosvenor Avenue

CITY. TOWN    Watkinsville    _ VICINITY OF    STATE    Ohio

## 5 LOCATION OF LEGAL DESCRIPTION

COURTHOUSE.
REGISTRY OF DEEDS, ETC    Green County Courthouse

STREET & NUMBER    Lemon Street

CITY. TOWN    Madison    STATE    Ohio

## 6 REPRESENTATION IN EXISTING SURVEYS

TITLE    Historic American Buildings Survey

DATE    1965    X_FEDERAL  _STATE  _COUNTY  _LOCAL

DEPOSITORY FOR
SURVEY RECORDS    Library of Congress

CITY. TOWN    Washington    STATE    D.C.

259

# 7 DESCRIPTION

| CONDITION | | CHECK ONE | CHECK ONE |
|---|---|---|---|
| __EXCELLENT | __DETERIORATED | __UNALTERED | X_ORIGINAL SITE |
| __GOOD | __RUINS | X_ALTERED | __MOVED    DATE_____ |
| X_FAIR | __UNEXPOSED | | |

DESCRIBE THE PRESENT AND ORIGINAL (IF KNOWN) PHYSICAL APPEARANCE

Situated near Calls Creek, the Thomas Miller House is a two-story rectangular building of broken course cut sandstone construction. Twenty feet wide by forty-nine feet long, it is five bays wide with radiating sawn-stone lintels above the windows. Two single stack chimneys, flush with the gables, straddle the ridge on either side of the house. Above the front door is a single transom light and a radiating wooden lintel. The roof is tin and in poor condition. The entrance hall is flanked by single rooms, which are of equal size, with fireplaces centered in the north and south walls. Floor to ceiling cabinets of pre-Victorian design can be found in the south room on the ground floor. Ca. 1850 mantles, dating from when Mott owned the house, are still intact in two rooms on the second floor.

Structurally the house has been altered by a one-story metal lean to shed which runs the length of the back and north side of the building. The structural integrity of the original exterior is not affected by the shed, which was built ca. 1940; it could be dismantled without injury to the house.

Also on the property is a barn with metal siding, built in 1954. Located twenty feet from the front of the house, it is used to store lumber.

# 8 SIGNIFICANCE

| PERIOD | | AREAS OF SIGNIFICANCE -- CHECK AND JUSTIFY BELOW | | |
|---|---|---|---|---|
| __PREHISTORIC | __ARCHEOLOGY-PREHISTORIC | __COMMUNITY PLANNING | __LANDSCAPE ARCHITECTURE | __RELIGION |
| __1400-1499 | __ARCHEOLOGY-HISTORIC | __CONSERVATION | __LAW | __SCIENCE |
| __1500-1599 | __AGRICULTURE | __ECONOMICS | __LITERATURE | __SCULPTURE |
| __1600-1699 | X_ARCHITECTURE | __EDUCATION | __MILITARY | __SOCIAL/HUMANITARIAN |
| __1700-1799 | __ART | __ENGINEERING | __MUSIC | __THEATER |
| X_1800-1899 | __COMMERCE | __EXPLORATION/SETTLEMENT | __PHILOSOPHY | __TRANSPORTATION |
| __1900- | __COMMUNICATIONS | X_INDUSTRY | __POLITICS/GOVERNMENT | __OTHER (SPECIFY) |
| | | __INVENTION | | |

SPECIFIC DATES  ca. 1815           BUILDER/ARCHITECT  Morris Bros., Masons

STATEMENT OF SIGNIFICANCE

The Thomas Miller House, built ca. 1815, is significant for its historic associations with the development of Watkinsville and early industry in Ohio. The house is a rare example of stone architecture common to this area, and is significant for the excellence of its craftsmanship and detailing.

Thomas Miller was one of the early settlers of the community, and numerous deeds show that Miller acquired a large amount of property in and around Watkinsville in the first two decades of the 19th century. It is not known precisely when the house was constructed, but the earliest deeds pertinent to the property show an increase from $2,250 paid by Henry Watkins, the founder of Watkinsville, to $12,000 paid November 1, 1815 by Thomas Miller for the same tract of land. This would indicate that the edifice was constructed during that time.

Miller and subsequent owners, James Mott and Charles Aston, were closely associated with the industrial development of Ohio and the Midwest. In 1815, Miller established a ropewalk and cloth mill on Calls Creek near the house. One of the earliest industries in Ohio, the mill was equipped to weave cotton, flax, and wool, and by 1820 it included two carding machines and one mule of 204 spindles. (The site of the early mill is now completely occupied by a factory.) Miller quickly expanded his industrial and commercial activities to Tennessee and Kentucky, and supplied provisions to the Army posts of the Southwest, such as Fort Smith, and to expeditions such as the one of Colonel Atkinson to the upper reaches of the Missouri River.

In 1884 the house and land were sold to James Mott who continued milling operations along Calls Creek. Managers of the mill lived in the house, after Mott and his family built an Italianate villa in Watkinsville. In 1902 the house and twenty acres of land were purchased from the Mott family by Charles Ashton. Ashton was responsibile for building an asbestos shingle factory on the land immediately adjacent to the house. For the past thirty years, the house has served as the office of a lumber yard, owned by a descendant of Ashton.

Architecturally, the house is similar in construction to Ohio's first Capitol building in Adena and consequently may have used the same masons, the Morris brothers, for the exterior stonework. The interior wood trim is in good condition, although not original to the house. No other house of this early period survives in Watkinsville. Despite the large factory buildings surrounding the house and its inappropriate present use, the Thomas Miller house retains much of its original fabric and character.

## 9 MAJOR BIBLIOGRAPHICAL REFERENCES

Evans, S. A History of Watkinsville  Green Acres: Farm Press, 1957

Lutz, M.C. The Early Architecture of Green County. Madison: Madison State College Press, 1970

## 10 GEOGRAPHICAL DATA

ACREAGE OF NOMINATED PROPERTY _____1_____

UTM REFERENCES

A |1,7|  |2|7,9|6,6,0|  |3,7|5,1|3,6,0|     B |_,_|  |_,_,_,_,_,_|  |_,_,_,_,_,_|
  ZONE  EASTING      NORTHING                ZONE  EASTING        NORTHING
C |_,_|  |_,_,_,_,_,_|  |_,_,_,_,_,_|         D |_,_|  |_,_,_,_,_,_|  |_,_,_,_,_,_|

VERBAL BOUNDARY DESCRIPTION

The property nominated is a rectangular lot 200' by 215', bounded on the north, west, and east by the Ashton Asbestos Company.

LIST ALL STATES AND COUNTIES FOR PROPERTIES OVERLAPPING STATE OR COUNTY BOUNDARIES

| STATE | CODE | COUNTY | CODE |
|-------|------|--------|------|
| STATE | CODE | COUNTY | CODE |

## 11 FORM PREPARED BY

NAME / TITLE    James Cliff

| ORGANIZATION | DATE |
|---|---|
| Watkinsville Historical Society | 10-25-76 |
| STREET & NUMBER | TELEPHONE |
| Nelson Street | 514/567-8901 |
| CITY OR TOWN | STATE |
| Watkinsville | Ohio |

261

262

# Appendix D

*Historic Site Surveys:*
*Sample Procedure and Form*

SOURCE: Carroll County (Indiana) Interim Report, Historic Landmarks Foundation of Indiana, the Indiana Department of Natural Resources: Division of Historic Preservation and Archaeology, and the Department of the Interior

# Survey Procedure

Before field surveying began, preliminary research and interviews with local historians provided surveyors with a basic orientation on the county's development. Early maps and historical accounts revealed date of settlement, early major industries, historic transportation routes, agricultural evolution, and original town boundaries. Evaluation of this information indicates which areas of a county might contain concentrations of historic fabric. Selected county roads were then driven for a general assessment of extant cultural resources. Any building types or styles unique to the area were noted and additional research was conducted where necessary.

Every road in the county was then driven and properties were selected using the criteria established for entering sites and structures in the survey. A revised "Indiana Historic Sites and Structures Inventory" form (fig. 1) was used to record information describing name, location, use, condition, integrity, alterations, date, descriptive information on the building and its surroundings, as well as a brief statement of significance. Black and white photographs were taken and contact prints attached to the form. The

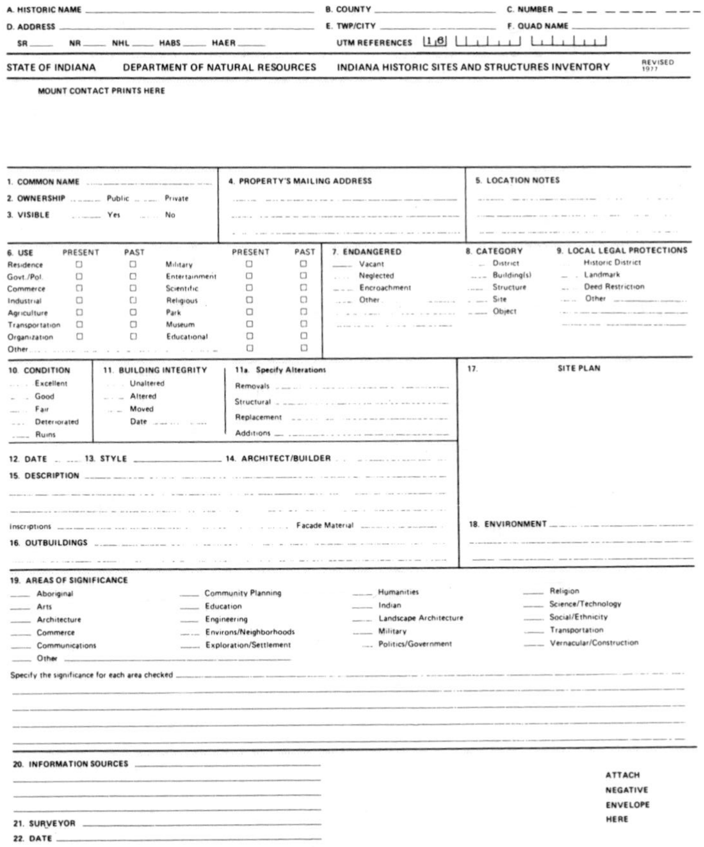
A. HISTORIC NAME ____ B. COUNTY ____ C. NUMBER ____
D. ADDRESS ____ E. TWP/CITY ____ F. QUAD NAME ____
SR ___ NR ___ NHL ___ HABS ___ HAER ___ UTM REFERENCES 1 6

STATE OF INDIANA DEPARTMENT OF NATURAL RESOURCES INDIANA HISTORIC SITES AND STRUCTURES INVENTORY REVISED 1977

MOUNT CONTACT PRINTS HERE

1. COMMON NAME
2. OWNERSHIP ___ Public ___ Private
3. VISIBLE ___ Yes ___ No

4. PROPERTY'S MAILING ADDRESS

5. LOCATION NOTES

6. USE PRESENT PAST: Residence, Govt./Pol., Commerce, Industrial, Agriculture, Transportation, Organization, Other; PRESENT PAST: Military, Entertainment, Scientific, Religious, Park, Museum, Educational

7. ENDANGERED: Vacant, Neglected, Encroachment, Other

8. CATEGORY: District, Building(s), Structure, Site, Object

9. LOCAL LEGAL PROTECTIONS: Historic District, Landmark, Deed Restriction, Other

10. CONDITION: Excellent, Good, Fair, Deteriorated, Ruins

11. BUILDING INTEGRITY: Unaltered, Altered, Moved, Date

11a. Specify Alterations: Removals, Structural, Replacement, Additions

17. SITE PLAN

12. DATE ___ 13. STYLE ___ 14. ARCHITECT/BUILDER
15. DESCRIPTION
Inscriptions ___ Facade Material
16. OUTBUILDINGS

18. ENVIRONMENT

19. AREAS OF SIGNIFICANCE
Aboriginal, Arts, Architecture, Commerce, Communications, Other
Community Planning, Education, Engineering, Environs/Neighborhoods, Exploration/Settlement
Humanities, Indian, Landscape Architecture, Military, Politics/Government
Religion, Science/Technology, Social/Ethnicity, Transportation, Vernacular/Construction

Specify the significance for each area checked

20. INFORMATION SOURCES
21. SURVEYOR
22. DATE

ATTACH NEGATIVE ENVELOPE HERE

fig. 1

surveyor usually spoke with the occupant to collect additional information. Each inventory entry was assigned a preliminary survey number and located on the appropriate Unites States Geological Survey (USGS) map. This map series was utilized because it conformed with the National Register program's mapping policies. In towns and villages with high density of outstanding, notable, or contributing structures, or a common theme between non-adjacent structures, areas were defined and inventoried as a district. Information was collected on each building within the district on a street-by-street basis. In general, all properties within the working boundaries of a historic district were entered in the survey including non-contributing buildings. If the density of eligible buildings was not sufficient to warrant a district, scattered individual sites and structures were identified within the city boundaries. Additional research was conducted by experts in local history who prepared a narrative on the historical and architectural development of the area. When the field survey was completed, research and reconnaisance was carried out to complete omissions and verify the accuracy of data collected.

# Evaluation

The significance of potential inventory entries was evaluated in terms of history, architecture, environs, and integrity and grouped into three general categories for township listings: "outstanding" (O), "notable" (N), and "reference" (R). In districts, entries were grouped into two additional categories: "contributing" (C), and "non-contributing" (NC) which supplement the reference category. While all entries merit attention, limited financial and organizational resources require that priorities be established to protect endangered properties immediately and develop long-range preservation plans.

## HISTORY

Historical information was evaluated less in terms of date than in the entry's national, state, or local significance. This included consideration of its association with famous people or events, social history, settlement, technology, and twenty other broad categories of significance. Entries of outstanding local importance could thus be more important than an entry only remotely associated with a state or national figure.

## ARCHITECTURE

Entries were next considered for their architectural merits as exemplary of either academic historical style, rare or unique design, vernacular techniques, representative types, or construction methods.

## ENVIRONS

The location of a building in relation to other structures, street layout, landscaping, and street hardware as well as overall environment of a place, affected its rating. Many buildings depend primarily on their sites within a district for their contributing rating to a district. This is especially relevant to the case of farm groups, small villages, neighborhoods, and business districts.

## INTEGRITY

In assessing integrity, an attempt was made to determine how much original building fabric remained. A structure in poor condition but retaining its original architectural features was evaluated based on its integrity, whereas a structure exhibiting extensive alterations by removals, structural changes, replacement, and additions was given a lower rating. The relocation of a building from its site also might lower an entry's rating.

265

# Appendix E

## Building Preservation:
## Local Ordinances

Federal laws on preservation are important, but it is often a local ordinance that makes a difference in saving buildings or districts. This municipal ordinance, which was instrumental in the preservation of a number of notable buildings in one community, provides an example of a measure other communities might consider.

### Article VI. Landmarks Commission

#### Sec. 2-113. Created; composition; terms of members.

The landmarks commission of the city is hereby established. It shall consist of nine (9) members appointed by the council. Of this number, one (1) shall be the owner of a landmark structure within the city limits, and one (1) person having at least ten (10) years previous experience in the business of buying, selling or dealing in real estate. The remaining seven (7) members shall be persons who, by training, experience or activity, have demonstrated an interest in preserving the landmarks of the city as the same are herein defined. Of those initially appointed, three (3) shall serve for a period of one (1) year, three (3) for a term of two (2) years and three (3) for a term of three (3) years. All persons thereafter appointed shall be appointed for a term of three (3) years.

#### Sec. 2-115. Duties and powers.

The landmarks commission is hereby authorized and directed to make a continuous study of all buildings, structures, parks, areas, sites, districts and items of natural or artificial phenomena located within the city and which are known to, or brought to the attention of, the commission for designation as possible landmarks under the provisions of this article.

#### Sec. 2-116. Authorized to officially designate and establish criteria for landmarks.

The landmarks commission shall have authority to establish criteria for and to designate those buildings, structures, parks, areas, sites, districts and items of natural or artificial

SOURCE: City of Florissant, Missouri. Provided by Rosemary Davison.

phenomena which in its judgment should be officially designated as landmarks under the provisions of this article. In determining what should be designated a landmark under this article, the commission shall take into account the age, design, period of construction, esthetic value, past use, historical significance, unusual nature, point of location or other recognized or generally accepted basis.

## Sec. 2-117. Rules and regulations in selection of items considered.

For the purpose of carrying out the provisions of this article, the landmarks commission shall have the authority to establish rules and regulations in order to evaluate and select items to be considered; to fix criteria to be followed when designating landmarks; and to provide the ways and means for the evaluation, selection and designation of possible landmarks.

## Sec. 2-118. Public declaration of officially designated landmarks.

Whenever a building, structure, park, area, site, district or other item of natural or artificial phenomena has been officially designated as a landmark within the meaning of this article, such fact shall be publicly declared by the commission and shall be transmitted to the building commissioner of the city, who is hereby charged with the duty of maintaining an official landmark register in which shall be entered all such designations, adequately described for proper identification. A statement of the considerations that formed the basis for such designation shall also be filed with the building commissioner, who shall maintain such statement for public use and inspection.

## Sec. 2-119. Notice of designation sent to owner of landmark.

Whenever a landmark has been officially designated by the landmarks commission, as herein described, notice of the designation shall be sent by registered mail to the owner of the landmark, as the name is disclosed by the city or county records. In the event any such owner shall feel aggrieved by such designation, he may, within thirty (30) days after such designation, appeal to the commission to revoke the designation. All such appeals shall be in writing and shall be considered informally by the commission. The person claiming to be aggrieved by such designation shall have an opportunity to appear and present reasons why such designation should be revoked.

## Sec. 2-120. Designated landmarks declared to be matters of public interest and concern.

(a) All buildings, structures, parks, areas, sites, districts and items of natural or artificial phenomena duly designated as landmarks and registered with the building commissioner of the city as herein provided are declared to be matters of public interest and concern.

· (b) The preservation of such landmarks is hereby recognized to have economic and aesthetic value and is held to be in the best interest of and to promote the general welfare of the city and its inhabitants.

267

### Sec. 2-121. Changes or alterations prohibited unless reviewed by commission.

No permit for the demolition, material alteration, substantial modification or other change shall be issued by the city for any designated landmark until the plans and specifications upon which the application for such permit is based shall have first been submitted to the landmarks commission for review.

### Sec. 2-122. Application for permit to be submitted to commission for review.

Upon submission to the landmarks commission of any such application for a permit, the commission shall have ninety (90) days in which to study and review such application and the plans and specifications upon which application is based and to confer with the owner, occupant or other person having an interest in such building, structure, park, area, district or other item of natural or artificial phenomena for the purpose of making suggestions and recommendations with respect to any and all means or methods considered feasible and proper for the preservation of such landmark. It shall be the duty of the commission within such time to make suggestions and recommendations whereby the landmark in question may be preserved and maintained in a state which will not deface, mar, materially alter or destroy, in whole or in part, the historical significance or aesthetic value of such landmark.

# Appendix F

## *Regional Branches of the National Archives*

The branches of the National Archives and Records Service hold federal government records relating primarily to activities within their region. In addition, they have microfilm copies of many records located in the National Archives in Washington, including the census. For specific information on holdings and access, inquiries should be directed to the appropriate branch.

For Connecticut, Maine, Massachusetts, New Hampshire, Rhode Island, and Vermont:

Archives Branch
Federal Archives and Records Center
380 Trapelo Road
Waltham, Massachusetts 02154
(617) 223-2657

For New Jersey, New York, Puerto Rico, and the Virgin Islands:

Archives Branch
Federal Archives and Records Center
Building 22—MOT Bayonne
Bayonne, New Jersey 07002
(201) 858-7251

For Deleware, the District of Columbia, Maryland, Pennsylvania, Virginia, and West Virginia:

Archives Branch
Federal Archives and Records Center
5000 Wissahickon Avenue
Philadelphia, Pennsylvania 19144
(215) 951-5591

For Illinois, Indiana, Michigan, Minnesota, Ohio, and Wisconsin:

Archives Branch
Federal Archives and Records Center
7358 South Pulaski Road
Chicago, Illinois 60629
(312) 353-0161

| | |
|---|---|
| For Alabama, Georgia, Florida, Kentucky, Mississippi, North Carolina, South Carolina, and Tennessee: | Archives Branch<br>Federal Archives and Records Center<br>1557 St. Joseph Avenue<br>East Point, Georgia 30344<br>(404) 763-7477 |
| For Iowa, Kansas, Missouri, and Nebraska: | Archives Branch<br>Federal Archives and Records Center<br>2305 East Bannister Road<br>Kansas City, Missouri 64131<br>(816) 926-7271 |
| For Arkansas, Louisiana, New Mexico, Oklahoma, and Texas: | Archives Branch<br>Federal Archives and Records Center<br>4900 Hemphill Street (building address)<br>P.O. Box 6216 (mailing address)<br>Fort Worth, Texas 76115<br>(817) 334-5525 |
| For Colorado, Montana, North Dakota, South Dakota, Utah, and Wyoming: | Archives Branch<br>Federal Archives and Records Center<br>Building 48, Denver Federal Center<br>Denver, Colorado 80225<br>(303) 234-5271 |
| For northern California, Hawaii, Nevada, and the Pacific: | Archives Branch<br>Federal Archives and Recores Center<br>1000 Commodore Drive<br>San Bruno, California 94066<br>(415) 876-9009 |
| For Arizona and southern California: | Archives Branch<br>Federal Archives and Records Center<br>24000 Avila Road<br>Laguna Niguel, California 92677<br>(714) 831-4220 |
| For Alaska, Idaho, Oregon, and Washington: | Archives Branch<br>Federal Archives and Records Center<br>6125 Sand Point Way, N.E.<br>Seattle, Washington 98115<br>(206) 442-4502 |

# Appendix G

## State Archives, Humanities Councils, Historical Societies, and Preservation Offices

These instititutions are good starting places when looking for advice, assistance, and information about nearby history. They can often help in finding more specialized aid.

## State Archives

*Alabama*
Alabama Department of
 Archives and History
624 Washington Avenue
Montgomery, Alabama 36130
(205) 832-6510

*Alaska*
Alaska State Archives
141 Willoughby Avenue
Pouch C
Juneau, Alaska 99801
(907) 465-2275

*Arizona*
Department of Library, Archives,
 and Public Records
1700 W. Washington Street
Phoenix, Arizona 85007
(602) 255-3701

*Arkansas*
Arkansas History Commission
300 West Markham
Little Rock, Arkansas 72201
(501) 371-2141

*California*
California State Archives
Office of the Secretary of State
1020 O Street, Room 130
Sacramento, California 95814
(916) 445-4293

*Colorado*
Division of Archives and
 Public Records
Department of Administration
1313 Sherman Street
Denver, Colorado 80203
(303) 839-2055

*Connecticut*
Archives, History, and
 Genealogy Unit
Connecticut State Library
231 Capitol Avenue
Hartford, Connecticut 06115
(302) 566-3690

*Delaware*
Bureau of Archives and
 Modern Records

Division of Historical and
   Cultural Affairs
Hall of Records
Dover, Delaware 19901
(302) 736-5314

*Florida*
Bureau of Archives and
   Records Management
Division of Archives, History,
   and Records Management
Department of State
The Capitol
Tallahassee, Florida 32304
(904) 488-1486

*Georgia*
Department of Archives and
   History
Secretary of State
330 Capitol Avenue
Atlanta, Georgia 33034
(404) 656-2358

*Hawaii*
Archives Division
Department of Accounting
   and General Services
Iolani Palace Grounds
Honolulu, Hawaii 96813
(808) 548-2355

*Idaho*
Idaho State Historical Society
610 North Julia Davis Drive
Boise, Idaho 83706
(208) 384-2120

*Illinois*
Illinois State Archives Division
Office of the Secretary of State
Archives Building
Springfield, Illinois 62756
(217) 782-4682

*Indiana*
Commission on Public Records
Indiana State Library
140 Senate Avenue
Indianapolis, Indiana 46204
(317) 232-3373

*Iowa*
State Historical Department
Historical Museum and
   Archives Division
Historical Building
E. Twelfth and Grand Avenue
Des Moines, Iowa 50319
(515) 281-5113

*Kansas*
Archives Division
Kansas State Historical Society
120 West Tenth Street
Topeka, Kansas 66612
(913) 296-3251

*Kentucky*
Division of Archives and Records
Department of Library and Archives
851 East Main Street
Frankfort, Kentucky 40601
(502) 564-3616

*Louisiana*
State Archives and Records
Office of the Secretary of State
P.O. Box 44125
Baton Rouge, Louisiana 70804
(504) 389-5256

*Maine*
Maine State Archives
Augusta, Maine 04333
(207) 289-2451

*Maryland*
Maryland Hall of Records Commission
Box 828
Annapolis, Maryland 21404
(301) 269-3915

272

*Massachusetts*
Archives of the Commonwealth
Office of the Secretary
State House
Boston, Massachusetts 02133
(617) 727-2816

*Michigan*
State Archives
Michigan History Division
Department of State
3423 North Logan Street
Lansing, Michigan 48918
(517) 373-0512

*Minnesota*
Minnesota Historical Society
Division of Archives and
    Manuscripts
1500 Mississippi Street
St. Paul, Minnesota 55101
(612) 296-6980

*Mississippi*
Archives and Library Division
Mississippi Department of Archives
    and History
100 South State Street
P.O. Box 571
Jackson, Mississippi 39205
(601) 354-6218

*Missouri*
Records Management and
    Archives Service
Office of the Secretary of State
P.O. Box 778
1001 Industrial Drive
Jefferson City, Missouri 65101
(314) 751-3319

*Montana*
Montana Historical Society
225 North Roberts Street
Helena, Montana 59601
(406) 449-2681

*Nebraska*
State Archives Division
Nebraska State Historical Society
1500 R Street
Lincoln, Nebraska 68508
(402) 432-2793

*Nevada*
Division State, County, and
    Municipal Archives
Secretary of State
1807 North Carson Street
Carson City, Nevada 89710
(702) 885-5210

*New Hampshire*
New Hampshire Division of
    Records Management and Archives
Department of Administration and
    Control
71 South Fruit Street
Concord, New Hampshire 03301
(603) 271-2236

*New Jersey*
Archives and History Bureau
New Jersey State Library
185 West State Street
Trenton, New Jersey 08625
(609) 292-6260

*New Mexico*
New Nexico Records Center
    and Archives
404 Montezuma Street
Santa Fe, New Mexico 87503
(505) 827-2321

*New York*
New York Department of Education
New York State Archives
Cultural Education Center
Albany, New York 12230
(518) 474-1195

## North Carolina
Archives and Records Section
Division of Archives and History
109 East Jones Street
Raleigh, North Carolina 27611
(919) 829-3952

## North Dakota
State Historical Society of
 North Dakota
Liberty Memorial Building
Bismarck, North Dakota 58501
(701) 224-2666

## Ohio
Archives—Library Division
Ohio Historical Society
I-71 and Seventeenth Avenue
Columbus, Ohio 43211
(614) 466-1500

## Oklahoma
Division of Archives and
 Records
Oklahoma Department of Libraries
200 N.E. Eighteenth Street
Oklahoma City, Oklahoma 73105
(405) 521-2502

## Oregon
Archives Division
Secretary of State
1005 Broadway, N.E.
Salem, Oregon 97310
(503) 378-4241

## Pennsylvania
Division of Archives and
 Manuscripts
Bureau of Archives and History
Pennsylvania Historical and
 Museum Commission
P.O. Box 1026
Harrisburg, Pennsylvania 17120
(717) 787-3051

## Rhode Island
Archives Division
Office of the Secretary of State
Room 43, State House
Providence, Rhode Island 02903
(401) 277-2353

## South Carolina
South Carolina Department of
 Archives and History
P.O. Box 11669, Capitol Station
1430 Senate Street
Columbia, South Carolina 29211
(803) 758-5816

## South Dakota
Archives Resource Center
Records Management Building
East Highway Bypass
Pierre, South Dakota 57501
(605) 773-3173

## Tennessee
Tennessee State Library and
 Archives
403 Seventh Avenue North
Nashville, Tennessee 37219
(615) 741-2451

## Texas
Archives Division
Texas State Library
Box 12927, Capitol Station
Austin, Texas 78711
(512) 475-2445

## Utah
State Archives and Records
 Services
Room B-4
State Capitol Building
Salt Lake City, Utah 84114
(801) 328-5250

Vermont
Public Records Division
Department of Administration
133 State Street
Montpelier, Vermont 05602
(802) 828-3288

Virginia
Archives Division
Virginia State Library
Eleventh and Capitol Streets
Richmond, Virginia 23219
(804) 786-2306

Washington
Division of Archives and Records
    Management
Department of General Administration
Washington State Archives and Records
    Center Building
Twelfth and Washington Streets
Olympia, Washington 98504
(206) 753-5468

West Virginia
Department of Culture and History
Science and Cultural Center
Capitol Complex
Charleston, West Virginia 25305
(304) 348-2277

Wisconsin
Division of Archives and
    Manuscripts
State Historical Society of
    Wisconsin
816 State Street
Madison, Wisconsin 53706
(608) 262-9580

Wyoming
Archives and Historical Department
Archives, Records Management and
    Centralized Microfilm Division
State Office Building
Cheyenne, Wyoming 82002
(307) 777-7518

# State Humanities Councils

Alabama
The Committee for the
    Humanities in Alabama
Box A-40
Birmingham-Southern College
Birmingham, Alabama 35204
(205) 324-1314

Alaska
Alaska Humanities Forum
429 D Street, Room 211
Loussac Sogn Building
Anchorage, Alaska 99501
(907) 272-5341

Arizona
Arizona Humanities Council
112 North Central Avenue, Suite 304
Phoenix, Arizona 85004
(602) 257-0335

Arkansas
Arkansas Endowment for the
    Humanities
The Remmel Building, Suite 102
1010 West Third Street
Little Rock, Arkansas 72201
(501) 663-3451

California
California Council for the
    Humanities
312 Sutter Street, Suite 601
San Francisco, California 94108
(415) 391-1474

Colorado
Colorado Humanities Program
601 Broadway, Suite 307
Boulder, Colorado 80302
(303) 442-7298

Connecticut
Connecticut Humanities Council
195 Church Street
Wesleyan Station
Middletown, Connecticut 06457
(203) 347-6888

Delaware
Delaware Humanities Forum
2600 Pennsylvania Avenue
Wilmington, Delaware 19806
(302) 738-8491

District of Columbia
D.C. Community Humanities
   Council
1341 G Street, N.W., Suite 620
Washington, D.C. 20005
(202) 347-1732

Florida
Florida Endowment for the
   Humanities
LET 360
University of South Florida
Tampa, Florida 33620
(813) 972-4094

Georgia
Georgia Endowment for the
   Humanities
1589 Clifton Road, N.E.
Emory University
Atlanta, Georgia 30322
(404) 329-7500

Hawaii
Hawaii Committee for the
   Humanities
2615 South King Street
Suite 211
Honolulu, Hawaii 96826
(808) 947-5891

Idaho
The Association for the
   Humanities in Idaho

1409 West Washington Street
Boise, Idaho 83702
(208) 345-5346

Illinois
Illinois Humanities Council
201 W. Springfield Avenue
Suite 205
Champaign, Illinois 61820
(217) 333-7611

Indiana
Indiana Committee for the
   Humanities
4200 Northwestern Avenue
Indianapolis, Indiana 46208
(317) 925-5316

Iowa
Iowa Humanities Board
Oakdale Campus
University of Iowa
Iowa City, Iowa 52242
(319) 353-6754

Kansas
Kansas Committee for the
   Humanities
112 West Sixth Street, Suite 509
Topeka, Kansas 66603
(913) 357-0359

Kentucky
Kentucky Humanities Council, Inc.
Ligon House
University of Kentucky
Lexington, Kentucky 40508
(606) 258-5932

Louisiana
Louisiana Committee for the
   Humanities
1215 Prytania Street, Suite 535
New Orleans, Louisiana 70130
(504) 523-4352

*Maine*
Maine Council for the
  Humanities and Public Policy
P.O. Box 7202
Portland, Maine 04112
(207) 773-5051

*Maryland*
The Maryland Committee for
  the Humanities
516 N. Charles Street,
  Rooms 304-305
Baltimore, Maryland 21202
(301) 837-1938

*Massachusetts*
Massachusetts Foundation for
  the Humanities and Public Policy
237-E Whitmore Administration Building
University of Massachusetts
Amherst, Massachusetts 01003
(413) 545-1936

*Michigan*
Michigan Council for the
  Humanities
Nisbet Building, Suite 30
Michigan State University
East Lansing, Michigan 48824
(517) 355-0160

*Minnesota*
Minnesota Humanities
  Commission
Metro Square, Suite 282
St. Paul, Minnesota 55101
(612) 224-5739

*Mississippi*
Mississippi Committee for the
  Humanities, Inc.
3825 Ridgewood Road, Room 111
Jackson, Mississippi 39211
(601) 982-6752

*Missouri*
Missouri State Committee for
  the Humanities

Loberg Building, Suite 202
11425 Dorsett Road
Maryland Heights, Missouri 63043
(314) 739-7368

*Montana*
Montana Committee for the
  Humanities
P.O. Box 8036
Hellgate Station
Missoula, Montana 59807
(406) 243-6022

*Nebraska*
Nebraska Committee for the
  Humanities
Cooper Plaza, Suite 405
211 N. Twelfth Street
Lincoln, Nebraska 68508
(308) 474-2131

*Nevada*
Nevada Humanities Committee
P.O. Box 8065
Reno, Nevada 89507
(702) 784-6587

*New Hampshire*
New Hampshire Council for
  the Humanities
112 South State Street
Concord, New Hampshire 03301
(603) 224-4071

*New Jersey*
New Jersey Committee for the
  Humanities
73 Eastern Avenue
CN 5062
New Brunswick, New Jersey 08903
(201) 932-7726

*New Mexico*
New Mexico Humanities Council
1712 Las Lomas, N.E.
The University of New Mexico
Albuquerque, New Mexico 87131
(505) 277-3705

277

*New York*
New York Council for the
Humanities
33 West 42nd Street
New York, New York 10036
(212) 354-3040

*North Carolina*
North Carolina Humanities
Committee
112 Foust Building
UNC-Greensboro
Greensboro, North Carolina 27412
(919) 379-5325

*North Dakota*
North Dakota Humanities Council
Box 2191,
Bismarck, North Dakota 58502
(701) 663-1948

*Ohio*
The Ohio Program in the
Humanities
760 Pleasant Ridge Avenue
Columbus, Ohio 43209
(614) 236-6879

*Oklahoma*
Oklahoma Humanities
Committee
Executive Terrace Building
2809 Northwest Expressway
Suite 500
Oklahoma City, Oklahoma 73112
(405) 840-1721

*Oregon*
Oregon Committee for the
Humanities
418 S.W. Washington
Room 410
Portland, Oregon 97204
(503) 241-0543

*Pennsylvania*
Pennsylvania Humanities Council
401 N. Broad Street
Philadelphia, Pennsylvania 19108
(215) 925-1005

*Puerto Rico*
Fundacion Puertorriquena de
las Humanidades
Box 4307
Old San Juan, Puerto Rico 00904
(809) 723-2087

*Rhode Island*
Rhode Island Committee for
the Humanities
463 Broadway
Providence, Rhode Island 02909
(401) 273-2250

*South Carolina*
South Carolina Committee for
the Humanities
17 Calendar Court, Suite No. 6
Columbia, South Carolina 29206
(803) 738-1850

*South Dakota*
South Dakota Committee on
the Humanities
University Station, Box 35
Brookings, South Dakota 57007
(605) 688-4823

*Tennessee*
Tennessee Committee for the
Humanities
1001 Eighteenth Avenue South
Nashville, Tennessee 37212
(615) 320-7001

*Texas*
Texas Committee for the
Humanities
1604 Nueces
Austin, Texas 78701
(512) 473-8585

*Utah*
Utah Endowment for the
  Humanities
10 West Broadway
Broadway Building, Suite 900
Salt Lake City, Utah 84101
(801) 531-7868

*Vermont*
Vermont Council on the
  Humanities and Public Issues
Grant House, P.O. Box 58
Hyde Park, Vermont 05655
(802) 888-3138

*Virginia*
Virginia Foundation for the
  Humanities and Public Policy
One-B West Range
University of Virginia
Charlottesville, Virginia 22903
(804) 924-3296

*Washington*
Washington Commission for
  the Humanities
Olympia, Washington 98505
(206) 866-6510

*West Virginia*
The Humanities Foundation of
  West Virginia
Box 204
Institute, West Virginia 25112
(304) 768-8869

*Wisconsin*
Wisconsin Humanities Committee
716 Langdon Street
Madison, Wisconsin 53706
(608) 262-0706

*Wyoming*
Wyoming Council for the Humanities
Box 3274-University Station
Laramie, Wyoming 82701
(307) 766-6496

# State Historical Societies

*Alabama*
Alabama Department of Archives
  and History
624 Washington Avenue
Montgomery, Alabama 36130

*Alaska*
Alaska Historical Society
635 Alder Street
Juneau, Alaska 99801

*Arizona*
Arizona Historical Society
949 East Second Street
Tucson, Arizona 85719

*Arkansas*
Arkansas History Commission
1 Capitol Mall
Little Rock, Arkansas 72201

*California*
California Historical Society
2090 Jackson Street
San Francisco, California 94109

*Colorado*
Colorado Historical Society
1300 Broadway
Denver, Colorado 80203

*Connecticut*
Connecticut Historical Society
1 Elizabeth Street
Hartford, Connecticut 06105

*Delaware*
Historical Society of Delaware
505 Market Street Mall
Wilmington, Delaware 19801

279

*Florida*
Florida Historical Society
University of South Florida Library
Tampa, Florida 33620

*Georgia*
Georgia Historical Society
501 Whitaker Street
Savannah, Georgia 31401

*Hawaii*
Hawaiian Historical Society
560 Kawaiahao Street
Honolulu, Hawaii 96813

*Idaho*
Idaho State Historical Society
610 North Julia Davis Drive
Boise, Idaho 83702

*Illinois*
Illinois State Historical Society
Old State Capitol
Springfield, Illinois 62706

*Indiana*
Indiana Historical Society
315 West Ohio Street
Indianapolis, Indiana 46202

*Iowa*
State Historical Society of Iowa
402 Iowa Avenue
Iowa City, Iowa 52240

*Kansas*
Kansas State Historical Society
120 West Tenth Street
Topeka, Kansas 66612

*Kentucky*
Kentucky Historical Society
300 West Broadway
Frankfort, Kentucky 40601

*Louisiana*
Louisiana Historical Society
203 Carondelet Street
New Orleans, Louisiana 70130

*Maine*
Maine Historical Society
485 Congress Street
Portland, Maine 04101

*Maryland*
Maryland Historical Society
201 West Monument Street
Baltimore, Maryland 21201

*Massachusetts*
Massachusetts Historical Society
1154 Boylston Street
Boston, Massachusetts 02215

*Michigan*
Historical Society of Michigan
2117 Washtenaw Avenue
Ann Arbor, Michigan 48104

*Minnesota*
Minnesota Historical Society
690 Cedar Street
St. Paul, Minnesota 55101

*Mississippi*
Mississippi Historical Society
100 South State Street
Jackson, Mississippi 39205

*Missouri*
State Historical Society of Missouri
Hitt and Lowry Streets
Columbia, Missouri 65201

*Montana*
Montana Historical Society
225 North Roberts
Helena, Montana 59601

*Nebraska*
Nebraska State Historical Society
1500 R Street
Lincoln, Nebraska 68508

*Nevada*
Nevada Historical Society
1650 North Virginia Street
Reno, Nevada 89503

New Hampshire
New Hampshire Historical Society
30 Park Street
Concord, New Hampshire 03301

New Jersey
New Jersey Historical Society
230 Broadway
Newark, New Jersey 07104

New Mexico
Historical Society of New Mexico
Box 5819
Santa Fe, New Mexico 87502

New York
New-York Historical Society
170 Central Park West
New York, New York 10024

North Carolina
Historical Society of North Carolina
c/o Southern Historical Collection
University of North Carolina,
   Wilson Library
Chapel Hill, North Carolina 27514

North Dakota
State Historical Society of North Dakota
North Dakota Heritage Center
Bismarck, North Dakota 58505

Ohio
Ohio Historical Society
I-71 and Seventeenth Avenue
Columbus, Ohio 43211

Oklahoma
Oklahoma Historical Society
2100 North Lincoln Boulevard
Oklahoma City, Oklahoma 73105

Oregon
Oregon Historical Society
1230 Southwest Park Avenue
Portland, Oregon 97205

Pennsylvania
Historical Society of Pennsylvania
1300 Locust Street
Philadelphia, Pennsylvania 19107

Rhode Island
Rhode Island Historical Society
52 Power Street
Providence, Rhode Island 02906

South Carolina
South Carolina Historical Society
100 Meeting Street
Charleston, South Carolina 29401

South Dakota
South Dakota State Historical Society
Soldiers' and Sailors' Memorial Building
East Capitol Avenue
Pierre, South Dakota 57501

Tennessee
Tennessee Historical Society
War Memorial Building, Ground Floor
Nashville, Tennessee 37219

Texas
Texas Historical Commission
Box 12276, Capitol Station
Austin, Texas 78711

Utah
Utah State Historical Society
307 West Second Street
Salt Lake City, Utah 84102

Vermont
Vermont Historical Society, Inc.
State Street
Montpelier, Vermont 05602

Virginia
Virginia Historical Society
428 North Boulevard
Richmond, Virginia 23221

*Washington*
Washington State Historical Society
315 North Stadium Way
Tacoma, Washington 98403

*West Virginia*
West Virginia Historical Society
Department of Culture and History
State Capitol Complex
Charleston, West Virginia 25305

*Wisconsin*
State Historical Society of Wisconsin
816 State Street
Madison, Wisconsin 53706

*Wyoming*
Wyoming State Archives and
   Historical Department
Barrett Building
Cheyenne, Wyoming 82002

# Historic Preservation Officers

*Alabama*
Director, Alabama Department of
   Archives and History
Archives and History Building
Montgomery, Alabama 36104
(205) 832-6510

*Alaska*
State Historic Preservation Officer
Division of Parks
Department of Natural Resources
619 Warehouse Avenue,Suite 210
Anchorage, Alaska 99501
(206) 583-0150
(Ask for Anchorage 274-4676)

*Arizona*
Chief of Natural and Cultural
   Resource Conservation Section
Arizona State Parks
1688 West Adams Street
Phoenix, Arizona 85007
(602) 255-4174

*Arkansas*
Director, Arkansas Historic
   Preservation Program
Suite 500, Continental Building
Markham and Main Streets
Little Rock, Arkansas 72201
(501) 371-2763

*California*
State Historic Preservation Officer
Office of Historic Preservation
California Department of Parks
   and Recreation
P.O. Box 2390
Sacramento, California 95811
(916) 445-2358

*Colorado*
State Historic Preservation Officer
Colorado Heritage Center
1300 Broadway
Denver, Colorado 80203
(303) 892-2136

*Connecticut*
Director, Connecticut Historical
   Commission
59 South Prospect Street
Hartford, Connecticut 06106
(203) 566-3005

*Delaware*
Director, Division of Historical
   and Cultural Affairs
Hall of Records
Dover, Delaware 19901
(302) 678-5314

282

*District of Columbia*
Director, Department of Housing
and Community Development
1133 North Capitol Street, N.W.
Washington, D.C. 20001
(202) 535-1282

*Florida*
Director, Division of Archives,
History and Records Management
Department of State
The Capitol
Tallahassee, Florida 32301
(904) 488-3965

*Georgia*
Chief, Historic Preservation
Services
Department of Natural Resources
270 Washington Street, S.W.,
Room 703-C
Atlanta, Georgia 30334
(404) 656-2894

*Hawaii*
State Historic Preservation Officer
Department of Land and Natural
Resources
P.O. Box 621
Honolulu, Hawaii 96809
Phone: Ask for Honolulu 548-6550

*Idaho*
Historic Preservation Coordinator
Idaho Historical Society
610 North Julia Davis Drive
Boise, Idaho 83706
(208) 334-2120

*Illinois*
Director, Department of Conservation
602 State Office Building
400 South Spring Street
Springfield, Illinois 62706
(217) 782-6302

*Indiana*
Director, Department of
Natural Resources
608 State Office Building
Indianapolis, Indiana 46204
(317) 232-4020

*Iowa*
Director, Iowa State Historical
Department
Division of Historic Preservation
26 East Market Street
Iowa City, Iowa 52240
(319) 353-4186 or 6949

*Kansas*
Executive Director
Kansas State Historical Society
120 West Tenth Street
Topeka, Kansas 66612
(913) 296-3251

*Kentucky*
Commissioner, Department of Arts and
State Historic Preservation Officer
Capitol Plaza Tower, 22nd Floor
Frankfort, Kentucky 40601
(502) 564-6683

*Louisiana*
State Historic Preservation Officer
Office of Program Development
P.O. Box 44247
Baton Rouge, Louisiana 70804
(504) 389-2567

*Maine*
Director, Maine Historic
Preservation Commission
55 Capitol Street
Augusta, Maine 04330
(207) 289-2133

*Maryland*
State Historic Preservation
Officer
John Shaw House

283

21 State Circle
Annapolis, Maryland 21401
(301) 269-2440 or 2433

*Massachusetts*
Executive Director, Massachusetts
  Historical Commission
294 Washington Street
Boston, Massachusetts 02108
(617) 727-8470

*Michigan*
Director
Michigan History Division
Department of State
Lansing, Michigan 48918
(517) 373-0510

*Minnesota*
Director, Minnesota Historical
  Society
690 Cedar Street
St. Paul, Minnesota 55101
(612) 296-2747

*Mississippi*
Director, State of Mississippi
  Department of Archives and History
P.O. Box 571
Jackson, Mississippi 39205
(601) 354-6218

*Missouri*
Director, State Department of
  Natural Resources
P.O. Box 176
Jefferson City, Missouri 65101
(314) 751-4422

*Montana*
State Historical Preservation
  Officer
Montana Historical Society
225 North Roberts Street
Veterans Memorial Building
Helena, Montana 59601
(406) 449-2694

*Nebraska*
Director, The Nebraska State
  Historical Society
1500 R Street
Lincoln, Nebraska 68508
(402) 471-3270

*Nevada*
State Historic Preservation Officer
Division of Historic Preservation
  and Archeology
Capitol Complex
Carson City, Nevada 89710
(702) 885-5138

*New Hampshire*
Commissioner, Department of
Resources and Economic Development
P.O. Box 856
Concord, New Hampshire 03301
(603) 271-2411

*New Jersey*
Commissioner, Department of
  Environmental Protection
P.O. Box 1390
Trenton, New Jersey 08625
(609) 292-2885

*New Mexico*
State Historic Preservation Officer
Department of Finance and Administration
  State Planning Division
505 Don Gasper Avenue
Santa Fe, New Mexic 87503
(505) 827-2108

*New York*
Commissioner, Office of
Parks, Recreation, and Historic
  Preservation
Agency Building #1
Empire State Plaza
Albany, New York 12238
(518) 474-0468

North Carolina
Director, Division of Archives
  and History
Department of Cultural Resources
109 East Jones Street
Raleigh, North Carolina 27611
(919) 733-7305

North Dakota
Superintendent, State Historical
  Society of North Dakota
Liberty Memorial Building
Bismarck, North Dakota 58501
(701) 224-2667

Ohio
State Historic Preservation Officer
The Ohio Historical Society
Interstate 71 at Seventeenth Avenue
Columbus, Ohio 43211
(614) 466-3852

Oklahoma
State Historical Preservation Officer
Oklahoma Historical Society
Historical Building
Oklahoma City, Oklahoma 73105
(405) 521-2491

Oregon
State Parks Superintendent
525 Trade Street S.E.
Salem, Oregon 97310
(503) 378-6305

Pennsylvania
Executive Director
Pennsylvania Historical and Museum
  Commission
P.O. Box 1026
Harrisburg, Pennsylvania 17120
(717) 787-2891

Commonwealth of Puerto Rico
Office of Cultural Affairs
La Fortaleza

San Juan, Puerto Rico 00905
9-809-724-2100
9-809-724-0700—Institute of P.R.

Rhode Island
Director, Rhode Island Department
  of Community Affairs
150 Washington Street
Providence, Rhode Island 02903
(401) 277-2850

South Carolina
Director
State Archives Department
1430 Senate Street
Columbia, South Carolina 29211
(803) 758-5816

South Dakota
State Historic Preservation Officer
Historical Preservation Center
University of South Dakota
Alumni House
Vermillion, South Dakota 57069
(605) 677-5314

Tennessee
Commissioner, Tennessee Department
  of Conservation
Tennessee Historical Commission
4721 Trousdale Drive
Nashville, Tennessee 37220
(615) 741-2371

Texas
Executive Director
Texas State Historical Commission
P.O. Box 12276, Capitol Station
Austin, Texas 78711
(512) 475-3092

Utah
State Historic Preservation Officer
Utah State Historical Society
307 West 200, South, Suite 1000
Salt Lake City, Utah 84101
(801) 533-5961

*Vermont*
Director, Vermont Division for
   Historic Preservation
Pavilion Office Building
Montpelier, Vermont 05602
(802) 828-3226

*Virginia*
Executive Director
Virginia Historic Landmarks Commission
221 Governor Street
Richmond, Virginia 23219
(804) 786-3143

*Washington*
State Historic Preservation Officer
111 West Twenty-First Avenue
KL-11
Olympia, Washington 98504
(206) 753-4011

*West Virginia*
Commissioner
Department of Culture and History
State Capitol Complex
Charleston, West Virginia 25304
(304) 348-0220

*Wisconsin*
Director, State Historical
   Society of Wisconsin
816 State Street
Madison, Wisconsin 53706
(608) 262-3266

*Wyoming*
Director
Wyoming Recreation Commission
604 East Twenty-Fifth Street
Cheyenne, Wyoming 82001
(207) 777-7695

# Acknowledgments

For permission to print or reprint the materials listed below and for the courtesy extended by fellow authors and others, as this book was being prepared, authors and publisher make the following grateful acknowledgments.

The University of Akron, for excerpts on pages 8–9, 65–66, 106, 112, and 207, from the university's Family History Collection, American Research Center. Reprinted by permission of John V. Miller, University Archivist, the University of Akron.

Pamela Bohlmann, for the excerpt on page 119, from her untitled essay for a family histories project (St. Louis, 1977).

The University of Chicago Press and E. McClung Fleming, for the excerpt on page 153 from "Artifact Study: A Proposed Model," by E. McClung Fleming, in *Winterthur Portfolio* 9 (1974): 156. Copyright © 1974 by the University of Chicago Press. Reprinted by permission of the University of Chicago Press.

The City of Florissant, Missouri, and Rosemary Davison, for "Building Preservation: Local Ordinances," on pages 266–268.

Harcourt Brace Jovanovich, Inc., for "A Worker Reads History," by Bertolt Brecht, from *Selected Poems* by Bertolt Brecht, translated by H. R. Hays. Copyright © 1947 by Bertolt Brecht and H. R. Hays. Copyright renewed 1975 by Stephan S. Brecht and H. R. Hays. Reprinted by permission of Harcourt Brace Jovanovich, Inc.

Indiana Department of Natural Resources: Division of Historic Preservation and Archaeology, the Historic Landmarks Foundation of Indiana, and the Department of the Interior, for excerpts on pages 263–265, from "Survey Procedure," Carroll County (Indiana) Interim Report, Historic Landmarks Foundation of Indiana.

Indiana University Northwest, James B. Lane, and Ronald D. Cohen, for excerpts on pages 17–18, from "The Greek Community of East Chicago," by Georgia Kollintzas; and on pages 204–205, from "The Explosion of Standard Oil, August 27, 1955," by Ruthie Williams, in *Steel Shavings*, edited by James B. Lane and Ronald D. Cohen (Gary, Ind.: Indiana University Northwest, 1976). Reprinted by permission of Ronald D. Cohen.

Guy Johnson, for excerpts on pages 46 and 178 from his manuscript "The Boy on Kiegley's Creek."

Michael Musick for information in the excerpt on pages 190–191.

The Missouri Historical Society, the Western Historical Manuscript Collection of the University of Missouri/St. Louis, and Katharine T. Corbett, for the excerpt on pages 130–131 from "St. Louis Garment Workers: . . . Photographs and Memories," in *Gateway Heritage*, Summer 1981, pp. 22–23. Copyright © 1981 by the Missouri Historical Society.

Mt. San Antonio College and William F. King, for the excerpt on pages 38–39, from *The Vintage Years: Our Valley before 1945*, by William F. King (Walnut, Calif.: Mt. San Antonio College, Department of Community Services, 1975). Reprinted by permission of William F. King.

*The New Republic* and Neil Harris for the excerpt on page 167, from "Spaced-Out at the Shopping Center," by Neil Harris, in *The New Republic*, December 13, 1975, p. 23. Copyright © 1975 by *The New Republic*. Reprinted by permission of *The New Republic*.

*Western Pennsylvania Historical Magazine* and Josephine McIlvain, for the excerpt on pages 98–99, from "Twelve Blocks: A Study of One Segment of Pittsburgh's South Side, 1880–1915," by Josephine McIlvain, in *Western Pennsylvania Historical Magazine* 60 (October 1977). Reprinted by permission of William F. Trimble, Editor, *Western Pennsylvania Historical Magazine*.

# Picture Credits

Authors and publisher make grateful acknowledgment here to the following individuals and organizations granting permission to reproduce, on the pages listed below, pictorial materials from their collections.

Pamela Bohlmann, cover, 119

The Chicago Historical Society, 69.

Peggy Creed, 141.

H. Roger Grant, 2 (top) and 158.

Eleanor Heishman, 104.

The Library of Congress, 34, 54 (top and bottom), 138, 169, 175, and 235. Illustrations on pages 74, 76, 77, and 81 (top and bottom) were photographed at the Library of Congress.

Missouri Historical Society and the Western Historical Manuscript Collection, the University of Missouri/St. Louis, 130–131.

Michael Musick, 191.

The National Archives and Records Service, 3 (top), 25, 31, 33, 57, 101, 150, and 190. The illustration on page 96 was photographed at the National Archives.

Roy L. Plunk, 50–51.

Summit County Historical Society Collection, American History Research Center, University of Akron, 2 (bottom), 3 (bottom), 24 (top and bottom), 79, 133, 139, 168, 170, 173, 214, and 221 (top and bottom).

Unity Lutheran Church, Bel-Nor, Missouri, 44, 45, and 172.

Lab work for the illustrations on pages 74, 76, 77, 81, and 96, as well as for pictures appearing on pages 44, 45, 50, 51, 135, 152, 154, and 172 was done by David Jackson.

Photographs on pages 71 and 136 are from the personal collection of David Kyvig; those on pages 20, 135, 152, 154, and 185 belong to Myron Marty.

# Index